Rural Congregational Studies

Rural Congregational Studies

A Guide for Good Shepherds

L. SHANNON JUNG
MARY A. AGRIA

Abingdon Press
Nashville

RURAL CONGREGATIONAL STUDIES: A GUIDE FOR GOOD SHEPHERDS

Scripture quotations are from the New Revised Standard Version Bible, copyright © 1989, by the Division of Christian Education of the National Council of the Churches of Christ in the United States of America.

Excerpts from "Nurses Promote Wellness," by Finn Bullers; "Farm Woes: Crisis Not Over; Tragedy Common," by Steve Webber; and "Green Island Dies, but Not Community," by Lyn Hanson, are © *Telegraph Herald*, a division of Woodward Communications Inc., 1992. Reprinted with permission.

Excerpts from *A Thousand Acres* by Jane Smiley are copyright © 1991 by Jane Smiley. Reprinted by permission of Alfred A. Knopf, Inc.

Excerpts from *Dakota* are copyright © 1993 by Kathleen Norris. Reprinted by permission of Ticknor & Fields/Houghton Mifflin Co. All rights reserved.

Excerpts from "Innovative Practices Allow Flexible, More Profitable Lives" and "Sustainable Farms May Mean Less Profit, but Better End Result," by James Walsh, are reprinted with permission of the *Star Tribune*, Minneapolis-St. Paul.

97 98 99 00 01 02 03 04 05 06—10 9 8 7 6 5 4 3 2 1

MANUFACTURED IN THE UNITED STATES OF AMERICA

To all those
members of rural and small congregations,
shepherds themselves, and to all
the pastors and priests
who serve them

Contents

Contents

About This Book

Rural Congregational Studies: A Guide for Good Shepherds is written for all laity and clergy who are or may be doing ministry in rural congregations. It focuses on the nature of congregational life in the rural context. The content of the book has been hammered out on the anvil of the experience of many rural congregations and pastors, especially our church partners in twelve community empowerment models in Illinois, Iowa, and Wisconsin and the seminary interns who served them over a three-year period. In sharing the learnings of this special coalition, our intent is to strengthen the training of pastors for service in the rural church, as well as to help experienced clergy as they work with their respective rural congregations.

By emphasizing rural congregational studies, we intend to help you capture the essence of what it means to live, work, and minister in rural America. Further, we believe that this sourcebook will encourage churches to build and sustain their vital, and in places endangered, rural communities. If we succeed in nothing else but holding up the important vision of being God's people in community, we will have borne witness to the power of the Spirit we have seen at work around us.

Our special thanks go to University of Dubuque Theological Seminary faculty members Lyle Vander Broek, Tom Albin, and Barbara Pursey, Wartburg Theological Seminary faculty member Norma Everist, and pastors Craig Bowyer, Don Dovre, and David Guetzsky for their patient and invaluable reading and critique of this manuscript. We are grateful also to the interns, pastors, and parishioners named throughout this book who shared with us their visions of the rural church and life in rural communities. In regard to the day-to-day insights and assistance of the staff of the Center for Theology and Land—including Patty Walker, Paul Peterson, Judy Shelly, Kris Kirst, and Claudia Krogmann—the authors can only say that without you this book would have never come to be. Warmest appreciation goes out also to the Pew Charitable Trusts of Philadelphia, Pennsylvania, in supporting the original research and to the administration of Wartburg and the University of Dubuque Theological Seminaries for their ongoing support and encouragement.

Putting This Book to Work

This book is designed as a resource for seminaries as they train students for the rural church; for administrators within seminaries and denominations as they reassess their policies toward the rural church; for clergy as they tackle specific problems related to their rural congregations; and for congregations and lay leaders as they wrestle with what it means to "do ministry" in rural communities. It is appropriate for classroom use and for self-study.

For use in seminary settings, the book is designed so that instructors in various traditional disciplines or departments can use it effectively as a supplement to other course materials. In addition to the text's obvious applications for courses in congregational studies, sections of the text are especially useful for classes in cross-cultural studies, ethics, evangelism, pastoral care, polity, preaching, spiritual formation, theology, and worship.

In congregational settings, this book is designed for use by both ordained and lay ministers. It is intended to be used in helping congregations think about how best to engage in evangelism and mission in the particular locations in which they find themselves. The chapters are organized around the four benchmarks of congregational studies:

1. CONTEXT: What are the features of the rural context in which the congregation is located? What is the history of the town? the region? What are the primary economic influences? What is the racial and ethnic makeup of the community? How representative of the community is the congregation? Attention to the national, regional, and local context is important. This focus suggests much about what has shaped the congregation and also the opportunities that a specific congregation has as it approaches its evangelizing and its community mission (see chapter 2).

2. IDENTITY: What is the style of the congregation? What are the congregation's distinctive characteristics? What stories, symbols, beliefs, values, and patterns does this particular congregation live by? What is the essence of its identity? The history and mission and stages in a congregation's life give important clues to its persisting character, which enables it to have a sense of purpose despite the changes it experiences (see chapter 3).

3. PROGRAM: What activities is the congregation engaged in? All the activities of the congregation and its members should receive attention. Many rural congregations will be surprised by the buzz of activity their churches generate. The *Handbook for Congregational Studies* defines programs as "those organizational structures, plans and activities through which a congregation expresses its mission and ministry both to its own members and those outside the membership"[1] (see chapter 4).

4. PROCESS: What are the dynamics of decision making, of leadership, and of polity that knit a congregation together? These elements of "the way we do things" affect the climate of the church and the way we feel about a particular congregation. One significant characteristic is the friendliness of the rural church: Does it make room for everyone? Can everyone find a place in the church? The degree to which the congregational processes allow participation is very important in smaller and rural congregations (see chapter 5).

Chapter 6 will focus on integrating the four aspects of the rural congregation that we have laid out in chapters 2 to 5. There we will also become particularly practical in that we will suggest various strategies or activities that might stimulate your thinking about ways to empower the congregation of which you are a member. This chapter will also encourage you to think about the future; what sort of congregation might you want to see come into being in ten years? What can be done in the next few years that will enable that to happen in your location? What are the futurists saying about rural America, and how might that affect your community? Such questions might increase your awareness of the ways God is seeking to use your congregation.

The book offers a bibliography of print materials, as well as other media such as videotapes, addresses of rural organizations, newsletters, and worship materials. Of central concern throughout the text is how the church as an institution—as well as pastors in those churches—fits into the picture.

We are using the framework for congregational studies that emerged from the efforts of Jackson W. Carroll, Carl S. Dudley, C. Kirk Hadaway, James F. Hopewell, Speed B. Leas, William McKinney, Mary C. Mattis, and Wade Clark Rook in their groundbreaking volume *Handbook for Congregational Studies,* which is in revision for a 1997 edition.

We are grateful for their pioneering work. The approach labeled "congregational studies" seems to have the considerable advantage of organizing all those attitudes, dispositions, idiosyncrasies, and activities that go into the culture that is a congregation. It keeps us from skipping over an important part of a congregation's life.

Materials in *Rural Congregational Studies: A Guide for Good Shepherds* are designed to help congregations do the following:

● Understand the rural context of the United States in basic terms that can be considered in relation to their community and congregational setting. Readers can and should give attention to their specific regional and local characteristics as well.

● Explore the human issues that can make or break a rural congregation, including concepts of power, prevailing attitudes in rural culture, leadership styles, and pastoral and lay leadership relations.

● Move from theory into practice, through modeling and role-playing strategies for empowering rural America and particularly the rural church, to address the problems and challenges ahead in their location.

● Point out further resources that can support rural clergy and congregations, as well as seminaries, their faculty, their students, and their graduates as they become more aware of and skilled in ministering within rural communities.

Enhancing the Teaching/ Learning Process

Note the pivotal role that seminarians played in developing the resources presented in this study guide. During a three-year research project, interns from Wartburg and the University of Dubuque seminaries in Dubuque, Iowa, were sent out into model communities with the goal of recording what they learned about rural life, small churches, and the community-building process. Some of these students had extensive rural experience and some had no previous rural experience. Their observations, then, were laid side by side with the perceptions of the field supervisors, lay leadership, and pastors also at work in those congregations. Powerful mutual ministry took place, enriching the experienced pastors and the seminarians alike.

We recommend that faculty or congregations using this book adopt a similar approach. The text should be treated, not as a definitive collection of materials about rural life, but rather as an approach to learning about rural ministry. Among the most valuable resources in any study of rural congregations are insights that participants bring into the discussions as they wrestle individually and collectively with their personal experiences with and exposure to rural culture. Among the materials that could serve as supplements to this guide are

● excerpts from personal diaries, journals, and position papers;

● materials related to the history and decision-making process of the congregation;

● annotated bibliographies and studies emerging during the course work;

● videotapes and audiotapes of participants discussing issues vital to their congregational experiences in rural settings.

The Center for Theology and Land and its Rural Ministry Program at Wartburg and University of Dubuque theological seminaries also functions as a valuable ongoing source of such materials.

For a congregation doing a self-analysis and self-assessment, it would be helpful to use the resource units numbered 2.8, 3.1, 4.6, 5.1, and 6.1.

For those in training to be pastors of rural churches, the expository chapters and excerpts from novels, diaries, and other sources provide windows into the rapidly changing and fascinating world of the rural congregation.

Chapter 1

Introducing Rural Ministry: Congregational Studies in Perspective

Ann Morrison's First Church

Judging by the response of her fellow classmates, the faculty, staff, and ecstatic seminary administration, Ann Morrison knew she had it made. With graduation two months away, she had been offered a position as associate pastor at one of the largest congregations in the state. It was "an incredible first pastorate," everyone told her. The other candidates, from seminaries all over the country, had been exceptional. So why, Ann found herself asking, was she so troubled?

Thirty-six, divorced, and the custodial parent of a four-year-old, Ann had struggled hard to complete her seminary education. Balancing parenthood, studies, and multiple jobs along with her required internships left little energy and time to reflect on her dream of serving in a large suburban congregation similar to the one in which she had worshiped as a child. Financially, the wolf was always at the door. She had reluctantly accepted help from her elderly parents, both after her divorce and through those three long years of seminary training that followed. But it was a debt Ann was determined to repay.

Despite all the obstacles, Ann had won the preaching prize two years in a row, and her academic record put her near the top of her class.

Her classmates had chosen her to be their representative on the administrative council. The dean had personally nominated her for the position in Pastor Jack Crayton's church. The two-thousand-member congregation was one of the strongest financial supporters of the seminary. Its members held key positions on the boards and committees of the national church.

Ann had been convinced that her chances of being chosen for the position were slim indeed. Much to her disappointment she had not been able to do her supervised ministerial training in a large congregation. Her personal and financial situation had forced her to take a church close to the seminary, a struggling rural congregation in Hayden, which the regional church governance had been threatening for some time to close.

Despite her worries about her limited experience in a large church, Ann felt she had given her best to the interview with Pastor Crayton and the congregation. Much to her surprise, within the week she was offered the position.

THE JOB OF A LIFETIME

"As youth pastor, you are going to be a highly valued member of the pastoral team," Pastor Crayton told her. He reminded her once again of the rich resources and backing she could expect in carrying out her ministry. The programming, facilities, and opportunities the congregation offered to its four-hundred-plus young people under age eighteen were the envy of other congregations in the community. In national church circles, the congregation had established a reputation as a dynamic model for urban ministry.

As to her status as a divorcée (something that had worried Ann during the interview), Pastor Crayton assured her, "You have a unique gift that you can bring to us. We especially need your insights into the problems that young people are facing in our urban situation—all the stress and pain that go along with divorce and parents out of work. You'll make a tremendous difference here, Ann."

Back at the seminary, Ann informed the dean of the offer. "This will be tremendous for the seminary as well," he beamed. "That church has been a strong source of support for us in the past. Jack Crayton has a powerful voice on the national educational committee; he could be even more help to us with you there. You'll be the first woman pastor to serve that congregation. It's something Jack has wanted for a long time. You're the perfect candidate."

Ann's conversation with the dean only confirmed her resolve. She was determined to accept the offer. But back in her apartment that evening there was a message waiting on her answering machine. It was the outspoken owner of the grain elevator in Hayden, Pete Wilton, who served as president of the church council throughout Ann's time as student pastor there.

"We need to talk," the message said. With a tightness in her throat, Ann dialed the number. She listened, anxious and with a growing sense of incredulity. Despite the seminary regulations discouraging placement of graduates full-time in churches where they had served as students, the congregation was petitioning the seminary to waive its policy in this case and allow her to serve as permanent pastor.

"The council is unanimous," Pete summed it up gruffly. Ann visualized those six stern male faces and the lone woman among them, recording secretary Mona Frieden, who farmed five hundred acres with her husband and who had seen far too much tragedy in her sixty-odd years. Pete's wife and Mona were the two women she had grown to know best during her year in Hay-

den. Winning their trust had meant a great deal to Ann.

The silence was heavy on the line. Painful as it was, Ann shared a carefully censored version of the offer from Pastor Crayton's congregation. Even then, the contrast could not be lost on Pete Wilton.

"We haven't got much to offer," he said finally. "But then I don't have to tell you that. The parsonage furnace needs replacing. Not much in the budget this year, but we'll work on it."

Ann promised to think about it. But the very prospect was disturbing, painfully so. It would have been so tempting to give it a tactful week—the time within which she was expected to respond to the offer from Crayton's congregation—and then express her regrets to Pete Wilton and the council. Instead, Ann shared the situation with those she most trusted.

"Do you know what that would entail?" Her supervised-practice-of-ministry professor dismissed the possibility when Ann shared her dilemma. Ann did know, all too well, but the professor told her anyway. "You would be bucking both denominational and seminary politics for that assignment—two powerful strikes against you right there."

LISTENING FOR GOD'S VOICE

Over the next several days, in subtle and not too subtle ways, other students made it plain that Ann would be foolish not to accept the offer from Pastor Crayton's congregation. "You've got to be kidding," one of her male classmates summed it up. "So far the only nibble I've gotten is Elk Hills, population 520 and shrinking. Not exactly the first call I had in mind. Even if I pay my dues, it might be years before anything turns up like Crayton's congregation. If I were in your shoes, I wouldn't hesitate for a minute."

More and more distraught, Ann found herself sharing her doubts with her faculty adviser. "I know this all sounds very irrational," she admitted. "I've always wanted a suburban church. So do most of my classmates. If we thought about places like Hayden, it was maybe in terms of a first pastorate, with the goal of eventually winding up in a church like Pastor Crayton's; provided that everything goes right. And I have that opportunity handed to me. Common sense tells me Hayden would be difficult, in so many ways."

Her adviser was cautious for other reasons. "Revenues and attendance at the Hayden church have been declining steadily. Plus the acceptance level for single women pastors in nearby rural communities hasn't been encouraging."

Ann started to protest, but her adviser was ahead of her. "Okay . . . I'll admit, you've done a wonderful job in Hayden. Several younger unchurched families began to attend on a regular basis during your six months there. But you'd be fighting an uphill battle, Ann. You're one of the best students I've ever had. You've had to face so much risk and uncertainty to get to this point. It's not selfish to put your personal interests on the line here as well. You really need to think about it. Hard."

Ann's parents said little, although her father's veiled questions about child care and the Hayden school district spoke volumes. They, too, were worried about her.

Amid all those voices, the only dissent came from her professor of missions, retired now, but crusty and uncompromising as ever, very much driven by his fifteen years in the mission field. "If it's safety you want, you're in the wrong business, Ann. But then you know that. Be faithful—and if Hayden is where God wants you, go for it! Blow the established seminary fathers, and everyone else who cannot understand it, out of the water!"

On Sunday Ann drove out to Hayden as usual, but with a heavy heart. Her sermon seemed lackluster to her, and she found it hard to make eye contact. As she stood outside the tiny church to greet the congregation, Mona Frieden's silent hug seemed awkward . . . strained. Pete Wilton was nowhere to be found. It was his wife who tackled the unspoken head-on.

"I know a lot of the wives out here haven't known what to make of you, a pastor and all," she admitted. "College education. Working with the men on the council like you do. But most of our daughters are doing that. If anyone can help us learn to understand, you could. We need that. We can't give you much compared to that big church that wants you. But one thing I do know. They've got a lot of folks. We've just got you. Maybe that counts for something."

Giving Ann a brusque hug, the woman turned and headed down the crumbling cement steps toward her pickup. Alone now, Ann watched the dust cloud billowing down the dirt street as the truck headed toward the soybean fields at the outskirts of town.

Is this what it meant to hear God's call to ministry? Ann wondered. But if she were to choose Hayden, how on earth would she justify that decision to her professors, her colleagues, Pastor Crayton, and her well-meaning family? Or even to herself?

Congregational Studies in a Rural Context

Ann Morrison's dilemma is not unique. Her doubts and uncertainties are echoed time and time again, not only by seminarians but also by experienced pastors contemplating the call to service in the rural church. Without an appreciation for the ambiguities inherent in the choices Ann was making, it is difficult to understand the nature of rural congregational dynamics and life.

Between the lines in debates about the future of rural congregations, for example, we often find a preoccupation with issues of fiscal viability and ideal congregation size; on a personal level, the prospect of service in rural congregations forces clergy to confront issues of the relative merits of urban versus rural lifestyles. Such considerations may make it appear that prevailing contemporary secular values are influencing the world of the church: in other words, "big" can sometimes be confused with "better," and geographic isolation can become interpreted as "unsophisticated" or "out of it."

We suspect that one reason seminarians and other pastors are apprehensive about serving a rural parish is because they have little experience in a rural congregation and community. This sourcebook is meant to alleviate some of that fear of the unknown.

From a biblical perspective, Israelite prophets and Christian messengers of the gospel were not immune to similar pressures or preconceptions about challenging locations in which God was calling them to serve. Consider the experiences of Samuel, Elijah, Jonah, Peter, and Paul, among others, in that context (1 Sam. 3:1-18; 1 Kings 17:2-7; Jon. 1:1-2, 3:1-2; Matt. 4:18-20; Acts 9:1-19). One rural Iowa pastor captures the essence of such struggles:

> Like so many of my colleagues, I wound up loving rural ministry more or less by default. It was the unspoken—and sometimes spoken—assumption in my seminary that all of us would wind up ultimately in suburban or urban pastorates. God had other plans for me, but it is unfortunate that I never even saw that particular "call" to ministry as a possibility worth pursuing. Even now I get the feeling that some people in the national church see rural churches as a dumping ground for pastors who for whatever reason are not "up to" the demands of ministry in larger congregations.

He goes on to say,

> If I had to single out the biggest single barrier to effective training for rural ministry, it would be the common attitude that the rural church is a great "first call" or first step for new pastors. Change that . . . and you'll change the whole attitude toward rural ministry. Rural ministry is among the most challenging and rewarding kinds of service I can imagine!

This Iowa pastor, like Ann, had come to recognize the immense power, potential, and joy of the rural mission.

However, for a pastor (or layperson) to serve confidently and effectively or to make ministry in rural communities vital and energizing, it is not enough to sense the need or feel a sense of vocation. High levels of congregational leadership and empowerment skills are essential.

Ministry is also limited by the vision one brings to the process. Another midwestern pastor reports:

> In 1988, former agriculture secretary Earl Butz visited our area supposedly to offer us hope. What we heard was a rationale for pastors helping parishioners mourn as their communities and churches died. That kind of cynicism is not what the courageous, pioneering spirit of these communities, or what a challenge to ministry, is all about!

The human ramifications of the Butz position are bleak indeed.

If many such small congregations did not exist, vast areas of the United States would not have access to a live pastoral presence, spiritual leadership, or an institutional focus for their spiritual lives. In many rural communities, the church is the one institution left to deal with major societal issues, as well as the mental, physical, and spiritual health of individual parishioners. That realization could either impel one to the ministry of a lifetime or seem like an intimidating and overwhelming task.

For many newly ordained pastors, such rural congregations are the church. Although percentages vary from denomination to denomination, openings in small and rural congregations are common options for graduating clergy each year. In some denominations, notably the Roman Catholic Church, rural congregations are reserved for late-career clergy placement. Whatever placement pattern prevails, coping with the transition to rural congregational life is a task that most ordained clergy will face at some point in their ministry.

Hence, rural congregational studies are important. By having some way of thinking about the rural congregation in its community, pastors who are new to rural settings can approach their ministry with a set of tools for making sense of their specific location. Even more important, however, is the recognition that the rural community and the smaller membership church *are* different. The clergyperson who realizes this will begin by asking and learning rather than by answering and telling; it is vital that all who would do ministry, lay or ordained, discover the distinctive, unique, and even wonderful world of the rural church. Congregational studies can help.

Rather than being a specialized and highly esoteric discipline, congregational studies incorporates an approach, an aid to observation, a way of finding out who and what this congregation in this place is. The first aspect of that study is the *context*—the rural terrain of this place in this region in this country.[1] Everything that a congregation has been, is, and will be is influenced by its social context. This includes the history of the church and region, the economic status of the congregation itself and as well as the community at large, the political stance of the community, the buying patterns of the people, the community's vision of its future, the age of the population, and the size of the congregation.

Although every region and every setting is different, we can nevertheless offer some generalizations about the context of rural communities (and hence rural congregations) in the United States in the last few years of the twentieth century. Though they are not the only questions, the following are important ones:

● What is it that makes a community "rural"? What goes into the notion of rural "community"?
● How is the rural economy doing? Specifically, how is an agriculturally based economy doing in rural areas?
● What can we say about the population in rural communities? In general, how does the population in rural locations compare to the rest of the United States in terms of age, stability, income, crime rate, and so forth?
● What values do rural men and women hold, in general?
● How do the economics and politics and distances characteristic of rural America affect life there? What opportunities and challenges does the overall context present for rural congregations?

Sometimes we forget that statistics about drug use or crime or average age or income level describe people and their activities. At issue are not just economic or physical concerns, but emotional, relational, and spiritual considerations as well, including contextual factors that influence strategies of leadership and the empowerment that makes community possible. Sensing a common rural frame of reference—connectedness that goes beyond numbers or socioeconomic forces to an underlying sense of shared community identity—will prove invaluable to seminarians and to pastors already in the field. Understanding context will not only guide church leadership, it can also assist in moving beyond a sense of loneliness and isolation.[2]

Helping Ann Morrison Serve Her Church

The real "Ann Morrison," it is refreshing to note, eventually chose the rural congregation. (For the rest of that story, see pp. 119-21.) Sustaining her was a deep faith, along with the capacity to respect and draw strength from proximity to the land, its peoples, and the resources of the earth—a respect that can be lost amid the concrete and steel of urban life. But shallow romanticism and nostalgia had no place in her decision, nor in her perspectives on or attitudes toward rural life. Anyone serving the rural church must start with a realistic sense of the problems and challenges that face its mission and stewardship.

From the outset, then, the goal of this text is to emphasize that rural congregational studies cannot be treated in isolation. In the rural microcosm, the immediacy of relationships makes sensitivity to context essential, more so perhaps than in any other congregational setting. Whereas larger urban churches commonly retain staffing with a variety of specialized tasks and constituencies, in smaller rural churches solo pastorates are more often the rule (and many solo pastors also hold other full-time jobs). Understanding, appreciating, and negotiating one's role as pastor becomes one of the most important and challenging aspects of ministry in rural churches.

RESOURCES FOR CLARIFYING ATTITUDES
TOWARD RURAL MINISTRY

The remainder of this chapter is devoted to helping rural church members, pastors, and seminary students put their attitudes toward rural ministry in perspective. This will include the exploration of attitudes within society and even the church that can affect the perception of rural ministry as a calling.

1.1   Reassessing the Rural Call: Case Notes—Ann Morrison's First Church
1.2   Ministry to a Living or Dying Community? Two Communities in the Heartland
1.3   A Denomination Revisions the Rural Church: Excerpts from the 1993 ELCA Resolution on Rural Ministry
1.4   The Politics of Renewal: Letters from an Iowa Pastor to the Bishop
1.5   Challenging the Assumptions: Five Reasons Why Most Rural Churches Should Be Closed

1.1 Reassessing the Rural Call
Case Notes—Ann Morrison's First Church

The case presented at the beginning of the chapter ("Ann Morrison's First Church") is intended to be a springboard into discussion. The teaching notes below are designed to promote conversation about the subtle factors that influence a new pastor's choice of calls.

The goals of the discussion are to encourage students and pastors in the field to reexamine their personal attitudes toward first pastoral assignments and toward urban versus rural ministry, and to sensitize them to the forces that shape those attitudes.

Secondary goals include the following: to raise the issue of calling versus job placement, as well as the question of whose church one is being led to serve (Ann's? the community's? or another paradigm entirely?); to encourage seminary students to become more sensitive to the issues of women pastors and their roles in the church; and to encourage seminarians (male and female) to examine their own values in relation to their pastoral career paths.

The instructor writes the group's short answers to the following questions on the board:

Brief Analysis:
  1. What is bothering Ann? (List responses under the heading DILEMMA.)
  2. Why is she so troubled? (List responses under the heading CAUSES.)

Personal Relevance:
  1. If Ann came to you, how would you have responded?
  2. Which church do you think she should take?
  3. Why?

Reality Testing:
  1. What is she likely to do?
  2. How are (a) the seminary, (b) fellow students, and (c) Pastor Crayton likely to respond?

ISSUES FOR DISCUSSION

1. Do students at this seminary (male and female) or pastors you know face problems or decision points similar to Ann's? (Note: Clergy in rural churches who field-tested the case identified closely with Ann's dilemma, reactions, and so forth.)

2. What biases do you perceive (if any) in your own or your seminary or denomination's attitudes toward rural versus urban pastorates?

3. What can the seminary or church do to deal more effectively with helping students (1) wrestle with the concept of career direction, and (2) cope with pastorates in small or rural church settings? (Write short responses on the board.)

1.2 Ministry to a Living or Dying Community? Two Communities in the Heartland

The *(Dubuque) Telegraph-Herald* and the AP articles included as resources on the following pages relate the stories of two communities—stories that serve as eloquent reminders of the fragility and tremendous strength of rural communities. The situations challenge us to put the issue of rural decline and rural renaissance into context.

One pastor facing a situation similar to the one in Green Island, Iowa, stated, "My task, as I see it, is to preside over the death of my church [and community]." He was speaking literally as well as figuratively—of burying the dead, discontinuing services for lack of numbers, and watching the quality of life for his parishioners erode. Does a pastor in such a situation have alternatives? How long could he or she deal with such a surfeit of grief before overloading? What would you have done in the pastor's place? What would you do to keep yourself from falling prey to that kind of burnout?

The incident involving the churches in Hamlet, Illinois, reflects a very creative and positive solution to some of the scarcities and problems facing rural communities. What are the key ingredients that turned those difficulties into triumph? What part did people play in the process? What are the key factors, as you see it, in this community's new beginning?

An interesting exercise also would be to imagine that you are a pastor called to serve a community like Green Island or Hamlet. How would you approach the following situations?

1. Your first week on the job. Where would you go, who would you visit, what would you do? Be specific about your goals for each of these activities.

2. Your first sermon. What topic would you choose, what scripture? (Assume you are not dealing with a fixed lectionary.) Outline the three main points you would try to make. Give your rationale for this approach.

Resource 1.3 offers a denomination's challenge to develop a new kind of ministry that could offer alternatives and hope to the Green Islands and Hamlets of rural America.

For Further Reading: Donald Harington, *Let Us Build a City: Eleven Lost Towns*. San Diego, Calif.: Harcourt Brace Jovanovich, 1986. Case studies of small, crossroads communities or abandoned towns in Arkansas.

GREEN ISLAND DIES,
BUT NOT COMMUNITY
by Lyn Hanson
(Dubuque) Telegraph-Herald

GREEN ISLAND, IOWA—The City of Green Island, 88, died Tuesday after a long illness. Friends said the cause of death was the disappearing railroad blues.

The town's residents voted 19-5 to dissolve Green Island's incorporation, ending a process that began a year ago. Every registered voter in town, save one, voted. Green Island has 26 voters. One of the 25 ballots cast was not counted because it was spoiled.

The end of the city, incorporated in 1904, will be final as soon as its accounts are settled and its assets sell—a one-acre park and a one-room city hall.

Mayor Francis Culver voted to keep the tiny Jackson County city, population 54 official.

Culver's convenience store and a tavern called No Place are Green Island's only businesses. Despite the city's shrinking population and tax base, Culver had hoped it could continue.

"If the vote had been taken a year ago, I don't think I'd have a doubt about the outcome," Culver said Tuesday as he and his wife, Donna, got ready to walk to city hall. "But now I think people have had time to think things through, and some of them want us to keep going."

Petrina Andresen voted to disincorporate. "There's nothing here," she said.

First in the alphabetical list of voters, Andresen was also the first to cast her vote in the musty, single-room city hall—cluttered with empty sandbags and a wheel-of-fortune from the last Home Town Country Days celebration. Among the debris was a yellowed 1984 newspaper clipping of Green Island receiving an Iowa Community Betterment award from Gov. Terry Branstad.

The next two voters to arrive agreed with Andresen.

"We just don't have the money," said Judy Marburger, wife of the city clerk. "Taxes will go up, and we can't make payments on the road leading into town. There's nothing we can do."

Her son, Robert Marburger, 18, cast the first vote of his life—to do away with the city where he'd grown up. "There isn't that much for young people to do here," he said.

Culver can remember when there were plenty of opportunities—working for the railroad. Almost from the beginning, Green Island was a railroad town.

Up to the 1950's, more than 35 passenger trains came through Green Island every day. The depot had three shifts. You could take a train from Green Island to Dubuque or Maquoketa.

The depot closed in 1979 and eventually was torn down—a victim of the decline in railroads. Soo Line tracks run near town, but trains haven't stopped in Green Island in years.

Today, Green Island is a small collection of homes at the foot of a scenic bluff.

Randy Robinson, wildlife technician at the Green Island Wildlife Area, said the community is not on an island, but it's located near plenty of water. . . . Railroaders dubbed it Green Island because it was the only visible green spot during a [Mississippi River] flood.

"There's a reason they keep all these sandbags in City Hall," said Nancy Kiel, who was watching the polls. "The river comes and visits us sometimes."

"Green Island may die as a city," Culver said, "but it will be a community as long as people want it to be."

> *Life and Times of Green Island, Iowa*
> 1839 - White settlers arrive
> 1901 - Railroad makes town a key transfer point
> 1904 - City is incorporated
> 1930s and 1940s - City has a dance hall, 3 general stores, 2 taverns, a school
> 1979 - Train depot closes
> 1990 - Pop. 54; post office closes
> 1991 - City petitions for disincorporation; church closes

Contrast the story of Green Island with the article that follows about the wedding of two rural churches. Rituals and traditions can become a measure of a community's pain and loss, or a source of hope for the future.

MARRIAGE UNITES
TWO RURAL CHURCHES

HAMLET, ILL. (AP) — The Rev. Keith Orr presided at an old-fashioned church wedding recently and it was one of the most satisfying of his 54 years in ministry. But there was no bride or bridegroom.

Orr orchestrated the marriage of two rural churches, which have shared pastors for 121 years and have even worshipped in the same building for the past 12 months, but kept separate identities all the while.

"It's been a great experience," Orr said, "I've been really excited about it."

Orr brought about a merger of the Hamlet and Perryton Presbyterian churches in rural Mercer County in extreme western Illinois.

The Hamlet parish was organized in 1870 in farm country about 15 miles east of the Mississippi River. The Perryton church, about five miles south, formed two years later.

"They shared a pastor for almost their entire history," said Orr, 75.

Orr retired from the ministry in 1977, returned to his native Iowa and has worked the past year as interim pastor in Hamlet and Perryton.

I served as pastor here in 1946 to 1949 and I never tried to get them together then," Orr said. "Both churches had very viable congregations for many, many years. There was very little program sharing. Both churches were strong enough to stand alone."

In those days, Hamlet was a self-sustaining little town with a country store, a garage, meat locker and blacksmith shop. The two churches had a combined membership of about 200 then, Orr said.

Today, only the churches remain to mark either village along Illinois 94. Before the merger, the Hamlet congregation stood at about 75 while Perryton's membership had dwindled to about 30.

"I'm sure Perryton would not have survived much longer," said Faye Eckhardt, an Aledo bank manager and Perryton church member who helped organize the merger.

"By the two churches coming together we've made a much stronger church," she said. "There's no doubt we'll survive now."

Orr said, "family traditions" made it hard for the church faithful to think about merging because they felt they were sacrificing the last remnant of their community's identity.

"Each church had its own pride," Eckhardt said. "It was hard to give up identity."

Orr said the merger creates the exciting opportunity for expanding ministry programs and attracting new members from nearby Rock Island and Moline to the north.

"Now, I can retire happy," Orr said. "Helping with this merger is the highlight of my career."

ISSUES FOR DISCUSSION

A major consideration is whether one views this story as being about the birth or the death of a church. What values and issues important to rural Christians did the pastor in this article take into account—knowingly or instinctively—in dealing with this potentially explosive and traumatic situation? How could such strategies be employed in communities like Green Island?

1.3 A Denomination Revisions the Rural Church

The following resolutions are excerpted from the Evangelical Lutheran Church in America Third Churchwide Assembly, preliminary minutes, Plenary Session Four, August 27, 1993, Kansas City, Missouri, Resolution on Rural Ministry.

RESOLVED, that
1. this church affirm its commitment to ministries in the rural setting;
2. this church assist congregations to move beyond congregational independence and biases toward better communication and cooperation among ministries in related communities, including ecumenical possibilities; and assist in developing creative responses to changing situations;
3. the seminaries of this church use instruction by extension and other instructional methods as ways for

developing pastors and lay leaders in rural ministry, and that synods coordinate communication of Lutheran and ecumenical opportunities for continuing education events related to rural ministry, and to inform rostered persons serving in rural ministries of those opportunities;

4. synods, in cooperation with churchwide units, develop and train teams of indigenous lay leaders to serve and provide leadership for worship, evangelism, community service, and Christian care;

5. resource materials in evangelism for and with rural congregations be developed;

6. this church provide resources to assist multi-point congregations in the development of "articles of agreement" for well-defined operations and relationships;

7. the publications of the Evangelical Lutheran Church in America, synods, and other entities of this church recognize and tell the story of multi-point parishes;

8. this church give encouragement to rural congregations to become more inclusive and to understand what gospel inclusivity and cultural diversity mean in the rural setting;

9. this church has an opportunity to foster a sense of community in the rural setting and should assist congregations in developing skills in the areas of community and economic development;

10. this church assist rural congregations to become active participants in working with others of good-will on environmental issues and to be advocates for the care of creation;

11. this church assist in the formation of partnerships of prayer, presence, understanding, and resource sharing between rural and urban congregations in particular; and

12. this church advocate for people suffering the effects of economic and social conditions that exist throughout the countryside.

ISSUES FOR DISCUSSION

1. What are some of the major issues raised in this document that influence reforming the rural church and denominational policies?

2. Note the seminary role proposed in the ELCA document. Does your seminary have a policy on these issues? Does it encourage debate on such issues? If not, discuss some of the possibilities.

3. How do you see the church and seminaries modeling these concerns? Explain how you see (or do not see) these priorities being implemented.

1.4 The Politics of Renewal: Letters from an Iowa Pastor to the Bishop

Community attitudes may play a role in congregational revitalization, but other forces affect the process, as the correspondence below shows.

PORTRAIT OF A CONGREGATION IN CHANGE: UNEDITED LETTERS FROM A HEARTLAND PASTOR TO THE BISHOP

September 14

Dear Bishop:
  January was like the sun coming out after a long rain. The attitudes here were so positive. We were beginning the year with no little loan to pay regular budget expenses. People in the congregation were talking about how we had changed; no longer were we the "bitchy" congregation that we had been. We really enjoyed being with each other. It was obvious and infectious.

Then came March. Giving was down, and by April the council had to borrow some money to pay bills. Almost instantly the attitude became pessimistic. The sun went back under the clouds.

I recently have done some short one-on-one interviews with key parishioners. I explored their thoughts about what this church can be. There is a pessimistic stand that doesn't think we can continue much longer without yoking. Our giving has gone from $38,000 in 1986 to over $70,000 last year. In the past six years we have lost about sixty people to death and moving, and have only gained eleven new active members. Some leaders were unexpectedly pessimistic. Since January they have regressed to a survival mentality.

Conversation of yoking irritates me to no end. We have no reason to do that. There are many people in the community who are unchurched.

Since the neighboring parish is vacant, and the interim pastor is preparing them for the next step, maybe this is a time to explore a different staffing configuration for the four congregations. Maybe we could look at something like two ordained persons and one or two laypersons in a staff.

I would rather keep things as they are here. I think we are healed enough to say we are back at zero, at the starting point. I think I can provide what is needed to help them start to move ahead. I can give them at least three more years, or longer. Maybe they need to go through the exercise of making a decision about full-time resident pastoral ministry at this time.

November 18

Dear Bishop:

In my letter of September 14 I brought you up to date on where I think the congregation is at this time. I write now because of the year-end report that you are asking us to return to you. I have been trying to evaluate whether I am the one to lead this church on to the next stage of its journey. Here is what I think they need.

They are healthy now, so they can consider growing spiritually and in ministry, but there is a tremendous resistance. Something like inertia, or a hump to get over. I think a spiritual renewal is needed. I can't think of anything else that will enable folks to have the courage to embark on the journey.

I have been teaching and preaching on discipleship. I think they are very clear on what it means to be a disciple. But we don't have the motivation. We are tied up by terror of sharing our faith.

One parishioner and I have begun to work for consensus, through a prayer group. Six people met with us by specific invitation last Sunday. We reviewed our history together, and came to the conclusion that we have moved from unhealthy things and are now a healthy congregation. We asked them to prayerfully consider four things: (1) Would they pray for the well-being of this church and for God's direction on where we need to be going? (2) Would they pray with us for ten minutes before worship, and during worship? Pray for their pastor, for the words that he is preaching—that they would be God's words—and for the Spirit to show us what ministries we need to be doing. (3) Would they be part of a pastor/spouse support group? (4) Would they pray together with us in person, or in Spirit if they can't be there, during the daily prayer services that we have? The group was enthusiastic about the ideas. We hope this group will be able to reach out and bring in many more.

I am trying to preach a little different type of sermon, grace sermons. I sense that is what I need to do, but I'm not sure I can do it.

I would like to stay here; they trust me, I trust them. My wife and I like the community, the congregation has been Grandma and Grandpa to our son. But, the way I understand call, there are two reasons to leave a call: (1) Another call is presented. I don't think looking for another call is appropriate unless (2) the present call needs someone different. It is not what I want, but what the congregation needs that is important. How is that decision made? I *think* I know the situation here, *but do I?* How do I fill out your form?

AN EXCERPT FROM THAT PASTOR'S SERMON
ON THE SECOND SUNDAY AFTER EPIPHANY, JANUARY

The management committee and I have not seen eye to eye. I appreciate them letting me know that my comments in my annual report were offensive to them. Now, the management committee are great people. I ask for their forgiveness if I was inappropriate. The issue needs to be raised and discussed, openly and earnestly. My identity is that of pastor; part of what I am called to do is to interpret Scripture for our situation. You decide what you will do with that interpretation, but I would be amiss if I didn't give it. The issue raised is about affording ministry here. A legitimate question, but Scripture says it is not the first or most important question. Trust is the first issue. Stewardship is the next.

This church may be at a crossroads. If we begin shutting down, pulling in, watching our dollars, it becomes a spiral downward that will have a life of its own. If we trust, stretch out, pay benevolences first, try to grow in our ministry, God will bless us. The direction will be up.

ISSUES FOR DISCUSSION

1. How would you summarize the challenges the pastor is facing within the local congregation? within the denomination itself?
2. How would you respond in that situation?
3. Relate this situation to other documents presented in this chapter (e.g., the denominational statement in resource 1.3 or the arguments for closing the church in resource 1.5).
4. Why the mood swings? What could be going on in that congregation to trigger such a wide range of responses?
5. Where is the bishop coming from in all this?
6. What could the regional denominational body do to support this pastor and congregation in this personal and collective time of crisis?

1.5   Challenging the Assumptions: Five Reasons Why Most Rural Churches Should Be Closed

Following is a "think piece" used in a seminar conducted by the Center for Theology and Land staff for students preparing for rural pastorates. The devil's advocate approach is intended to stimulate discussion and raise issues about personal vocation, attitudes about the relationship between individual congregations and the denomination, and personal assumptions about rural congregations.

WHY CLOSE RURAL CHURCHES?

1. There are too many!
In most mainline denominations, small churches—generally rural—make up about 50 percent of the total number of churches in the denomination. Yet they usually only provide about 20 percent of the membership.

2. They are a financial drain!
Many small churches are subsidized or, if unsubsidized, do not provide much money to denominational mission programs. Realistically a congregation needs to have 150 members to support a full-time pastor. Without a full-time pastor they lack the necessary leadership and theological guidance.

3. Most rural churches practice civil religion!
Tradition is so entrenched in rural communities that churches are just extensions of civil life. It is often more important to have an American flag in front of the sanctuary than it is to have Bibles in the pews. Church confirmation class is a cultural rite, not a faith experience.

4. Denominational competition in rural communities is sinful!
Small communities were built on cooperation. Given the pressures on small communities from the outside world, congregations that squander precious resources on simply keeping a building open, instead of pooling resources, are sinful. Rural churches should embrace the parish concept.

5. Most rural churches are patriarchal/matriarchal, not inclusive!
Often, one or two families dominate a rural church. Power is not shared, and defending family control is more important than providing ministry to the community. Denominations should not waste resources supporting dysfunctional families.

ISSUES FOR DISCUSSION

1. Based on the other documents in this chapter and on your past experiences, do you agree with these arguments or disagree? Explain your reasons.
2. When debating these issues, seminarians tended to give economic and sociological reasons for closing the rural church, and spiritual and theological reasons for keeping it open. Analyze your own responses in that context.

Chapter 2

UNDERSTANDING THE RURAL CONTEXT

THAT night the Great Prairie stretched herself voluptuously; giantlike and full of cunning, she laughed softly into the reddish moon. "Now we will see what human might may avail against us! . . . Now we'll see!" . . .

And now had begun a seemingly endless struggle between man's fortitude in adversity, on the one hand, and the powers of evil in high places, on the other. . . . The devastation [the plague of grasshoppers] wrought was terrible; it made beggars of some, and drove others insane; still others it sent wandering back to the forest lands, though they found conditions little better there, either. . . . But the greater number simply hung on where they were. They stayed because of poverty, that most supreme of masters, had deprived them of the liberty to rise up and go away. And where would they have gone? In the name of Heaven, whither would they have fled?

. . . Beautiful out here on the wide prairie—yes, beautiful indeed!

—*O. E. Rolvaag,* Giants in the Earth, *349-50*

The Boone Brothers Auction House was plenty busy that spring, and for years to come, riding on the surging waves of the land as it rolled and shifted from farmer to farmer. I wasn't told where our dishes and our couches and our tractors and our pictures and our frying pans washed up. . . . No lives are lived any more within the horizon of your gaze.

[My sister] and I did share a legacy, our $34,000 tax bill on the sale of the properties. . . . I think of it as my "regret money," and though what I am regretful for mutates and evolves, I am glad to pay it, the only mortgage I will ever be given. . . . At any rate, regret is part of my inheritance.

. . . [A]lthough the farm and all its burdens and gifts are scattered, my inheritance is with me. . . . Lodged in my every cell, along with the DNA, are molecules of topsoil and atrazine and paraquat and anhydrous ammonia and diesel fuel and plant dust. . . .

. . . I think of the loop of poison we drank from, the water running down through the soil, into the drainage wells, into the lightless mysterious underground chemical sea. . . . I drive in the country, and see the anhydrous trucks in the distance, or the herbicide incorporators, or the farmers plowing their fields in the fall, or hills that are ringed with black earth and crowned with soil so pale that the corn only stands in it, as in gravel, because there are no nutrients to draw from it. . . .

. . . And when I remember that world, I remember my dead young self . . . remembering what you can't imagine.

—*Jane Smiley,* A Thousand Acres, *368-70*

Rural America: Utopia or Wasteland?

One cannot imagine a sharper contrast than that between O. E. Rolvaag's description of farming in the Heartland in the late 1800s (during the grasshopper infestation) or Jane Smiley's Pulitzer prize–winning novel about the farm crises of the 1980s and popular portrayals of rural life in contemporary video culture. Programs ranging from *Green Acres*, *The Beverly Hillbillies*, and *Mayberry R.F.D.*, at one end of the spectrum, to *The Waltons* and *Little House on the Prairie*, at the other, depict rural Americans either as amiably bumbling folk rooted in a laid-back, pastoral way of life or larger-than-life families who exhibit superhuman moral fiber and who triumph consistently over horrendous obstacles. Any random hour spent analyzing the images of rural life on a country music radio station offers yet another view entirely.

After reading Smiley's novel—which casts midwestern farm life in the dark framework of Shakespeare's *King Lear*—one member of an urban Iowa book club commented, "It bothered me, more than I can say. This is not the image that comes to mind when you pass those green fields and neatly kept farmyards. You might expect this in an urban ghetto or slum. But out here? This is not what I think about when I think of rural." The kinds of problems and issues apparent from even these brief excerpts from rural fiction have profound theological as well as socioeconomic ramifications. Note the deliberate use of biblical language by Rolvaag in the references to plague, scourge, and evil in high places. Similarly, as Smiley's central character shares her reactions to her father's incest and to the sale of her family's farm (the thousand acres they had fought so hard to accumulate, the ultimate measure of economic success), she evokes Old Testament biblical imagery of judgment raining down upon multiple generations.

Understanding the interconnectedness between economics, social issues, and theological underpinnings is essential for any pastor serving rural families as they respond to the realities of their lives—not only from a congregational studies perspective, but from the point of view of faith formation and spirituality.

As one rural farm woman asserts, "If there is a drought or a crop fails, that's fate . . . or the way it is. Stuff happens. But if the farm fails, that failure is highly personal. God's back must be turned somehow in judgment." Proclaiming a gospel of loving forgiveness and hope in such a context assumes an urgency and imperative all its own.

Toward a Definition of Rural: Setting the Parameters

At first glance, the culture of a small church in the hills of West Virginia may seem very different from that of a crossroads community on the Great Plains or from that of a small, heavy industry–based community in the Northeast—just as these popular and literary views of rural life diverge from one another. But the premise behind this text is that there are common qualities of "ruralness" that can be extrapolated from these settings, qualities that affect the life of parishioners and hence the role of pastor in various communities throughout the United States.

Numerous secular rural specialists and theologians share that view. Books such as Anthony G. Pappas's *Entering the World of the Small Church: A Guide for Leaders* analyze some of these factors:

1. Geography/Demographics. Community size and population density are factors that distinguish rural areas from urban areas. The positive side of the smaller scale associated with rural life is a potential for greater intimacy. But when it comes to standard governmental, welfare, and other social program guidelines, communities of fifty thousand or less tend to fall off the bottom of the charts and are often neglected. Isolation—or distance from other population clusters or major metropolitan centers—is another demographic, geographic characteristic associated with the rural experience, and here again, that quality has both positive and negative aspects.

2. Economy. (a) Land-centeredness contributes to what makes a community rural or urban, although, occupationally, agriculture may not necessarily be the predominant factor in local economic life. Classic examples are the small, rural, industrial towns of the Northeast where agriculture-related items are still prominent in the local hardware stores and a feed mill may still be marginally viable. (b) Economy-of-scale is an issue, in that maintaining services that are dependent upon volume can be difficult where the population is sparse: hence, the difficulty many rural communities have in funding schools and infrastructure, viable retail diversity, and human social services such as health care. (c) There is dependence, in many cases, on a single primary industry, such as agriculture, fishing, lumbering, mining, or—increasingly—retirement and recreation industries.

3. Population Characteristics. Stability is yet another factor that enters into the definition. Although there may be some urban immigration, that influx is relatively modest or has little impact on the power structure. Power tends to issue from a core of longtime or lifelong residents, many of whom have roots in the area for several generations. Witness Southampton, Long Island, New York where members of all dozen or so original families still play a decisive role in political and civic life—despite the huge influx of tourists and summer residents annually from Manhattan and New England population centers. In some rural communities in the Midwest and elsewhere with stagnating or declining economies, the population also may be aging disproportionately to other areas of the country; at the other end of the spectrum, where tourism is growing, the rapid influx of "outsiders" can radically alter the traditional character of a rural area and create tensions that overshadow tourism's economic benefits to the community. In some communities there is both a settled population and an influx of transient or welfare-dependent families.

4. Mind-set or Values. Values may be harder to measure or quantify than statistical or demographic indicators, but these in fact may be more significant than geography, socioeconomic factors, or population in defining what makes a community rural. Although the analogy needs to be taken with some caution, Pappas likens the operating value system and structure in small or rural American societies—and churches—to those of folk societies in developing nations, citing the following shared characteristics:

- Tradition (maintenance of the status quo) is more important than innovation or so-called progress (change). A stable population is going to have a relatively long, multigenerational memory, in which an individual (as well as the church) is viewed, not just in terms of the present, but through a whole series of past events and relationships.

- Life roles—for example, work and leisure—are more integrated or holistic than they are in complex, bureaucratically oriented urban environments.

- The land is a powerful factor in people's lives and identities. At heart, as one southwestern Iowa pastor put it, all rural residents are farmers. Even if they themselves are no longer actively farming, their lives are intrinsically bound up with the land.

- Experience and time are perceived as cyclical rather than linear. Seen through the lens of collective memory and tradition, innovation tends to be viewed with suspicion, as an unproductive reinventing of the wheel.

- Little value is placed on introspection or self-analysis, since custom (habit or ritual) tends to be accepted dogmatically as the best possible state of being.[1]

Rural sociologist Gary E. Farley focuses also on the importance of a similar culture or set of values as a measure of rural identity. Within that framework he stresses relational factors in particular (e.g., well-defined roles; "characters," all of whom have their unique niches in community life; a set of common rituals; and shared stories and experiences). He adds to that what he calls a strong sense of place and a unique kind of boosterism—partly affirmative and partly defensive—which maintains that "smaller" is somehow "better."[2]

Yet another specialist in the field of rural issues, Cornelia Flora, describes the essence of rural life in terms of (1) food security, (2) land stewardship, (3) connectedness to land and human relationships, and (4) protection of diversity.[3] Common identity is as important as economics and geography in defining a particular rural community or context. Efforts to maintain traditions amid external pressures for change are sources of strength as well as potential weakness. Although, as Flora writes, "Our society has become so deeply urbanized that we almost assume urbanization to be a natural law," when dealing with rural life, it is important to remember that crowding, fast-paced lifestyles, and constant innovation are not necessarily economically desirable any longer in a postindustrial age. The rural experience reminds us that "change should not be taken for granted."[4] (The toll of fast-paced urban life on health, the impact of high-density development as in south Chicago and elsewhere, and similar factors also can be cited to argue the case that faster and bigger are not inherently better.)

In *Dakota: A Spiritual Geography*, Kathleen Norris sets forth a poetic, spiritual view of the geography of rural America:

The land and sky of the West often fill what Thoreau termed our "need to witness our limits transgressed." Nature, in Dakota, can indeed be an experience of the holy.

More Americans than ever, well over 70 percent, now live in urban areas and tend to see Plains land as empty. What they really mean is devoid of human presence....

Dakota is a painful reminder of human limits, just as cities and shopping malls are attempts to deny them....

...The city no longer appeals to me for the cultural experiences and possessions I might acquire there, but because its population is less homogeneous than Plains society. Its holiness is to be found in being open to humanity in all its diversity. And the western Plains now seem bountiful in their emptiness, offering solitude and room to grow.[5]

Norris shares the vision of the monk who also has chosen this particular rural setting for his home, as "the stimulus to develop an inner geography." She writes that we are "really speaking of values when [we] find beauty in this land no one wants."

Still other scholars focus on "church types" as a primary tool of analysis in defining rural dynamics and identity. Works by Lyle Schaller *(The Small Church Is Different)* and Nancy Foltz *(Religious Education in the Small Membership Church)* offer important insights. In using church-type models based on size, however, it is essential to remember that numbers alone are not determinate in discussing the rural church, since some congregations in nonurban settings are larger than their urban counterparts, especially congregations in the inner city, where the resident population base is small.

All these factors—geography, economics, demographics, values, and lifestyle issues—suggest an inherent tension in rural life, a tension that influences the capacity or resistance of the rural community or church to respond to the enormous problems facing it. Economic and other factors in many rural communities are urging change. At the same time, the people who advocate such change are often considered suspect. If the impetus for change is internal, it can be perceived as disloyalty; if external, as an outright threat.

The sense of continuity and holism in rural communities, in short, can be a source of both great strength and potential weakness. If a pastor (as "outsider") perceives his or her role in prophetic terms—in other words, the pastor sees himself or herself as the resident agent of social change, with his or her own agenda—the pastor's efforts may encounter enormous resistance (see chapter 6, especially resource unit 6.6). Yet it can be frustrating (and may even be unscriptural—note, for example, Josh. 1:6-9 or 2 Tim. 4:1-5) to go into a rural setting with only a caretaker or chaplain model in view.

Such attitudes toward change do not necessarily suggest that rural America is doomed—or that the rural church is powerless, static, or incapable of growth. However, church development specialists (Pappas) and community development specialists (Cornman and Kincaid, *Lessons from Rural America*) concur that change must come from within. Revitalization may be interpreted as a dramatic call to action on the part of civic or congregational leadership; another alternative is to serve quietly as leaven in the lump—modeling values and behavior that can, over time, become infectious.

For both community and church, the essence of change may lie, not merely in innovative programs or activities, but in a different kind of relational journey. The Christian experience in such a context can become a vital force in renewal. Subtly and lovingly, the church can help rural

Americans gradually stretch and redefine their personal, congregational, and community roles.

Myths and Realities of Rural Life

If it ain't broke, don't fix it!" popular folk wisdom urges. Despite that adage, as well as the persistent myth that the rural America of our past was part of a kinder, gentler Golden Age that somehow needs to be revived, the realities of rural life are harsh.

Some novels, such as those of Rolvaag, depict pioneers on the western frontier who knew their share of hardships, poverty, isolation, and loneliness. Farming has always been a dangerous business. Technology has reduced some of the brutality of the labor itself and has increased yields for the amount of human energy expended. But the hazard to life and limb remains very real. Technology cannot totally predict, much less change or control, the weather. These are forces against which farm families have struggled since the first of our human ancestors harvested the fields.

Other perils facing rural America are economic in origin. As society becomes more complex—demanding survival in a global arena, not just a local or regional one—rural America needs to cope with problems of economic diversity that were not relevant a century ago. Economic units, rural or urban, built on a single base (be it agriculture, heavy industry, tourism, or something else) are operating at a distinct disadvantage. While some diversification has taken place in rural settings, most rural areas still rely primarily on agriculture.

Barriers to economic vitality in rural America may vary from region to region, but the pattern of problems is basically identical:

● Tax revenues are inadequate (based in part on the low population density) to maintain basic services or deal with socioeconomic problems.

● Services, infrastructure, and other indicators of quality of life erode.

● There is a decline in population and income

(related in many cases to deteriorating economic bases). In some areas, there is a related aging of the population as young people leave to pursue job opportunities elsewhere. That can further strain already diminished social services and tax revenues.

● Rural communities are politically isolated, and the government is unresponsive to the problems and diversity of rural America. In a society where "bigger" is frequently equated with "better," rural communities are at a disadvantage in competing for their share of attention, funding, and policy influence.

Attempts to grapple with some of these issues in recent years have met with varying degrees of success.

During the 1970s—after several decades of population decline and a decade before the so-called farm crisis—both the agricultural sector and rural population showed signs of stabilization, if not a modest revival:

● Population actually grew somewhat faster in rural areas (15.7 percent) than in metropolitan areas (9.9 percent), primarily in the West. Areas such as the Plains, the Corn Belt, and the South meanwhile experienced an ongoing decline.

● Nonagricultural wage and salary growth was higher in rural areas than in metropolitan areas. Median family income in rural areas had increased to nearly 80 percent of that for metropolitan families.

But for all the hopeful signs that rural America's economy was becoming more integrated and diversified, problems remained. A disproportionate percentage of the U.S. poor live in rural areas (39 percent compared to 28 percent for the population at large).

Some of the issues that face a rural resurgence are these:

● Overall, the problems of rural America are not a high national priority.

● Rural areas can best build coalitions around very specific issues such as housing, health, or other services, rather than large policy considerations such as community development or poverty.

● Some studies maintain that in the end, rural Americans in many cases do not press hard enough for their voices to be heard.

● It is counterproductive to use federal funds rather than grassroots resources to develop rural agencies and programs.

If a rural resurgence is to succeed, its viability lies in the ability of individuals and communities to empower themselves to build their futures.

The question becomes not just one of saving farms as viable economic units or even saving "rural life" as it existed in the past. The issue is not just a nostalgic yearning for green space or fears that rural America is destined to become a gigantic suburb or mass parking lot. What is at stake is whether there will be a healthy and distinct rural culture in the future, and what shape that rural life and lifestyle will take in the years ahead.

The Economic Geography of Rural America

The economic configurations of rural America are highly complex. Although it is an important part of that structure, *agriculture is by no means the only economic factor in rural America.* Consider some of the emerging business and industrial trends affecting rural communities. Regions that had, in the past, been highly agriculturally based have diversified their industrial base to include tourism and retirement communities.

In the Northeast, particularly the New England states, where agricultural production had been highly varied, tourism and cottage industries are now the primary economic support. In the Southeast and Appalachia, where tobacco production as an industrial base is still viable to some extent and where mining has been on the decline since the 1940s, cottage industries and tourism and retirement industries have strengthened the economy. In the Northwest, where

there has been a decline of the raw materials industries, tourism has been an important factor in strengthening the economy. In other regions, particularly the Midwest, where farming has become more mechanized and larger scale, localized agriculture-related manufacturing has suffered, particularly farm machinery manufacture. In the western states, Oklahoma, Texas, Colorado, and Wyoming have strong economies because of diversification; Utah, Nevada, and Idaho are more dependent on natural resources; the Southwest relies heavily on tourism and retirement industries; and California, the prime fruit and vegetable producer (along with Florida) has also overtaken Wisconsin and eastern Minnesota in dairy production.

In *The Nine Nations of North America*, Joel Garreau identifies geographic blocks of a different sort, based around cultural diversity patterns as well as economic factors. His divisions encompass the territories of the United States, Canada, Mexico, and the Caribbean Islands.

Even from such brief overviews, it is apparent how strongly geography and natural resources affected the way in which rural America developed. But these forces alone cannot explain the changing rural socioeconomic landscape.

Other Factors Affecting the Rural Economy

Ethnic and historical factors also shape what *rural* means in a given region. Five such areas and influences are (1) the Native American approach to land and land usage; (2) the New England covenant communities of the early English settlers, with their villages and farms neatly organized around common central squares and greens; (3) the southern model of plantations, based on European feudalism; (4) the inland crossroads communities of the Scottish settlers; and (5) the upper midwestern multiethnic rural areas, which adapted so quickly to the emerging agricultural technology of the mid- to late-1800s. In this model, both the ethnic origin of rural Americans and the date of settlement determine attitudes toward development, toward approaches to agriculture, and toward the community structure itself.

A word of caution is in order, however. Although such regional grouping has some validity, it is important not to lose sight of the great diversity of rural life. For example, missing from the foregoing list are such unique settings as Appalachia, the cattle and sheep cultures of the Rocky Mountain areas, the timber and fishing communities of the Northwest's industrial-agricultural regions, or the relatively late-developing rural economy of California.

Regardless of where one looks or how one carves up the rural landscape, one of the tragic trends in rural development over the past forty years has been the tendency for industries to relocate from one rural area to another, following the lure of cheaper labor. The lack of a national development policy has sometimes further encouraged piracy by one region of another region's companies and industrial resources. Some companies have found that labor force costs equalize rapidly, negating any financial advantages of moving their facilities. Still other entrepreneurs have learned to exploit the system. They milk or bilk an area's tax and other relocation incentives, then pull up stakes and move on before they are required to begin paying back some of that investment through long-term tax contributions. The real losers are the communities themselves; witness the numbers of abandoned plants and empty industrial parks in many rural areas, which represent economic investment and dashed hopes.

Agriculture: Upsizing or Downsizing?

Though agricultural production is not necessarily a definitive criteria for what makes a community rural, it is difficult to understand rural community in many regions of the country without some knowledge of the factors that shape contemporary farm life. Most debate centers on (1) the status of the family farm and the rise in corporate farming; (2) causes of the so-called farm crisis; and (3) environmental issues and agricultural productivity.

Table 2.1 documents the consolidation that has been taking place in recent decades in agricultural production in the United States—specifically the dramatic decrease in small, family-owned farm operations. Government, banks, and others have been blamed for this decline. Among the policies cited to explain this trend are

● subsidy policies that reward corporate farmers and penalize smaller landowners for holding land inactive.

● policies that encouraged small farmers to expand—during times of high land values—and overinvest in technology, increasing their debt burdens beyond a viable level. Then as land values declined, the lenders began to tighten credit and squeeze farmers into foreclosure.

● farming policies including use of chemical inputs, fall plowing, and so forth, which poison the groundwater, erode the soil, and otherwise damage the environment and harm the basic resources needed to sustain long-term farm production.

Currently there is much debate in the United States about discontinuing some forms of subsidy that discriminate against smaller farmers. Farmers themselves are taking proactive steps toward creating smaller-scale, more labor intensive agriculture that relies less heavily on expensive chemical inputs to boost yields that can be hazardous not only to soil and water resources, but also to the food products themselves.

Sustainable agriculture is one term used for this approach to farming. Other approaches to enhancing the viability of family farming include choosing products that lend themselves best to small-scale rather than large-scale production (e.g., specialty crops, organic foods) or combining entrepreneurial activities (e.g., rural bed-and-breakfasts) that can coexist well with traditional agriculture.

Farmers and agricultural specialists alike are sharply divided over the future of farms and farming in the United States. Some maintain that the demise of the small family farm is inevitable. Others argue that families who use multiple jobs off the farm, combined with specialized farming, will be able to keep small farms operating, while the real at-risk agricultural producers are those

Table 2.1 Number of Farms[6]

State	1980	1985	1990	1991	1992
AL	59,000	52,000	47,000	46,000	46,000
AK	450	660	580	560	540
AZ	7,500	8,500	7,800	8,000	8,000
AR	59,000	53,000	47,000	46,000	46,000
CA	81,000	83,000	85,000	83,000	81,000
CO	26,500	26,700	26,500	26,000	25,500
CT	4,200	4,100	3,900	3,900	3,900
DE	3,500	3,500	2,900	2,900	2,700
FL	39,000	39,000	41,000	40,000	39,000
GA	59,000	50,000	48,000	46,000	46,000
HI	4,300	4,600	4,600	4,600	4,500
ID	24,400	24,600	21,800	21,400	21,000
IL	107,000	93,000	83,000	82,000	81,000
IN	87,000	81,000	68,000	65,000	65,000
IA	119,000	111,000	104,000	102,000	102,000
KS	75,000	72,000	69,000	69,000	67,000
KY	102,000	100,000	93,000	91,000	91,000
LA	37,000	34,000	32,000	30,000	30,000
ME	8,300	7,500	7,200	7,100	7,100
MD	17,500	17,500	15,200	15,400	15,600
MA	6,200	6,500	6,900	6,900	6,900
MI	65,000	61,000	54,000	54,000	54,000
MN	104,000	96,000	89,000	88,000	88,000
MS	55,000	48,000	40,000	38,000	38,000
MO	120,000	114,000	108,000	107,000	107,000
MT	23,000	24,300	24,700	24,700	24,600
NE	65,000	60,000	57,000	56,000	56,000
NV	2,900	2,700	2,500	2,500	2,500
NH	3,400	3,400	2,900	2,900	2,900
NJ	9,400	9,100	8,100	8,300	8,500
NM	13,500	14,000	13,500	13,500	13,500
NY	47,000	47,000	38,500	38,000	38,000
NC	93,000	79,000	62,000	60,000	60,000
ND	40,000	35,500	34,000	33,000	33,000
OH	95,000	90,000	84,000	80,000	78,000
OK	72,000	73,000	70,000	70,000	71,000
OR	35,000	37,000	36,500	37,000	37,500
PA	62,000	58,000	53,000	53,000	52,000
RI	860	770	740	700	700
SC	34,000	28,000	25,000	24,500	24,500
SD	38,500	37,000	35,000	35,000	35,000
TN	96,000	95,000	89,000	87,000	88,000
TX	196,000	194,000	186,000	185,000	183,000
UT	13,500	14,000	13,200	13,300	13,200
VT	7,700	7,300	7,000	6,900	6,900
VA	58,000	56,000	46,000	45,000	44,000
WA	38,000	38,000	37,000	37,000	38,000
WV	22,000	22,000	20,500	20,000	20,000
WI	93,000	86,000	80,000	79,000	79,000
WY	9,100	9,100	8,900	9,000	9,200
TOTAL	2,433,110	2,311,330	2,127,220	2,093,060	2,003,940

in the medium size range: in other words, only small and large farms are going to survive.

Still others contend that corporate farms and family farms are not mutually exclusive terms. A model is emerging in which some huge corporate farms, in the West in particular, operate under a structure in which *financing* is large-scale and sometimes external to the community, while the *day-to-day production* is still in the hands of families indigenous to the area.

Others raise the interesting parallels between the farm crises in America and in the former Soviet Union. At the very point that the large, centrally operated collectives in the lands of the former Soviet Union are breaking up, some specialists in the United States are pressing for large, corporate farming as the wave of the future. However, in light of the successes of some small, low-input farming, if all the costs (water, chemical inputs, machinery, land, etc.) are factored into the mix, large farming may have gone beyond the scale of efficiency and viability.

Where production and processing have been subsumed under nearly monopolistic conglomerate ownership, others warn of the dangers of allowing our nation's food supply and policies to be governed by or dependent upon a handful of multinational corporations.

According to figures released by the Agricultural Statistics Board in July of 1992, both the number of farms in the United States and the acres of land in farms was decreasing.

The number of farms in the United States in 1992 is estimated at 2.096 million, down less than one percent from 1991. Total land in farms is 980 million acres, down 2.7 million acres from last year. The rate of decline in number of farms and land in farm acreage slowed while the average farm size increased from 467 acres in 1991 to 468 in 1992.

Texas remains the state with the most farms, 183,000, down 2,000 from a year earlier. Missouri is second with 107,000 farms, the same as last year, followed by Iowa with 102,000 farms, also unchanged from 1991. In addition to Texas, Ohio and Kansas experienced the largest decrease in farm numbers with each down 2,000 farms from a year earlier.

Seven states showed increases in number of farms: Oklahoma, Tennessee, and Washington, up 1,000 each to 71,000, 88,000, and 38,000, respectively; Oregon up 500 to 37,500; and New Jersey, Maryland, and Wyoming up 200 each to 8,500, 15,600, and 9,200, respectively. Twenty-eight states remained the same as a year ago, and the other fifteen states showed a decline from last year.

Texas continued to lead the nation in land in farms, 130 million acres, down 1 million from 1991.

The number of farms in the economic sales class between $1,000 and $9,999 increased from 1.003 million in 1991 to 1.006 million in 1992. Those with sales in the $10,000–$99,999 group decreased from 775,100 to 763,200. The $100,000 and over group declined from 327,060 to 326,340 farms.

Estimates for the number of farms and land in farms refer to June 1. A farm is defined as "any establishment from which $1,000 or more of agricultural products were sold or would normally be sold during the year."[7]

Problem or Opportunity?

I s the economic picture for rural America a uniformly bleak one? Not at all. Certain economic growth possibilities have emerged in recent years.

The emergence of the Information Age has opened an economic window of opportunity for rural America. Small rural businesses can compete internationally by utilizing computer technology. Areas with access to interstate highway systems are finding that they can successfully compete for certain kinds of new business development, including (1) wholesaling and warehousing, and (2) mail- and telemarketing-related service and sales businesses. In these types of businesses, infrastructure such as sewers and high levels of energy output (electricity in particular) are not crucial. Hence a small town or cluster of towns with an adequate regional labor supply can be as good a site as any urban area.

Among the positive options, some rural communities are finding growth potential in specialized agriculture. Gourmet and health food items (such as pesticide-free crops, herbs, and "baby vegetables") in some cases can bring far higher prices than traditional grains and similar products. Traditional rural crafts and handiwork produced large-scale can result in lucrative cottage industries. In both these cases, marketing is a key to make such specialized ventures profitable.

Still other rural areas are discovering that opening their doors to tourism or serving as retirement communities for urban refugees can stem declining populations and bring in new revenues and jobs. Even communities that do not boast natural wonders or recreational facilities have discovered ways to market themselves: small-town-USA tours, bed-and-breakfasts, weeks on a working family farm. Tourist business, however, can be seasonal or very economy-dependent. Attracting large numbers of retirees can put enormous strains on rural social services and lead to unanticipated tax burdens.

Other proposed directions for the rural economy are less promising. Among the most controversial prospects is the growing trend of using rural America as a dumping ground for the toxic wastes and garbage generated by major urban centers. Despite some potential for growth, the economies of rural America are still anything but booming. How to revitalize the rural economy is a question that has remained ignored or unanswered since the heyday of the rural awareness movement in the 1970s.

The Politics of Population

I f we were to compare maps describing population density and poverty levels in our country, the economic patterns of urban and rural America would emerge clearly. *Isolation and low population correlate with economic malaise, as well as contribute to a political powerlessness that makes it difficult for rural needs to be heard and addressed.* Given the high national debt and limited resources available for national economic programs, what voice can rural America realistically have in calling attention to its problems and issues?

In analyzing the results of a recent presidential election, at a national conference of mayors, Maynard Jackson, mayor of Atlanta, called for an aggressive new urban policy to help the cities of the United States: 80 percent of the American population, he reminded CNN viewers, live on 2 percent of this country's land. Yet, he added, the problems plaguing the cities are not unique, but are experienced in communities large and small all over the United States, particularly a deteriorating infrastructure that makes not only daily life but also any kind of job development difficult. Factories and companies need adequate roads, bridges, and water and sewage treatment plants in order to operate.

Though acknowledging that such needs are not unique to urban America, leaders such as Jackson couple such appeals with the not-so-subtle reminder that numbers in American cities justify prioritizing their plight. In our democratic system, numbers talk. The terrible dilemma facing rural America is that it may have more miles of roads, more tiny and decaying sewage systems, and more bridges with which to cope than its urban counterparts; but those necessities are also more spread out and affect—individually, at least—fewer people.

Even if politics did not play a role in targeting money and resources where the population is concentrated, the sheer logistics of rebuilding rural America's infrastructure are formidable. On a limited scale, innovative efforts have been made in recent years to cope with some of these problems. Is steel too expensive a replacement for deteriorating rural bridges that see relatively little traffic? In Pennsylvania, a coalition of educational institutions and the lumber industry have been experimenting with hardwood bridges as a possible alternative. To some, a return to the wooden bridge is more than just a nostalgic symbol of rural America's past. The Pennsylvania example may signal to other states and regions that "appropriate technology" may prove far more practical in some instances than recent, high-tech options. After decades of building better mousetraps, we may yet discover that tradition and simplicity, not advanced technology, hold the key to a rural revival. Sustainable agriculture is making some of the same claims by appealing both to environmental concerns and to dollars and cents.

There is no one standard definition of what makes a community or area *rural* demographically. The 1990 U.S. Census offers the following parameters for what constitutes *urban:*

The urban population comprises all persons living in (a) places of 2,500 or more inhabitants incorporated as cities, villages, boroughs (except in Alaska and New York), and towns (except in the New England States, New York, and Wisconsin) but with low population density in one or more large parts of their area; (b) census designated places (previously termed unincorporated) of 2,500 or more inhabitants; and (c) other territory, incorporated or unincorporated, included in urbanized areas. An urbanized area comprises one or more places and the adjacent densely settled surrounding territory that together have a minimum population of 50,000 persons.

By default, everything else is considered *rural*.

Complex? Yes. So much so that in terms of population density, some rural sociologists argue that it may be most realistic to skip over arguments that try to define "how small is small?" and designate as rural any county that is nonmetropolitan according to census statistics—bearing in mind that some nonmetropolitan areas are growing increasingly close to metropolitan areas.

Rural: More Than a Numbers Game

In the end, defining "ruralness" has as much to do with quality of lifestyle as size or demographics. But to the extent that numbers affect relative political power or powerlessness and the self-esteem of a particular community, an effective pastor in a rural setting cannot afford to ignore such considerations. The resource units that follow are challenges to develop a greater sensitivity to how geography, economics, and demographic factors can influence the congregation and shape the community empowerment process. The questions for discussion, in particular, set the stage for consideration of other elements of congregational studies later in the text.

RESOURCES FOR UNDERSTANDING THE CONTEXT

The units listed below can be used to encourage problem solving and discussion around key rural issues. For use in educational contexts, suggested materials to be placed on reserve in the library or assigned as text supplements are also listed.

2.1 Biblical, Literary, and Popular Tools for Analyzing Rural Life
2.2 The Media Looks at Rural Life
2.3 Poverty and Population: A View from the Pulpit
2.4 Advocacy from a Client's View
2.5 The Rural Community at the Crossroads: The Business Community
2.6 Issues Affecting the Agricultural Community
2.7 Community Development and the Church: Secular Venture or a Matter of Mission?
2.8 Assessing Your Congregation's Context

2.1 Biblical, Literary, and Popular Tools for Analyzing Rural Life

● **Study the passages** from *Giants in the Earth* and *A Thousand Acres* quoted at the beginning of chapter 2 in the context of the full chapters of those novels. Other possibilities and sources can be drawn from the recommended resources listed at the end of this book.

● **Now, listen to a country music radio station.** Based on the songs you hear (Garth Brooks, Wynona, Vince Gill, and others), what factors and problems would seem to be of importance to rural Americans? Do the songs idealize or portray a balanced view of rural life? How do the lyrics differ in songs recorded by men when compared to those recorded by women country singers? How do these perceptions differ from those in the novels?

● **Interpret these views in a biblical perspective.** For example, discuss the undercurrent in the Rolvaag and Smiley excerpts that establishes a link between devastation related to the land and divine judgment in light of the following passages from the Old Testament:

You shall not make for yourself an idol, whether in the form of anything that is in heaven above, or that is on the earth beneath, or that is in the water under the earth. You shall not bow down to them or worship them; for I the Lord your God am a jealous God, punishing children for the iniquity of parents, to the third and the fourth generation of those who reject me. . . . (Exod. 20:4-5)

Parents shall not be put to death for their children, nor shall children be put to death for their parents; only for their own crimes may persons be put to death. (Deut. 24:16)

Based on such sources, which view of human/divine interaction appears to prevail in rural communities, the one in Exodus or the one in Deuteronomy? How does the New Testament address this subject? How could a pastor address these issues of guilt and judgment in the context of Christian education, preaching, or counseling of parishioners in times of crisis such as the ones Rolvaag and Smiley describe? (In a survey in eastern Iowa following the summer floods of 1993, more than half the population interpreted the devastation as "an act of God"—i.e., a divine judgment of some sort.)

2.2   The Media Looks at Rural Life

The selection "Farm Woes," on the plight of the farmer in the Midwest, is excerpted here as a check on your stereotypes of what rural ministry is like. Before you read it consider these exercises:

● Select a geographic area (one of interest to you or in which you might be likely to serve) and then consider the following: (1) If you were to receive a call or appointment to a rural or small-town church in that region, what kinds of economic and related social problems would you expect to find in your congregation? (2) What would you expect your ministry to be like during the course of your first month? Year? (The introductory material in this chapter can also be used to support your perceptions.)

● Test your predictions against these observations by Kathleen Norris in her book *Dakota: A Spiritual Geography:*

[M]any of South Dakota's new jobs are on the low end of the pay scale. . . . As a friend put it, "If we don't watch out, we'll become a Taiwan on the Prairie."
    . . . Less visible than the poor in urban areas, they are afflicted by physical isolation in particularly severe ways. People who are laid off in my town have to travel one hundred miles to a Job Service office in order to register for benefits, and there is no public transportation on the route.
    . . . [M]any Dakotans retain an appalling innocence about what it means to be rural in contemporary America. The year we lost our J. C. Penney store, young people were quoted in the town's weekly newspaper as saying they'd like to see a McDonald's or a K Mart open in its place. . . . Since there is no market here, nothing that counts demographically, we don't exist.[8]

Farm Woes

Crisis Not Over; Tragedy Common
  by Steve Webber, *(Dubuque) Telegraph-Herald*
  September 20, 1992

- Divorce.
- Spousal rape.
- Incest.
- Child abuse.
- Suicide.
- Stress-related sickness.

Evidence of the disintegration of families in Chicago?
Maybe. But not in this case.
Oh, then Detroit? The inner city?
No. Closer to home. A lot closer.

This is the tragic checklist on some farmers in the Dubuque area who are not coping with the '90s, farmers too embarrassed about the tatters of their lives to talk to a reporter, even with the promise that their name will be omitted. Farmers who are not just forsaking their barns, fields and cows, but are leaving their wives and kids. Some even take their lives.

The Rev. Norm White knows the pain of the average farmer. For 10 years, his flock has been farmers on the edge—hard-working, self-reliant people who swallow their pride and ask the church for help.

Wait a minute, you ask White, haven't we left the farm crisis behind? Aren't things a lot better down on the farm in the '90s?

For some, says the rural life director of the Archdiocese of Dubuque, but for many farm families in the tri-state area the crisis remains. . . .

"They feel that if the farm crisis is over and I'm in trouble, it must be me," White says.

Charlotte Halvorson also knows the anguish of the average farmer. She's been counseling farm families for five years as rural health coordinator for Mercy Center St. Joseph's Unit in Dubuque.

. . . What makes things more difficult for farmers is the misconception that the farm crisis is over. . . .

"From my perspective the mid-'90s are going to be just as bad or worse than the '80s," Halvorson said. "And the sad reality is that to survive, some are going to have to get out."

"Politicians are yelling about family values when our strong family values in the Midwest on the family farm are vanishing," she said.

Two-thirds of the people Mercy treats for stress or mental illness "are farm families and rural folks." High blood pressure, depression and diabetes lead the parade of farm family maladies.

Last year, Halvorson answered three different suicide calls within one month. . . .

"I wish every politician could go with me for a week and see and hear the actual struggle these families are going through," [Roberta] Hinman [outreach worker and farm development specialist with Iowa State University] said. . . .

. . . The signs of a farm family under stress are easy to see.

"The living quarters are not well kept, the dishes are not done, the children are dirty—or not as clean as they should be—or it's just the opposite."

Hinman said some farm families are so embarrassed that they try to hide the symptoms.

"The cupboards are usually pretty bare. They've got canned vegetables, but they can't buy meat."

Now, you might think it ironic that a farm family would be short of food, she said, but farmers can't just butcher their cattle for meat if that animal has been pledged as security on a loan. . . .

Hinman said it's not unusual for a farm family of five to have only $90 a month for living expenses. . . .

So what can be done to help?
First . . . get rid of some of the misconceptions.
Such as?

- They're young. They'll make it. . . . Younger farmers are giving up much quicker than their parents. . . .
- It is wrong to assume that a struggling farmer "is someone who has made some major mistake," said Halvorson.

"When you're a farmer who loses a farm, you're considered a bad person or a bad manager, but when a businessman loses his business, he's considered a victim of the times."

● It is wrong to believe that modern farmers are growing and making everything they need for themselves.

"In the 1960s, they got $2.40 for a bushel of corn and they paid $25,000 to $30,000 for a combine," Hinman said. "Today, they're still getting $2.40 to $2.50 for a bushel of corn, but the combine costs $100,000. We're not gaining." . . .
Then what?

● Get money from food subsidies to the small farmers who need it.
● Get food for farmers.
● Get medical assistance for farmers.
● Get them better education.

That's the laundry list of ideas from these farm experts.
White argues that farm subsidies should be given to small- and medium-size farms, rather than spread across all farm operations, regardless of size.
"We need a sense of community, learning from each other, supporting each other," White said.
White questions politicians who say they are helping farmers by expanding markets. "What does that do for prices?" . . .
Struggling farm families are cutting corners on essentials and looking elsewhere for the income.
That's cutting into safety for young people and older people left to keep the farm going and it's causing a rash of health problems, Halvorson said. . . .
And the job in town, often for minimum wages, is no guarantee of insurance.
"In some cases, they're both working off the farm. They're going without insurance," White said. "Mom and Dad are putting off medical care."
Halvorson said that causes a domino effect.
"They're working with less rest and little, if any, recreation time," Halvorson said. "The No. 1 effect is safety, because they're always tired. And No. 2 is health hazards, because they're not taking care of themselves." . . .
As farm parents do more off-farm work, Halvorson sees retired relatives pitching in. But they have "hearing loss, slower reflexes and all the things that go with the natural aging process, and account for 25 to 30 percent of all farm accidents."
She also worries about farm children who take on more responsibility.
"On a family farm that's very much what it is—a way of life . . . but they're operating very powerful equipment, and what you know and can do at 15 and 16 isn't the same as what you know when you're 30 to 35."
Farm children suffer the most, evidently from the stress of keeping a family farm going, Hinman said. You see it in their eyes, she said.
"They're not wearing Nikes," she said. "Some haven't worn new clothes to school for a couple of years.
"I see a lot of acting up, withdrawal and behavioral problems, because they were used to doing things after school," Halvorson said.
"If they don't have money, that means no sports—no extra-curricular activities." . . .
Then there's the matter of affording health care.
. . . Sue Welu, a social worker for Mercy's Rural Outreach Program . . . said many farm parents are forgoing the care they need so they can afford it for their children. . . .
Hinman said anyone who takes up farming these days "has got to be God-sent.
"They've got to be a swine expert, a dairy expert, a crops specialist, a chemical specialist, and a financial manager. . . ."
And many farmers would benefit from more education about how to break into "niche markets for chemical-free, value-added farm products," White said. That education is not easy to come by. . . .
Word spreads "pretty quick when a farm family is in trouble," Hinman said. "All of a sudden nobody wants to talk to you at church. Friends and business people no longer want to talk to you. Some won't even take your personal check. They could know you for 20 or 25 years, but now . . . all of a sudden they don't feel like belonging to our church anymore or they quit completely because of strictly financial reasons—that should never be."

ISSUES FOR DISCUSSION

1. If you were serving as a new pastor in a congregation in an area similar to that described in "Farm Woes" or in *Dakota*, what strategies would you consider to begin helping your parishioners deal with the issues and problems these farm experts discuss? What role could the church itself play in these strategies?
2. Consider how passages such as Matthew 2:6 and Luke 15:8-9 treat these issues of poverty, numbers, and political power.

2.3 Poverty and Population: A View from the Pulpit

The following excerpt from "The Least of These," a sermon by Mary Lee Daugherty of the Appalachian Ministries Educational Resource Center (AMERC) at Wartburg/University of Dubuque theological seminaries in September 1992, puts issues of rural poverty in a global context.

As an Appalachian woman, permit me to share with you a vision for the church's mission and future theological education as we enter the twenty-first century. As we listen to the Gospel of Matthew [25:31-46], we realize that this passage connects us with the nitty-gritty issues of daily life. It's about food, water, clothing, sickness, and imprisonment.

Jesus repeats the central message four times in fifteen verses to be sure we get the point. According to Matthew's Gospel, this passage was given during the *final week of Jesus' life*, when his words were highly focused as he moved toward his own physical death.

We are perhaps surprised by the *criteria* God uses for judging the nations of the world. The question is not, "What we have believed doctrinally—or how well have we preached the gospel?" The question is, *"How have we treated and taken care of the least of these?"* Have we provided food, water, and clothing for them? Have we seen that they received proper treatment for their sicknesses?

. . . In other words, what have we done to relieve the physical human suffering which is so broad in our land? That's the question.

In 1960, after I graduated from the Presbyterian School of Christian Education and from Union Seminary, I went as one of your Presbyterian missionaries to Brazil. . . . You need to know that the conditions I observed and lived among in that "third-world" country are now to be found in our own country.

The "third world" is today in cities like Washington, D.C., New York, and Richmond, Virginia. And in the 399 rural counties of Appalachia—where . . . I live. . . . Counties of poverty are found in (1) the thirteen-state Appalachian region; (2) the Black belt of the South; (3) along the lower border counties of Texas (where many Hispanics live); (4) in the West among those counties where mostly Native Americans live; and (5) yes, they are also in Alaska (where the American Eskimo lives). They are all rural counties and they are all counties of hard-core poverty. They are our own U.S. "third world." The 1990 census revealed that *there are now more [such poverty-stricken] counties—more poor living in rural America—than in our largest cities.* Since the rural poor are more dispersed, they are harder to identify and locate than the poor in our inner cities.

The rural poor are hidden by interstate highways—upon which we speed by so swiftly. They are found up the "hills and hollers" of Appalachia. At the end of dusty roads where coal trucks park. Or at the end of a dirt path leading to a small farm.

In October 1989, the University of Kentucky released a new study on the Appalachian region. It is a heart-rending study which reveals that in all of our coal producing counties of Appalachia, 50 percent of our children now live below the poverty level. This is every other child. And in all of rural America, 25 percent (one out of four children) now live below the poverty line.

. . . Do you also know that in rural America today Blacks are 11 percent poorer than they are in our inner cities? Do you know that Appalachia's Native Americans—the Cherokees living on the Cherokee Indian

Reservation in North Carolina—are even poorer than Blacks in rural America? As terrible as this is for Blacks and Native Americans, do you know that 75 percent of all the poor in rural America have white faces?

The only difference is that poverty still affects more total lives in Brazil than are yet affected in our nation. When I graduated . . . and went to Brazil—I experienced the real beginning of my own conversion experience as a Christian and educator. As I witnessed the poverty of so many of God's people, I began to experience what I now call, "REVERSE EVANGELISM." The poor began to convert me—to teach me. . . . Are you in the conversion process?

1. Jesus Christ is Lord; and we are in ministry because of the gospel message of hope.

2. Appalachia is a precursor for what we all now observe happening in the rest of our nation. We believe we are witnessing the "Appalachinization" of America.

3. Fundamental economic shifts going on in our nation are resulting in further bifurcation (i.e., more gentrification) and at the same time, more welfare. Therefore, many more people in our country will be 50 percent dependent on some form of transfer payment.

4. There is a loss of cultural identity in Appalachia. We, like others, are being co-opted by the dominant North American culture.

5. We, as poor Whites, see on TV what we don't have—thus despair and a sense of the internalization of self-hate is greater than ever before. As poor Whites, we can't blame race and a history of slavery—nor do we speak a different language (such as Spanish)—so what is wrong with us? We can't make it either.

6. Secularization will mean that we will be less effective in our evangelistic task of reaching the unchurched, unless we learn to not only preach but also to *act*, together as Christians, in new and different ways.

7. In many rural counties after school consolidation, the church is the only . . . remaining social institution left where the poor may turn for help.

8. . . . Values placed on indigenous or old religious forms and expressions native to the region may mean pastors will not be easily interchanged from other parts of the nation unless they are specifically trained and have an understanding and appreciation of the local history, the culture of Appalachia, and rural values.

9. Outmigration of thirty- to sixty-year-olds will continue for economic reasons—resulting in increasing parochialism. The "brain drain" will continue.

10. Rural "shopping malls" will become commonplace every thirty miles or so. We might well call this the "Wal-Marting" of America. Rural churches will also increasingly be on thirty-mile grids rather than the six-mile grids of the horse-and-buggy days.

11. Rural poverty and fewer resources will force the churches to work in more ecumenical fashion in order to survive . . . (e.g., more multidenominational community churches).

12. There will be more trained lay preachers [and "second career" pastors and Christian educators who can work bivocationally].

13. Ministry will increasingly be understood as empowerment and enablement of the poor.

14. Clergy of the twenty-first century must see themselves as servants of the poor—not as specialized professionals. They must be willing to work and live among the poor at minimal salaries.

One of the most distressing questions I have repeatedly heard at [seminary graduations] is "How much is your total package?" We all need to survive—but how much is "enough"? How do we, as Christians, measure success? If we are only willing to serve the educated middle class we will continue to find our numbers shrinking, our churches closing. . . . We cannot afford the elitist theological structures we have created in the past.

ISSUES FOR DISCUSSION

1. How does Daugherty's analysis square with concepts of the United States as one of the wealthiest countries in the world?
2. How does Daugherty's analysis square with our views of urban and rural needs?

2.4 Advocacy from a Client's View

W here a numbers-oriented mind-set prevails, rural areas are at a distinct disadvantage. That applies both to the voice an individual community has in affecting policies and to a community's ability to attract external support and funding. In short, lack of numbers makes small communities a low priority—in other words, powerless. Such biases often prevail not just within secular agencies, but within the church as well, despite Christ's pointed reminder that every sparrow is precious in God's order of things.

Bureaucratic structures also function as barriers to economic, political, and social justice for rural communities. Although metropolitan areas are relatively cohesive as geographic service units, rural people may find themselves literally all over the map depending on which agency or organization is involved. *Where does one turn for help?* The solution to accessibility is rarely straightfoward. Geographic and economic factors can result in rural pastors experiencing similar neglect. With limited incomes and professional travel budgets, geographic isolation can cut them off from meaningful contact with both peers and the national church.

Multiple factors work against rural residents in accessing support: (1) lack of privacy in small towns, which leads people to fear confiding in others; (2) an ethos of independence and self-reliance that interprets outreach as meddling and receiving aid as weakness; (3) lack of local services; and (4) overlapping jurisdictions that confuse individuals about where to turn.

EXCERPTS FROM AN IOWA COUNTY HUMAN SERVICES DIRECTORY

Agricultural agencies:
Department of Natural Resources
Environmental Protection Agency
Groundwater Hotline (EPA)
Horticulture Answer Line
Iowa Agricultural Development Authority
Iowa Agricultural Statistics
Iowa Cattleman Hotline
Iowa Department of Agriculture
Iowa Farm Unity Coalition
National Pesticide Network
Rural Concern Hotline
Rural Outreach—1440 program
State ASCS
USDA Fraud and Abuse Hotline
USDA Meat and Poultry Hotline

Employment:
Dislocated Farmers—JTPA
Dislocated Homemakers—JTPA
Iowa Department of Employment Services
Iowa Vocational Rehabilitation
Job Service of Iowa
Proteus (migrant/farm workers)

Food/Shelter:
County Relief (housing/rent)
County Food Pantry

Human Services (food stamps/AFDC)
Northeast Iowa Housing Authority
Operation: New View (food/clothing)

Business agencies:
Disaster (SBA)
IDED Small Business Help Line (start-up)
Small Business Administration (aid)

Emotional support/Counseling
1440 Outreach Worker (in-home support)
AIM Teen Line
ANEW (Assurance Network Easing Widows)
Catholic Charities
Child/Dependent Adult Abuse
County Substance Abuse Agency
Domestic Abuse Hotline
Gamblers Anonymous
Lutheran Social Services
Parents Anonymous
Regional Mental Health Center
Rural Life Office

Families:
Child Abuse Prevention
Child Abuse Reporting
Domestic Abuse Hotline
Home Economics Answer Line
Iowa Commission on Status of Women
Parents Anonymous
Services for Abused Women
Social Security Hotline

Government:
Social Security
State Fire Marshall
Governor, Legislators (state/federal)

ISSUES FOR DISCUSSION

1. Look at this excerpt from a family resource directory for one Iowa county from the point of view of the average citizen needing help, a local agency staff member, a rural pastor, and a staff member from the regional or national church. Where would you go if you needed help? If such a directory did not exist, what would you do? How could the church cut through the bureaucracy? Given the fragmentation, what impact might unified advocacy from the religious community play in empowering rural Americans?

2. Now, look at the list as a set of opportunities for partnership in ministry. How could you find out which agency provides which services? Two places to start: (a) Visit the closest extension office and ask about their services. (b) Visit the human services (welfare and social services) office nearest you and ask them about their services and where you might go to find out more about these essential partners.

2.5 The Rural Community at the Crossroads: The Business Community

Some rural sociologists and economists have advanced the theory that the Wal-Mart store phenomenon—placing discount stores in magnet mid-sized rural communities—has been responsible for the destruction of the indigenous local retail and commercial community in many rural areas. Nationwide buying by such chains enables them to undercut pricing, offer wider variety, and compete so effectively as to drive smaller locally owned stores out of business. As more and more empty storefronts have appeared along Main Street Rural U.S.A., fewer customers have bothered to patronize the few remaining commercial establishments. Regional supermarkets and regional gas station/food shops have driven local groceries, restaurants, and gas stations out of business. Usually, the neighborhood bar has been the last remaining commercial institution to hang on. In short, Wal-Mart has been cast as the villain.

Interestingly enough, similar arguments were raised in the sixties concerning the suburban shopping malls that put pressure on urban downtown shopping areas. Statistics, however, revealed a different picture. When urban downtown merchants repositioned themselves—carved out specialized areas of the commercial market—their business did not decline, but rather *increased* after mall construction.

It can be argued that the demise of rural retail communities is a function of ineffective leadership from merchants and business associations, *not* an *inevitable* result of the chain stores.

Problems, Misconceptions	Underlying Issues
1. Merchants misunderstood the relationship between store and customer.	1. Customers do not owe a store loyalty. They base their buying decisions on convenience, price, and service.
2. Merchants failed to position themselves effectively.	2. If a store cannot possibly carry the same variety that a chain can, the merchant needs to (a) analyze her or his customers and identify items the store can stock that would be more easily purchased locally (i.e., not worth a fifteen to twenty minute drive) or that generic chains would not be likely to carry; and (b) offer services (repair, longer hours, unusual combinations of merchandise, return policies, etc.) that give customers individualized help and support that a chain is not likely to provide.
3. Merchants failed to reinvest in their businesses and in their communities. As one store owner we interviewed in a crumbling turn-of-the-century building put it, "For three generations, my family made a terrific living in this one-horse town. I can't wait to sell this place and move to Florida."	3. A town can only be as progressive as its leadership. Time does not stand still. We either change to meet changing conditions or we stagnate and decline. Without reassessment and reinvestment, no business is going to be successful.

Kathleen Norris describes how resistance to change can damage the rural community:

As [local business people's] frame of reference diminishes, so do their aspirations and their ability to adapt to change.... But the sad truth is that the harder we resist change, and the more we resent anyone who demands change of us, the more we shortchange ourselves.... When such attitudes come to prevail in a town, family is still important but community may not be.[9]

The material in this section will demonstrate that retail decline in the face of competition is not inevitable. It is clear that the arrival of discount giants destabilizes local businesses. Whether that is eventually negative is open to debate.

PUTTING WAL-MART IN PERSPECTIVE

Is Wal-Mart a corporate Goliath? a boon to rural consumers or a town-killer? a wake-up call for rural business to revitalize itself?

● The downtown of Waverly, Iowa, lost eight businesses in the first year Wal-Mart came to town because Wal-Mart's prices were often lower than local merchants' wholesale rates. Hardware stores and supermarkets were hardest hit. But, as *U.S. News and World Report* found, Wal-Mart's

competitive hammering . . . gives some businesses a needed jolt, forcing them to develop special niches or services. . . . Merchants who survive the first few years of coexistence . . . usually end up flourishing. Iowa State's survey found that per capita sales in Wal-Mart towns increase faster than the state average because the discount giant lures shoppers from a larger geographic area. . . . Noncompeting businesses stand to benefit . . . however, merchants in smaller towns nearby often suffer.[10]

● In "Flight or Fight: The Town That Took on Wal-Mart—and Won," an article for *American City & County*, Patrick Rains raises the question of whether Wal-Mart obstructs or proactively stimulates development in small communities.

As the nation's largest retailer, Wal-Mart has almost 1,700 locations across the country, with many in small towns. . . . Wal-Mart's philosophy of large discounted prices has sounded the death knell for many "mom and pop" operations.

A study of 15 small Iowa towns with Wal-Marts notes that 80 percent of their business comes at the expense of local retailers. . . .

However Fred Nelson, the owner of Nelson Mill & Agri-Center . . . did not wait to be run out of business. [He chose to] stock better brands, offer more service, ease his return policy, extend his store hours and open on Sundays.

Other downtown merchants soon followed Nelson's lead but unfortunately soon after Wal-Mart's arrival, stores began to close—hardware, sporting goods, jewelry, dime stores, even J.C. Penney.

. . . So 34 concerned citizens and merchants held a strategy meeting. . . .

. . . The town raised almost $180,000, a huge sum for such a small town [the smallest town in the county to apply], to apply for a national Main Street preservation program . . . and hire a project manager to oversee their revitalization campaign.

. . . [Their] spunk impressed the judges enough to admit the town to the select winners.

[After the beautification program that followed] most town folks believe Wal-Mart is not a villain. Rather the discounter actually helped save downtown by teaching businesses to streamline and compete. . . .

A study by the University of Missouri-Columbia College of Business supports this theory as well. The report found that the longer a Wal-Mart was in a county, the more positive the impact on all economic indicators. With Wal-Mart, for example, retail employment grew 76 percent and non-farm self-employment increased in 99 percent of the counties.

Wal-Mart is also noted for its participation with local communities. . . .

In the battle between David and Goliath, sometimes the outcome is not determined by who wins or loses but rather if co-existence is possible.[11]

● In an article in *Inc.* magazine, Edward O. Welles discusses what happened when one town in Maine hired an outside consultant to help them respond to the Wal-Mart challenge. The prognosis may have seemed grim: for example, hardware stores on average lose 30.9 percent of the market share faced with the retail giant's competition. But the consultant gave the town some straightforward advice:

Don't compete directly with Wal-Mart; specialize and carry harder-to-get and better-quality products; emphasize customer service; extend your hours; advertise more—not just your products but your business—and perhaps most pertinent of all to this group of Yankee individualists, work together.

. . . Jayne Palmer increased her advertising budget by 30%. She computerized her inventory and tied her system to General Electric Credit, enabling her to order GE products direct from the company and save money by getting better terms. She extended her hours and eased credit to customers. She created a room in her store where people could watch TV while their children played on the floor. She cut back on the low end of her inventory, knowing Wal-Mart could always undersell her there.

Craig Burgess extended the hours of the family market and stepped up promotions. . . . He claims that Wal-Mart creates the illusion that it always undersells the market, based on a handful of heavily marketed items at rock-bottom prices, but that the rest of Wal-Mart's inventory is not all that competitive on price.

The [town's] merchants also came together for the Christmas 1992 shopping season, . . . to fund a campaign promoting downtown as a shopping destination, the first time that had ever happened.[12]

ISSUES FOR DISCUSSION

1. Imagine that you are a pastor in a town of about one thousand, which used to have a movie theater, a hardware store, a grocery store, a clothing store, a gift store, a gas station, a doctor's office, an insurance office, a café, and a bar. Now only the bar is left. Parishioners come to you about the possibility of using an abandoned school to somehow revive the retail, commercial, and services sector of town. What would you do? Why?
2. Imagine yourself serving in a similar town, with half of its services still intact, but facing stiff competition from a new chain variety store in a town fifteen miles away. As pastor you are asked to serve on the downtown merchants association. What would you do? Why?
3. The central location of many churches in rural communities physically places them in a position to "turn around" a deteriorating community. What strategies might a congregation use to assist in the revitalization process?

2.6 Issues Affecting the Agricultural Community

This unit is designed to stimulate discussions about the kinds of economic, social, and ethical choices facing American farmers today. Begin by studying quotations from farmers reflecting different perspectives. The first excerpt comes from a farmer who is reflecting on the loss of his farm. The second comes from a farmer who has managed to keep his farm, partly by making the transition to chemical-free farming in 1967.

You get seduced into it [borrowing to buy more land using your land as collateral], you seduce yourself into it: it's always worked before, why shouldn't it go on that way? You had faith in yourself and so did the money people: that was the business they were in, to make loans.

. . . Your own home town, where everyone knows you and's known you from a child . . . can be the cruelest place in the world when you walk down the street and you know everyone's looking after you, everyone's seen you make all your mistakes, one by one. You feel you've got like some contagious disease. . . . People won't stop to shake your hand . . . like they was afraid of catching failure from you.

. . . But what I don't like is when folk you thought might give you sympathy . . . come to you knowing the pressure you're under, and it's only to see if they can get a bargain off you in machinery or a parcel of land. . . . All it's going to do . . . is drive you further each time into the ground.[13]

I realized that I was caught up with material things—building my kingdom with sheds, silos, cement floors, and more land. Enough was never enough. . . .

We consulted our "owner's manual," the Bible, which taught us we are to be led by the Spirit. . . . Living in the Spirit is a normal, natural way of life, not something spectacular or spooky. We still have problems, but one of our guiding principles is that if we have the right attitude, problems can turn into opportunities.

. . . In our push to get bigger and better and to farm easier, we have transformed the physical anguish of the past into a mental anguish of the present. . . . What a farmer won't do to beat his neighbor by one bushel per acre!

This kind of lifestyle is violent. It exploits our own beings, our fellow humans, and, last but not least, our environment.

We don't have to live this way. . . . Let's change our lifestyle from within because we want to. Let's not wait until we have no choice because somebody says we have to change.

. . . Agriculture business was properly named because it surely has given grassroots agriculture the business!

The idea of borrowing more money, buying more inputs, and pounding the soil harder to make it produce more bushels is not working. The "top yield" myth, the "get the last nickel" syndrome, and the "efficiency fairy tale" are a big part of recent farm bankruptcies and foreclosures.

Our farm probably would be for sale today if we hadn't felt led by God to change our thinking in 1967.[14]

ISSUES FOR DISCUSSION

1. Role-play that you are called or appointed as pastor to a rural community that has been through wrenching economic crises, such as the widespread foreclosures in the 1970s and 1980s or the ongoing problems exemplified by the first excerpt. One of your parishioners is committed to sustainable agriculture strategies (like the family from Boone, Iowa, quoted in the second excerpt); numerous others are rumored to be facing bankruptcy and are afraid of trying anything different that would jeopardize yields.

   ● How would you conceive your task as pastor?
   ● How would you address these issues
      a. during your first month of ministry?
      b. at a Bible class? at a church council meeting?
      c. during your first year? What would you expect your ministry to look like at this point? What are your goals?
   ● How would you deal with parishioners—especially low-input and high-input farmers—who all see their different approaches as faithful stewardship of the land (i.e., making the most productive use of the acreage with which they are working)?

2. The other two documents in this unit—"Portrait of a 'Sustainable' Farm," and "Corporate Farming: Villain, Necessity, or Dinosaur?"—will help guide your discussions further. Which of the arguments about the future of agriculture is most compelling for you? Defend your choice.

PORTRAIT OF A "SUSTAINABLE" FARM
Small-Farm Principle: Big Isn't Best

**Innovative Practices Allow Flexible,
More Profitable Lives**
by James Walsh
(Minneapolis) Star Tribune
December 4, 1994

Dave Minar is going against the grain.
   The first sign? His 78 cows are outside. In a foot of snow. Munching hay. And they seem to like it.

Though the major push in agriculture today is to become huge, Minar doesn't believe in giant dairy farms, the ones where 1,000 cows move from hangar-sized barns to gleaming milking parlors without ever stepping outside. Where the cows munch expensive feed, are injected with artificial hormones and are milked on a computer-tracked, production-driven schedule that would make an industrialist proud.

On Minar's 230-acre farm near New Prague, MN, cows graze on pasture grass eight months a year and eat hay in the winter. The buildings are a little dog-eared, the silos unused. No computers record production. No syringes line the cooler. Minar doesn't even milk his herd in the winter. All the cows have their calves in late spring, and Minar allows their lactation period to end in midwinter. In a more standard operation, the breeding is staggered throughout the year to allow year-round milking of the herd.

Profit—not production—is the name of the game. And adjectives such as small, quiet, and relaxed fit like a soft leather glove. "We've got to step back and try to get back to the notion of simplicity in life," he said. "I think I spent more time in a tree this fall [deer hunting] than ever."

Minar is part of a growing counter-culture that is seeking another way to keep farmers on the land and bring prosperity to rural areas.

These farmers resist the urge to expand. To them, staying small is better for their lifestyle, their families, their neighbors and their land. And, they insist, better for their bank accounts.

Some call themselves "sustainable farmers" and continually seek ways to cut costs and increase profit while making the soil and water cleaner. Others are more conventional in their methods for producing milk, pork, grain and vegetables.

They share a philosophy, however: Big doesn't mean best.

Dan and Muriel French

It's pretty here, among the rolling hills of southeastern Minnesota. . . . But French said he never really had time to enjoy it. He was too busy raising bigger crops, breeding better hogs and trying to produce more and more milk. Yet he was making less money every year.

Feed costs, veterinary bills, costs for seed, electricity, fuel, equipment—it all keeps draining the farm's profits. In 1988, after continued bad years and a drought that caused a feed shortage, French changed his thinking.

He also changed his farm.

He quit planting corn and oats and alfalfa. He stopped raising hogs. And he sold off much of his equipment, which needed almost constant repair. And French said he's never done better. He said he is making 25 percent profit; his goal is 50 percent. And he's working less.

Instead of milking 60 cows year-round, French and a hired man milk 120 in the spring, summer and fall. French said he's working less, having more fun and saving $60,000 a year in feed and energy costs.

Like Minar's herd, French's cows graze for their supper.

It's called rotational grazing. Pasture is divided into 2- or 3-acre paddocks, and cows are moved from one area to another every 12 hours or so over the course of the grazing season. Electric fences keep them out of areas that have been previously grazed so grass can recover.

"There's more than one alternative," French said. "And I don't think a lot of people are hearing that."

Rotational grazing is part of a larger idea called Holistic Resource Management. Under HRM, farmers make plans based on what kind of life they want, how much money they need, what their land can support and how they want their farms to look hundreds of years from now.

"It's a decision-making process. It allows you to achieve a goal in the most economically, ecologically, and socially sound way," said Judy Butterfield, an official with the Center for Holistic Resource Management in Albuquerque, NM. "It's actually quite simple. But it's so different from the way we've been doing things that it seems difficult."

French said planting grasses and eliminating the need to store manure has helped the ecology of his farm. He and others say that giving animals room to roam is healthier for the livestock and that their veterinary bills are lower than they used to be. French also says he believes farms like his contribute to the economic health of communities because they can survive for generations.

The Frenchs insist that factory farms—with their heavy debt, high risk and overproduction—cannot.

"What if you have all big producers and one of them goes out of business?" said Muriel French. "The industry is a lot worse off."

Dan French said their son recently bought his own dairy farm, using the low-cost grazing and management methods his father has used since 1988. It's the only way he could have afforded to buy into the business, French said. . . .

Full-Circle Co-op

With an eye on the environment and an interest in rural development, Steven Schwen and a group of growers decided to form the Full-Circle Co-op in 1985. Meant as a way to allow several organic farmers to combine efforts at marketing, education and labor, the co-op has become a support tool for about a dozen small southeastern Minnesota farms.

Schwen's farm has only 14 acres, 5 of which are used for intensive vegetable production. Through the co-op and individually, the growers of Full-Circle sell to Twin Cities–area residents through direct delivery and at farmer's markets. . . .

Dave Serfling

Dave . . . a 35-year-old hog farmer, has the numbers to prove that small guys can succeed. He pays 30 percent less for feed than the 13 best hog farms in southeastern Minnesota . . . [and] 70 percent less for veterinary bills and less than half . . . for equipment and fencing.

"We're not losing money, even at 26 cents a pound."

. . . "It's a way for me to live out my Christian beliefs. . . . I'm not buying my neighbor's farm, and I'm helping strengthen rural communities."

Steve Albers

. . . "I really think the smaller farm is the glue that keeps the community together," he said.

Think about it, Albers said. What is better for the enrollment of rural schools, the membership of rural churches and the fellowship of rural communities—two farms milking 1,000 cows each or 20 farms milking 100 cows?

Sustainable Farms May Mean Less Profit, but Better End Result
by James Walsh
(Minneapolis) Star Tribune
April 12, 1994

It's as if two evangelists from opposing faiths were competing. . . . Even as more farmers, educators and legislators look to large-scale agriculture to keep more people farming . . . sustainable farming [advocates] are raising the revival tents. Their gospel? A new seven-state study funded by the St. Paul–based Northwest Area Foundation showing that small, sustainable farms . . . may be better for long-term rural development.

. . . "There are no good guys and bad guys," said James Ridgeway, owner of Minnesota's largest dairy farm. . . .

But those who are pushing sustainable agriculture say no compromise exists when the soul of agriculture is at stake.

. . . The study found that conventional farmers generally earn more [gross incomes]. But sustainable producers come closer to—and sometimes surpass—their conventional counterparts, when net profit is calculated.

CORPORATE FARMING: VILLAIN, NECESSITY, OR DINOSAUR?

As you think about the religious, ethical, and pragmatic aspects of corporate farming, consider the following passages. The first is drawn from *Sacred Cows and Hot Potatoes: Agrarian Myths in Agricultural Policy*, by William P. Browne and others.

Corporate farms account for less than 5 percent of all income generated by farms. For the more typical industrial farm, a family owns the capital resources, but hires a manager, who in turn selects . . . hired laborers. An increasingly common industrial farm is one where a farm management firm contracts with former farm kids who continue to own the land but do not wish to manage it themselves. . . .

Whether or not *big* farms are bad for rural communities has been a hotly contested issue for some time. As is often the case with farming issues, it all depends.

. . . [S]tudies generally suggest that it is not so much the scope of operation but the social organization of the farm that influences rural communities. Large farms with industrial-type relationships tend to have negative influences, while owner-operator farms generally have positive influences.[15]

From *The Corporate Reapers*, by A. V. Krebs:

Michael Pertschuk, former Federal Trade Commission chairman, speculates only half jokingly [that] the way tobacco companies are accumulating cash and diversifying, "by the year 2000, there will be two consumer goods companies in the United States: RJR Nabisco will be selling all the consumer goods west of the Mississippi, and Philip Morris will be selling all the consumer goods east of the Mississippi."

. . . Pertschuk's words are more than food for thought.[16]

From *Alternative Agriculture*, a resource compiled by the National Research Council and others:

Successful alternative farmers often produce high per acre yields with significant reductions in costs per unit of crop harvested. A wide range of alternative systems . . . deserves further support and investigation. . . . With modest adjustments in a number of federal agricultural policies many of these systems could become more widely adopted and successful.[17]

From an article by Marty Strange in *The Des Moines Sunday Register*:

The fawning arguments of those who favor corporate farming . . . [rely on] loaded questions that presume (1) corporate farms are more efficient, (2) family farms are protected while corporations are not, (3) adding corporate hogs to the state's economy is the only way to grow, and (4) if hog numbers grow, packing plants will come (or stay) and family farmers will be better off than if the large operations are kept out. None of them stands tall in the face of facts or reason. . . . [Iowa] needs tough controls on corporate farming to force these enterprises from the cozy corner of protectionism into the tough and competitive world of farming.[18]

From an article by James Walsh in the *(Minneapolis) Star Tribune*:

Government programs are the reason why many sustainable farmers make less money. In a 1989 survey, Minnesota conventional farmers received an average payment of $9,214 . . . sustainable farmers received an average of $3,597. The study calls for a major shift in farm policy toward a more diverse agriculture that rewards farmers for sound environmental practices, not just production. . . . But large-farm advocates argue that . . . meatpackers and dairies would go elsewhere if only the small guys remained. . . . "If you want to survive . . . you either have to get bigger—or get smaller."[19]

2.7 Community Development and the Church: Secular Venture or a Matter of Mission?

The first table below includes samples of grassroots development models described in *From the Grassroots: Profiles of 103 Rural Self-Development Projects*.[20] The second table describes similar projects by rural churches. What do the ventures have in common?

"SECULAR" MODELS

Community	Goal	Project
Mars Hill, N.C.	To develop a specialty agricultural, marketing, and retail industry	Project Herbs: workshops led to a minimum of twenty-five new jobs in agricultural sales
Frederick, S.D.	To save the town's remaining grocery store	Community for-profit corporation more than doubled inventory value; store ran in the black
Hiawassee, Ga.	To establish a high-tech niche in agriculture business	The high school started a hydroponic lettuce greenhouse grossing $85,000 per year, employing 30 to 40 full-time, 150 seasonally

Other projects include community loan funds, worker-owned firms, business incubators and assistance centers; business retention programs, value-added businesses (involving additional processing of a local product, hence more jobs), tourism, and downtown revitalization.

CONGREGATIONAL MODELS

Community	Goal	Project
Rewey, Wisc.	To rebuild the community's medical and retail sector	Presbytery backed loan to buy old school; congregation converted school to housing; plans include possible convenience store, café, recreation center.
Lost Nation, Iowa	To restore lost medical services	Three churches fund ecumenical parish nurse program
Fisher, Ill.	To provide youth services in the face of a growing drug problem	Church works with FORWARD, a Fisher nonprofit organization, to establish day care

2.8 Assessing Your Congregation's Context

There are many instruments for describing the context in which your congregation lives, but one of the best we know comes from Gary Far- ley, who is an officer with rural ministry portfolio in the Southern Baptist Convention's Home Mission Board. We thank him for his permission to reprint the following material.

THIRTY QUESTIONS TO ANSWER CONCERNING A RURAL COMMUNITY

To be effective in a town and country community one must learn about its history, its peoples, its structures, its everyday life, its expectations for pastors, its hopes and fears, and the place of the churches in the place. This list is not a questionnaire one would ask congregational leaders to fill out or write down answers to. Nor is it an interview schedule to be given in a single setting. Rather, it is suggestive of some topic areas around which one can engage community residents over several months as opportunity presents itself. Over time one can come to experience a sense that he or she is at home in this place.

YOUR PLACE AS A PLACE AND ITS PEOPLE

1. How did the community come to be? What was the founding dream? What was the covenant upon which the community was built—utopia, commerce, resource exploitation, safety, freedom, or the good life? . . .
2. What is its focal symbol—courthouse square, grain elevator, mine tipple, or some other image of community function?
3. What is/are its chief economic function(s): farm trade, marketing, mill or factory, fishery, timbering, governmental service, recreation/retirement, college, transportation, bedroom community, or institution? Often this is integrated with the dream and the symbol.
4. Who are the honored, the despised, the loveable characters, and the "marginal" people of the town?
5. What world views, values, and norms inform the everyday life of the residents? What do people in your place believe about—Time (e.g. past present or future oriented). Nature of people. Interpersonal relations. Purpose of activity. Character of nature and supernatural? (A study of *Ministering Cross Culturally* by S. G. Lingerfelter and M. K. Meyers can be very useful in identifying world view issues.) [Grand Rapids, Mich.: Baker Book House, 1994.]
6. What cultural/racial/ethnic groups are present in the community?
7. What are the barriers that separate people/groups of people: race, religion, education, social status? Are they visible or invisible?
8. What are the sins/hurts of the community: the loss of an industry, a disastrous flood, a lynching?
9. What has become of its sons and daughters? Often people and communities in decline feel vindicated by the success of the children in the larger world.
10. What is the people's perception of the place; awareness of other's perception of it?
11. Does the community have distinct "sub-communities"? In a larger small town, some folks will not attend a big "first" church for social and cultural reasons.
12. What seems to be the future of the community—its dreams, who is responsible for dreaming/implementing?
13. In sum, what is the "story" of the community? You need to know and appreciate the story of the community. You need to come to "own" it and become a part of it, because for good or ill, you will.

YOUR PLACE AS PROCESS

1. What are the magnets of the community? What places, activities and events draw people?
2. What is the rhythm of everyday life? Daily, weekly, seasonally, annually?
3. What are the corridors/patterns of movement around the place? When can one "pastor" at the coffee shop, the post office, the ice cream parlor, and the sale barn?
4. How are decisions made? Who are the power brokers? Who are the major "get things done" people in the town? What is the route or career path to leadership positions? Who retains veto power?
5. What are the "routines" of everyday encounters/conversations: greeting, teasing, conducting business, courting, making requests, leave taking? What are the taboos?
6. How do people make a living? What is the routine/rhythm of their work?
7. How does the community relate to other communities in its region—dominance, conflict, subordination?
8. When, where, and how do the residents play? What are the annual events?
9. How does the community assimilate new people?

THE PLACE OF YOUR CHURCH IN THE PLACE

1. What role does your church play in the place—leader, cooperator, secondary? Dominant, denominational representation, or distinctive?
2. What kind of reputation does it have—friendly, aloof, rich, middle-class, poor, formal, ordered, informal, loving, conflicting, combative, community-serving, self-serving?
3. What is the relationship between your church and the other congregations in the community?
4. What community resources are available to assist your church in doing ministry?
5. What ministries, programs, events, and activities in the community receive the support of your church?
6. What community leadership roles are filled by active members of your church?
7. How does the community relate to your congregation? Embraces, holds at a distance, rejects?
8. Does your church seek to serve or to dominate the life of the community?

For a congregation interested in finding out more about itself and its mission, we suggest using this resource (2.8) and also 3.1, 4.6, 5.1, and 6.1. We think you will enjoy that!

Chapter 3

Who Are We?
Identifying the Spirituality
of Rural Congregations

The second component of congregational studies is that of identity. Who does the congregation think it is? What stories, patterns, symbols, distinctive Christian virtues, beliefs, or events in this congregation are lifted up over and over again so powerfully that they not only summarize our past but also shape our present and future?

Obviously, context has a lot to do with the shape of the congregation, as we saw in chapter 2. However, it is not only socioeconomic status or geography or agricultural base that makes a parish what it is. It also involves spiritual and religious dimensions. Congregational studies is built on the premise that God is alive and well in the local church, and that rural congregations are the carriers of the faith. Indeed, the promise of congregational studies in the American church context is that "it may become a means of indigenizing our theological heritage in the first world in the way that base communities are doing in the third world. As such it could be the salvation of liberation theology which now admires the application of the Gospel abroad but cannot imagine what shape the church should take at home."[1]

One way of talking about identity, then, is to ask how the congregation thinks God is acting and has acted in and through the congregation. How is God active in this context?

The local congregation that thinks of itself as part of the Jesus movement following Christ's call to discipleship, located in a rural community in the United States on the cusp of the twenty-first century, has had its identity formed in certain ways. If one's context includes the common features of being Christian, rural, and American, there are certain elements of identity already in place. But, as James Hopewell and others have reminded us, every congregation is different; every congregation is a distinct culture with its own life force. Every congregation has features of identity that people have chosen and held to be important and worth saving and living out of.

In an effort to mirror both the *commonalities* and the *distinctiveness* of a congregation's identity, we begin this chapter by exploring the commonalities at the heart of Christian spiritual and biblical identity. Then we suggest some ways of thinking about the distinctive nature of each congregation. Yet we realize that ultimately only the members of a congregation can say what is distinctive about their congregation.

Our Commonality: A Biblical Understanding of Rural Congregational Spirituality

What rural congregations hold in common, besides their rural context, which we have already examined a bit, is their commitment to an understanding of God derived from the Scriptures and from their experience of God alive and active in the world today. Thus we will concentrate attention here on that part of their identity that rural congregations point to when they call themselves Christian. Biblical images are especially prominent in defining who the rural Christian congregation is.

Two centuries ago, in Christ's time, Nathanael asked, "Can anything good come out of Nazareth?" (John 1:46). Many modern people, even rural residents, wonder the same thing about their smaller communities and congregations. It seems that the same societal views prevailing in Christ's time are alive and well today.

The theology of the Old and New Testaments turns society's conventional ways of looking at things upside down. There is power in what seems like powerlessness. The preponderance of rural images in the Bible are positive ones. Poetry and prose alike celebrate the majesty of the rural environment; parables and stories view moral issues in terms derived from rural life and lifestyles.

Like the portrait of rural America drawn in chapter 2, community life for the children of Israel was anything but idyllic. Economic, social, and political problems were everyday realities. Families struggled with the same problems facing modern rural communities. The role of the faith community in responding to those problems was called into question then, as it is now. And God's people today, as they were then, are challenged to work out their faith in loving community and fellowship with one another.

While exploring such biblical perspectives on rural life in detail is beyond our scope here, the purpose of this chapter is to touch on some of the major biblical themes that have become part of the identity of rural congregations. These include the following basic beliefs:

1. Life in community is relational; in all our relationships God is present. From God's leading the people out of Egypt, to God's dwelling among the Israelites in the Ark of the Covenant, to Christ's assurance that "I am with you always" (Matt. 28:20) human history in Scripture is tied to the living presence of God among us.

2. Covenant and redemption are underpinnings of our relationship to God, one another, and indeed all creation. The biblical story traces the emerging vision of a loving God bent on redeeming humankind along with the rest of creation, which was alienated in the rebellion of Eden. There are many detours and milestones along the way in that journey—among them, the brokenness that resulted not only in the Flood but in the promise of the rainbow, leading ultimately to Christ's death on the cross and the promise for all creation in the Resurrection. It is here, even in the face of suffering and struggle, that rural congregations find their greatest source of hope.

3. The creative act of ministry is at the core of congregational response to redemption. The work of community, in biblical terms, is not an act of penance, but one of joyful, loving affirmation and thankfulness. Rigid concepts of duty are swept away by a God who seeks and finds—who reaches out to us lovingly where we are in our daily lives and who admonishes us to go and do likewise. This changes duty into joy.

4. Pain, suffering, and struggle are taken up and understood through the vision of a healthy existence with God. The God of the Old and New Testaments, especially as embodied in the ministry of Christ Jesus, is involved with congregations in the tragedies and sorrows of human existence. By choosing to become flesh and dwell among us, God assumed the form of a servant—offering healing to those experiencing physical and emotional suffering, and finally taking that same suffering upon himself. Through the anguish of the Cross comes the triumph of the Resurrection. In that paradox, Christ offers the promise of new life to all of us as God's people.

5. Land- or earth-centeredness is integral to achieving right relationships between humankind and God. It is no accident that humankind's act of rebellion in the Garden of Eden was tied to abuse of the natural world. The imagery of the Scripture stresses time and again the interconnectedness of all creation. In the

New Testament especially, Christ's teachings link right use of human gifts to responsible relationships with the gifts of the earth. Where better to understand such values than in rural congregations, where economic and physical existence is so closely tied to creation in the broadest sense of the word?

6. Jesus Christ has given rural congregations a mandate to go out into their world, preaching, teaching, baptizing, and calling all people to life in God's grace. The church has a commission to represent God's truth in its internal life and its outreach. Congregations are to build the sort of community that exists in the kingdom of God, communities of peace and justice.

Congregational Identity and a Biblical Understanding of Community

Community is at the heart of the biblical experience and thus essential to congregational identity. We see that priority unfolding in the Garden of Eden, where God desired that humans live in fellowship with one another and in harmony with creation.

Community in the Old and New Testaments is a process that emerges in the linkages between being and doing, humanity and the divine, and humankind and the whole of creation. Through a series of highly personal encounters, the God of the Old and New Testaments forges relationships not just with humankind, but with all creation. The community of God is the household in which we are invited to live. God lives with us as an active member of that community.

That emerging relationship is a covenantal one. Living in right relationship in God's righteousness means that we are to treat one another justly. God's intentions in creation are that all life is to flourish. We in the church are called to mirror the justice of God's kingdom in our congregational life and in the world. Community is characterized by inclusiveness, embracing not only Jews and Gentiles, but all creation. Nature and the physical world, as well as humankind, experience the bountiful grace and hope that ties us in love to our Creator.

As it emerges in the pages of Scripture, commu-

nity cannot be visualized and experienced apart from informed, deliberate moral action. Human response to redemption is bound up in the conscious modeling of the kind of unqualified love Christ showed on the cross—life-transforming love that forms the foundation for right relationships.

True community depends upon congregational nurturing of spiritual values. In 1 Corinthians 12:1-11, Paul lays the foundations for such a community dynamic by describing the spiritual gifts that are central to the life of the church. Among these are the utterance of wisdom and knowledge, faith, gifts of healing, prophecy, and discernment of spirits. In contemporary language, these are encapsulated as the preaching, teaching, healing, and prophetic functions of clergy and laity within the Christian community. These, too, are part of congregational identity.

Congregational Identity and Ministry

Experienced rural pastors consistently express the importance of the ministry of the Word—teaching and preaching—as an important underpinning of congregational identity, reminding us of the distinctive nature of the community we are building. Pastor John Peshek of Pelican Lake, Minnesota, asserts:

> In all we say and do, we need to preach Jesus. There are too many sermons without that—it's appalling, really. You must be spiritually healthy in order to change. If Jesus is not lifted up in relationships, a lot of trouble can follow. You have no basis for relationships. Social justice is nothing apart from Jesus—his death and resurrection have to be in everything. You need to stress that over and over as pastor, one-on-one, in sermons, and in council meetings—lift it up over and over again. It is the only healthy motivation in volunteer organizations in the church. Otherwise there will be nothing but sinfulness, evil, and struggles for power. Jesus needs to be held up in front of us *always* and in *all ways*.
>
> Safety is a big issue that you need to work on in order to build community within a congregation, starting with the church council. It is important for the pastor to help parishioners see that God is in people—the theological fisher-folk

idea is where vitality and evangelism need to begin. This must be intentional. The church must become a small sanctuary with an atmosphere of intimacy. Trust is the key: (1) Do people trust the pastor? (2) Is the reverse true? (3) Do people trust each other? If not, there are going to be political power plays.

[Change and ministry in rural settings aren't] hopeless. But spiritual health has got to become the basis of any change. We have to be working with more than a Sunday school theology—and I say that lovingly. It is sad how many adults haven't thought through grace, sin, salvation, justification, and so on. These things are not very meaningful to them. They need to be challenged and questioned in the context of a class. And the pastor needs to model vulnerability: to confess and demonstrate forgiveness. There is safety for people in this.

Clergy and laity alike can come to rely on the power of a preaching and teaching ministry as a vital source of personal, community, and congregational renewal.

When asked about what they see as the source of the vitality of their congregation, rural parishioners concur with those priorities:

We are fortunate to have a pastor who prioritizes preaching and teaching. Sermons and Bible study need to stress how to treat one another. Our pastor, from the pulpit, continually admits his humanness—about slighting people and so on and other typical things we all do. Our pastor just finished a series on the seven deadly sins and admitted to all of them. That makes it easier for us to admit our problems. Pastor, people, place, and faith are the keys to trust. This is a Christian community. People here feel safe to forgive, knowing that we're all sinners.

Here lies an important clue to how pastors can utilize the teaching and preaching process in the building of community.[2] Vulnerability—modeled by the pastor and reinforced from pulpit and across the church council table—creates the climate in which community becomes possible.

Along with preaching and teaching the Word, liturgical expression is an important expression of congregational identity. When asked about the vitality of her particular church, one North Dakota parishioner gave credit to the nature of the act of worship itself:

Church is not a pastor or organist, but they certainly help. They make you want to come back. From the music, you know you are in a living church. Live music programs in worship (organ, choir, piano, or whatever you have) makes music more meaningful for me and it attracts others also. Youth are involved, too, not just in Sunday school but also in worship. The sermons seem like our pastor is following us around in our daily lives. He really connects. This is probably the main factor for me.

People are so involved in the community that they are stretched to the limit. Maybe that's why there are no "big" church events here. Church is more a safe harbor to get away from all that. Maybe that is an important role of the church for kids, too—a place to center yourself again. Maybe that's bound to be true in a town of our size.

Variety and diversity, opportunities for participation, and an atmosphere of safety that sets the church as an institution apart from the society around it are factors that can make liturgics a source of identity for the worshiping community. At the same time, it is important for church people to challenge themselves to move out of their comfort zones.

Rural congregational life demands a high level of individual participation and involvement. Time and time again God calls the people of Israel to act—to break out of their traditional ways of doing things, to recognize a need or problem situation that requires attention, and then to assume personal responsibility for that call to service. In 1 Corinthians 12, Paul focuses on identifying individual gifts and assuming personal responsibility for using these gifts in the service of others as central to building up the community of faith. Healing, prophecy, teaching, and preaching are not the sole responsibility of clergy, but the responsibility of all Christians as they live and work together within the church.

Another aspect of the congregational identity of many rural churches is that their outreach is activated through neighborliness and through affirming gifts more often than challenging or confronting. Pastors can build on this identity by using the Pauline strategy of identifying people's gifts, by lifting up needs, as well as by encouraging the structures through which laypeople ask one another to become involved. The prophetic

Table 3.1 Scriptural Material in the Rural Bible Study Series *Planting the Seeds of Community* (available from the Center for Theology and Land, 2000 University Avenue, Dubuque, IA 52001, phone 319-589-3117).

OLD TESTAMENT

Genesis	11 (Work); 3:13–4:20 (Ministering); 19:12-13 (Tomorrow)
Exodus	16:17-18 (Work)
Leviticus	19:13 (Economics)
Deuteronomy	15:10-11 (Building); 5:4-9 (Learning)
2 Kings	2:19-22 (Earth)
1 Chronicles	21:19-27 (Ministering)
Nehemiah	2:17-18 (Building);
Psalms	65:9-13 (Earth); 48:9 (Celebrating)
Proverbs	13:1 (Learning)
Ecclesiastes	11:3-4 (Change)
Isaiah	53:4-5 (Healing); 11:1-9 (Good News); 58:6-7 (Stress)
Jeremiah	32 (Economics); 29:10-14 (Tomorrow)
Daniel	1:9-17 (Change)
Amos	5:21, 23-24 (Celebrating)
Habakkuk	3:17-19 (Stress)

NEW TESTAMENT

Matthew	13 (Good News); 11:28-30 (Stress)
Mark	4:31-32 (Building); 9:23-24 (Healing); 6:6-13 (Ministering)
Luke	15:8-9 (Good News); 16:23 (Work); 12 (Work); 21:1-4 (Economics); 15:11-32 (Family); 14:13-14 (Celebrating)
John	21:4-6 (Good News); 19:25-27 (Family); 21:15 (Learning)
Acts	4:32 (Building); 3:1-16 (Healing)
Romans	8:19-21 (Earth); 12:9, 12-13 (Celebrating)
1 Corinthians	3:6-9 (Learning); 12:4-5, 7, 31 (Ministering); 3:21-23 (Tomorrow)
Ephesians	2:19-21 (Economics); 6:1-4 (Family)
Philippians	1:7-9 (Stress)
Colossians	1:15-16 (Earth)
Philemon	10–12 (Change)
Hebrews	8:6-7 (Change)
James	1:19-20, 26 (Family)
Revelation	21:5-6 (Tomorrow)

wisdom of the pastor lies not in confronting, but in affirming. As one Minnesota parishioner expressed it:

Through the prayer chain and announcements about people's needs during the course of worship and in church newsletters, our pastor is helping us learn to be more aware of one another's needs. You need to listen all the time. Also, when you pray for one another, it's safer to share your problems. When people know there is a need, they'll respond. We're good at that in the rural community—responding in a crisis. But we need to be better about asking for help.

Experienced rural pastors continually stress that successful evangelism or living out one's beliefs is not determined by a congregation's money or age or tangible assets. At a grassroots level, a successful congregation is one whose ministry incarnates Christ's mission.

Perhaps nowhere is it more important to conceptualize salvation as an experience that embraces the whole of creation or to recognize this truth as central to Christian theology than it is in rural settings. Rural congregations recognize that the land is part of their identity as well. As one rural parishioner expresses it, "Land is at the heart of everything we do and believe. As a parish health nurse I see every day how closely the health of rural people and communities is tied to the health of the land."

Scripture in both the Old and New Testaments reinforces such a view of the roots of community and spirituality. Passages such as the following affirm in powerful language the bonds between the human and nonhuman creation in God's plan of redemption:

> How long will the land mourn,
>   and the grass of every field wither?
> For the wickedness of those who live in it
>   the animals and the birds are swept away,
>   and because people said, "He is blind to our
>   ways." (Jer. 12:4)

The health of creation and of human society are inextricably bound up with each other. Viewed from the biblical perspective of connectedness between humankind and the natural world, the business of farming in rural areas—like any endeavor in the human community—takes on new significance. Use of land must be interpreted not just in terms of personal environmental concern, but as an issue integral to the life and health of Christian community itself. The kind of mutual dependence within creation described in Scripture goes beyond the notion of stewardship of soil, water, and land that many rural (as well as urban) dwellers traditionally have evoked to interpret their interaction with the natural world; it points to our dependence on one another and ultimately on God.

Our Distinctiveness: Ways of Thinking About Our Particular Identity

At this point we have examined the aspects of identity that most rural Christian congregations share. Some of those aspects—the biblical images—are ones that almost all rural churches understand as central to their identity. Others are not as universally shared but still have a fair probability of being shared. In this section we begin to explore our distinctiveness as congrega-

tions. That is more difficult to do since there are as many distinctive configurations of identity as there are congregations.

It will be particularly valuable for the congregation to articulate its own identity. The members of a congregation should think about what stories, symbols, physical objects or structures, history, doctrines, and experiences are especially significant to them. Resource unit 3.1 is designed to help you begin to do this.

Perhaps the best we can do here is to suggest some ways in which congregations embody unique characteristics.

The *Handbook for Congregational Studies* lists seven elements that together constitute a congregation's identity:

1. History: The way a congregation remembers its past and anticipates its future.
2. Heritage: All those aspects of tradition, such as ethnicity, that integrate and transform it.
3. World View: How it perceives the world—its order and threatening crises.
4. Symbols: Both religious symbols—the cross, the altar rail—and pictures or articles that stand for something else.
5. Rituals: Often-repeated ceremonies that mark special occasions and reinforce the meaning of congregational life (e.g., Thanksgiving services or spatial patterns of seating or the location of the baptismal font).
6. Demography: The age, income, ethnicity, and educational level of the congregation's members.
7. Character: The traits of the congregation and the ways in which it has developed by having adapted to changing circumstances.[3]

The most important aspect of identity is the way the congregation thinks of itself, but not too far behind is the way the broader public of the rural community thinks of it. The latter is particularly significant in terms of evangelism and mission, which are central aspects of the church's task.

David Ray offers us one list of ways a rural church can think of itself. It might see itself as a *dominant church*—a prestigious congregation whose members are very influential in the community. It might consider itself a *subordinate church*—a second, somewhat less wealthy church, which attracts people who may be a rung or two down on the income or status ladder. It might see itself as an *exclusive* (or *niched*) church—serving a particular, limited group of people defined on the basis of ethnic heritage (e.g., Norwegian Americans or Latvians or Laotians) or a particular denomination in a community that is dominated by another denomination (e.g., Presbyterians in a Roman Catholic community). A church might define itself as a *newcomer church*—one that attracts recent arrivals in the community. A church may identify itself as an *indigenous church*, composed of long-term residents of the area. It may celebrate the fact that it is a *culturally-mixed church*, which has attracted newcomers and long-term residents perhaps with many different values and styles of belief.[4] Another list of Ray's that articulates some of the elements of congregational identity includes the *always small church*, the *once large or remnant small church*, the *not-yet-large small church*, the *schismatic small church*, the *intentionally small church*, the *clan* or *family church*, and the *ethnic small church*.[5]

Many rural congregations have never made a conscious effort to put their identity into words, spoken, much less written. It can be helpful to do so, but we can understand the reluctance of a church centered around one or two extended families to articulate its identity when to do so would make people who are not members of those families question their place in the church.

There are several other possible identities. Here are a few that may spark your thinking about any given congregation that you serve:

1. There are many churches whose identity centers around the location of the church. Location may include both historical and geographical aspects, and it may say something about the missional outreach of the church. Examples include The Plains Presbyterian Church (in an area known as "the Plains," outside Zachary, Louisiana), Jefferson Prairie Lutheran Church, or Fennimore United Methodist Church.

2. There are churches that express their particular identity in terms of doctrine, belief, or virtue. At Dilworth Presbyterian Church in Minnesota, where Shannon Jung served as pastor, the session decided to include on the sign for the church a bronze figure of a dove descending, a prominent feature of the symbol of the national Presbyterian Church. Forever after that, Pastor Jung felt constrained to remember the Holy Spirit in his preaching and teaching. The symbol of the dove began to enter the life of the church.

The identity of some churches is embodied in their names: for example, countless Grace Lutheran Churches. Other churches incorporate the belief and virtue of Hope; others Community; others Holy Trinity. Others take their names from one of the saints; often stories of that saint parallel stories of the congregations they name.

3. Often, the identity of the congregation is not evident in the name. People in the church remember, for example, "the great fire that almost wiped us out in 1955, but which ended up strengthening our resolve to become the church we were capable of being." Or the story may go, "Remember the time when we all got together and . . . ?" Or it may focus on a decision whether to move the church.[6]

4. There may be less positive aspects of the church's identity as well. The church may think of itself as "The-Last-Great-Defender-of-the-True-Faith" or Garrison Keillor's "Our Lady of Perpetual Responsibility" or "God's Frozen Chosen" or "The Andersons' Church" or "Pastor Rossiter's Church" or any number of others less-than-positive, but nonetheless real, expressions of identity.

5. Perhaps most important in terms of evangelism is the identity or reputation of the church in the community. This is, of course, different from the self-identity of the church that we have been concentrating on thus far. The church gets a certain reputation and visibility in the community; for too long mainline Protestant churches have been hiding their light under a bushel; Roman Catholic churches are only slightly better about this. Both could learn a lot from their more conservative, evangelical brothers and sisters who have developed ways of becoming visible and accessible.

Whatever the name, churches gain a reputation; they become known as "the church that is always doing things in the community," "the church that is so cold and impersonal that it's amazing anyone goes there," "the Boltons' family church," "the friendliest church in town," "the church that always puts on such a great cherry pie supper" (or fish fry or steak fry or chicken salad or you-name-it). They may be "the church you can always count on to cooperate with the fund drive" or "the community church" (where many of the members are so involved in community issues that their opinion counts for a great deal). Sometimes the external reputation and the internal identity match; sometimes they do not.

Identities develop slowly and, indeed, almost unnoticed in many cases. They also change over time. It may be quite helpful and uplifting to celebrate the goodness of the identity of the church you are affiliated with. You may also explore ways of strengthening those aspects of identity that do not express the name "Christian" as well as they can.

The following resource units set a framework for the rural congregational studies issues that have been raised: (1) asking how rural parishioners see themselves spiritually, (2) suggesting how liturgy and the Word can be used to revitalize community, and (3) challenging congregations to draw on the policy and mission statements of their own denominations as a resource in rebuilding themselves in the context of human needs.

RESOURCES FOR DISCOVERING CONGREGATIONAL IDENTITY

The resource units in this chapter are designed to help pastors new to rural ministry as well as members of congregations determine the identity of the congregations and communities in which they are doing ministry. What is the history of this congregation? What is the role of the church in the community? How does the community view your congregation? How do members view themselves as people of faith?

3.1   Locating the Identity of the Rural Congregation
3.2   What Would the Community Say About Your Congregation?
3.3   How Rural People View Their Faith
3.4   How Does the Church View Itself As Part of the Larger Community?

3.1   Locating the Identity of the Rural Congregation

It would be helpful for congregations as a whole, perhaps at a potluck supper, an adult or intergenerational Sunday school event, or a series of informal gatherings, to spend some time thinking about just what its identity is. Much could be gained from following the entire procedure described below, but much could be gained from abbreviated modifications of it as well. A provocative procedure might begin with individual reflection on the questions below; then, in small groups, people could share their answers and impressions; then each group could share the most significant elements of identity their group located. This conversation would be very helpful to a pastor who is new to the rural scene or to a particular church. It would be instructive to long-term church members to consider how differently other members perceive the congregation's identity.

1. How was the church founded? Who were the leaders of the church during its early years? Has the church always been in the same building? How do you perceive the future of this church? What will its identity be in five years? What will its identity be in ten years?

2. Why was the church founded? Were there particular stresses, needs, or opportunities that led to the church's being located where it is? Is there a distinctive heritage that the church seeks to pass on? What sorts of traditions does it have?

3. The church may gather part of its identity from the beliefs that it lifts up as significant for its life: for example, forgiveness, fellowship, creation, hope, reconciliation. What Christian beliefs, virtues, or

guidelines are especially meaningful to your church? How does it view the world—optimistically, tragically, stoically, neutrally? What is the church's relation to its world?

4. What material symbols (such as the building, an organ, a memorial gift, a painting, or a pulpit) do people in the congregation think are meaningful? Why? What memories or events or people do they call to mind? What does the church as a whole mean symbolically? What feelings do you have when you think about your church as a whole? What is its significance to you?

5. Are there particular ceremonies or ways of doing things—for example, baptisms, Easter Vigils, orders of service for the Lord's Supper—that the church has adopted? Does the church have ritual practices?

6. What about the people in the congregation? Are they predominantly of a certain age or race or income level? How does that enter into the church's identity? Do they celebrate any particular ethnic identity?

7. What about the character of the church? If the church were an individual man or woman, how would you personify it—friendly, courageous, grumpy, outgoing, happy, sad, optimistic?

8. How does the church think of its relationship with the community? Is it a community institution? A leader in the community? Only occasionally involved in the life of the community? Other?

9. Overall, given the list of questions you have struggled with, what features surface as being most characteristic of your rural congregation's identity? What would you say is the mission of your church in the community, given your answers to the questions above?

3.2 What Would the Community Say About Your Congregation?

We often travel to different towns and crossroads and often have to stop at the local gas station or tavern or convenience store to ask directions to the church we are visiting. It is always instructive to hear what the attendant says about the church. Many times the answer is, "Sure—you go down to the stop sign and turn right; it's about three blocks down on your left." Sometimes the answer is, "Betty, where is that Baptist church again? Is that the one near Hansons?" Whatever the response, it tends to say something about the reputation of the church and how well known it is in the community.

Imagine that you are just coming into town and asking a bit more than directions to the church. What would the attendant at the local convenience store, gas station, or shoe store tell you about the church? What would other people in the community have to say?

Try to imagine that you have asked the question, "What is the Disciples/UCC church (or other) here like?" What response would you get from

- a high-school boy and girl you meet at the coffee shop?
- the attendant at the convenience store?
- the police officer you see on Main Street?
- the funeral director?
- the local booster club or Chamber of Commerce or Rotary Club or other civic group?
- the County Board of Supervisors?
- the School Board?
- a group of fifth-graders?
- a group of young women?
- a group of middle-aged women?
- a group of older men?

Thinking about particular individuals and how they perceive the identity of the congregation is a helpful exercise. We have been thinking of identity essentially as how the congregation perceives or understands itself, but how others perceive it (what we have been calling its reputation) is an element of identity as well.

What do your answers to these questions say about the evangelism of the church? What do they say about the mission of the church? Are there ways in which the church could become more visible and welcoming and engaging in the community?

3.3   How Rural People View Their Faith

Below are some of the responses Pastor Don Dovre, of Peace Lutheran Church in Ryan, Iowa, received in response to a survey he administered to his congregation during a sermon one Sunday. The survey asked the question, "If a friend, coworker, or relative asked you, 'Why do you go to worship? Why do you believe in God? Tell me about Jesus,' how would you answer?" Respondents included adults and children in the congregation.

Who else would think of animals? Or how everything is made up of atoms? Or who else would have the power to provide us with all that we need to live, grow, and reproduce? There is only one that could possibly do it and that is God. He knows where the universe starts, ends, and what it does. He's one smart dude.

God's son died for me. This saves me from my sin. I was baptized and will keep this faith forever.

I go to worship God because on Sunday after worship I feel refreshed and renewed and ready to tackle another week. If I miss a Sunday of church I feel like the day isn't complete. It feels void.

The Lord is our hope. When I think of the Lord it brings me peace of mind and happiness. He's always there to listen to me. He is my life!

I believe in God because he helps me in many ways, and I know that I'll see him some day. God is a Holy Spirit that lives in our hearts, but also in heaven. God hears our prayers and answers them.

I believe and worship God because I was brought up in the faith. I have found that I need someone stronger than me to lean on who is always there. God stands for good values and that makes it easy to feel good about believing in him.

Worship makes life's enjoyments more meaningful because they are rewards from God.

I believe in God because he is my savior from this world of sin. When I see in awe all of nature and its beauty, I know there is a creator, a God. I feel in my heart the peace of God at Christmas and Easter, especially. I believe in God because without him there would be no purpose or reason for living this life.

Because he died for our sins. I look outside and see God all around me. God loves us. He's always with us no matter what. I go to church to listen to the word of God with others. It gives me a lift for the week ahead.

He is our savior.

I believe and worship God because it gives me inner peace. It makes me a better person and helps me understand other people better and maybe help them deal with some of their problems.

I believe in God because he died for my sins. I come to worship because he is my savior. I can come to him in prayer.

The Lord has taken good care of me during all my trials in life. I was brought up to worship God. I feel he is always near me.

Because there has to be more to life than just the body.

Because of the miracles in life—giving birth, being able to heal (humans and animals)—beauty of nature, etc. There must be something responsible for these things.

Because he saved Moses and the Israelites and died on the cross for us and in the end he will save us too.

Jesus has taken me through many trials. He has been there to comfort me when I needed him. Going to church helps to keep this faith strong and gives explanations of the life of Christ. "Footprints" to me is a very good way to describe what the Lord does for me.

I always have believed in God because of the way we live and how plants grow.

Jesus is God's son who lived on earth and showed us how to love our neighbors then died on the cross and rose to heaven to show believers he was truly God's son.

I worship God by going to church and by praying.

For eternal life. Something I grew up doing and what my family does also.

God created heaven and earth. If you ask in prayer, God will answer you. I go to worship to thank him for what he has done for me. To guide me to—to make the right decisions.

Because he is always here no matter what. Good or bad, war or peace, till the end of time.

ISSUE FOR DISCUSSION

What patterns emerge in this tapestry of faith statements? As a pastor, how would you work with such a congregation to deepen specific understandings essential to building community?

3.4   How Does the Church View Itself As Part of the Larger Community?

The following excerpts from denominational statements give some indication about how the larger national bodies view issues that are significant to rural congregational identity.

EVANGELICAL LUTHERAN CHURCH IN AMERICA

"Resolution on Rural Ministry," adopted at the 1993 Churchwide Assembly. (An unabridged list of resolution items appears in resource unit 1.3.)

WHEREAS, the projected shortage of ordained pastoral leadership and lack of available financial resources . . . may require lay leaders to assume the responsibilities formerly performed by clergy; and
WHEREAS, this church needs to recruit ordained and lay leaders who will see rural ministry as an opportunity for service and will make long-term commitments to this ministry . . . , be it

RESOLVED, that
1. this church affirm its commitment to ministries in the rural setting;

2. this church assist congregations to move beyond congregational independence . . . toward better communication and cooperation among ministries in related communities, including ecumenical possibilities . . . ;
3. the seminaries of this church use instruction by extension and other instructional methods as ways for developing pastors and lay leaders in rural ministry . . . ;
4.-5. synods . . . develop and train teams of indigenous lay leaders to serve and provide leadership . . . ;
6. this church . . . assist multi-point congregations [in developing yoking agreements];
7.-10. [promote work of multi-point parishes and encourage inclusivity, as well as foster economic development and land stewardship in rural communities.]

PRESBYTERIAN CHURCH (U.S.A.)

The Church Responding to Rural America: A Report Approved by the 203rd General Assembly (1991) Presbyterian Church (U.S.A.) (available from Distribution Management Services, phone 1-800-524-2612)

● The theme of God as Creator and human beings as the stewards of creation has special meaning for those who live in the rural context. The care of the land is far more than a theological principle. The neglect and destruction of the land has direct long term consequences for those who, through daily work, know . . . sustenance comes from the land.

● Community as a gift of God's grace to humanity has also been a traditional assumption of life in rural areas. Persons who live in small towns cherish the experience of knowing neighbor and working together for the common good. As rural and small town communities undergo disintegration, the sense of loss is acute. The New Testament emphasis on God creating the new community is a biblical theme that can give [rural America] hope.

Community Ministry
● The Christian life also results in caring for one's neighbor. That mission is a particularly pressing one for rural communities where the economic well-being of people has declined over the past decade.

Common Issues
● Participants . . . identified eight common issues to be addressed by the church . . . :
A. Corporate Agriculture: Land Ownership and Control; B. Environment and the Stewardship of Creation; C. Rural Poverty; D. Education; E. Health Care; F. Rural and Small Town Racism; G. Alcohol and Drug Abuse; and H. Disintegration of the Rural Community.
● The issue cited in item H is economic decline; the imposition of a "growth-oriented value system that emphasizes bigger is better, competition is the only sensible human motivation for life, and 'survival of the fittest' as a proper human economic expression of natural selection."

The Response of the Church
● One practical model for rural, small town ministry could be the establishment of ecumenical church and community centers. Such centers could develop ministries of worship, community celebration, biblical reflection on issues, reconciliation among groups, and programs for service and justice.

Pastoral Leadership
● Rural ministry calls for pastors, church workers, and laity to be community leaders.
● Pastors need to be able to articulate a theology of hope and lead the people of the church toward a positive vision of mission. . . . In addition, the rural pastor needs to build team ministry with the laity and provide necessary resources.

ROMAN CATHOLIC CHURCH

From U.S. Bishop's Pastoral Message and Letter, "Economic Justice for All: Catholic Social Teaching and the U.S. Economy," Origins 16, no. 24 (27 November 1986): 409-55

Paragraphs 242-47 recommend limiting subsidies that favor large landholders at the expense of moderate-sized family farms, reforming tax policies that encourage similar trends, redirecting research toward small- and medium-sized farm productivity, and protecting wage levels.

Paragraph 248 is aimed at farmers:

The everpresent temptation to individualism and greed must be countered by a determined movement toward solidarity in the farm community. Farmers should approach farming in a cooperative way, working with other farmers in the purchase of supplies and equipment and in the marketing of produce. It is not necessary for every farmer to be in competition against every other farmer.

Paragraphs 356-58 are aimed at the church:

The church has a special call to be a servant of the poor, the sick and the marginalized, thereby becoming a true sign of the church's mission. . . . True Charity leads to advocacy.

Yet charity alone is not a corrective to all economic social ills. . . . Grass-roots efforts by the poor themselves, helped by community support, are indispensable.

Also see *Strangers and Guests: Toward Community in the Heartland. A Regional Catholic Bishops' Statement on Land Issues,* May 1, 1980; and *Report of the Ad Hoc Task Force on Food, Agriculture, and Rural Concerns, National Conference of Catholic Bishops,* United States Catholic Conference, November 15, 1988. For copies, call the U.S. Catholic Conference at 202-541-3291 or 202-541-3287.

UNITED CHURCH OF CHRIST

A Pronouncement of the Twelfth General Synod of the United Church of Christ, 1979

This pronouncement calls attention to four major areas of rural life and recommends policy statements that

- call for stewardship of natural resources.
- support the strengthening of rural business economics while similarly affirming the right of workers to equity and justice.
- renew support of the small- and medium-sized family farm as the predominant unit in American agriculture.
- call for greater effort by government and the private sector to improve community services, cultivate human resources without discrimination, and encourage community organization and development.

THE UNITED METHODIST CHURCH

Policy Recommendations: Aiming at the Grass Roots (from "Faithful Witness on Today's Issues: Agricultural and Rural Life Issues," a report of the 1988 Quadrennium of The United Methodist Church)

VI. A Call for Change: What Needs to Be Done?
Complex problems that have developed over long periods of time have no quick and simplistic solutions. We call upon the church, local communities, state and federal governments to make the following changes:

A. We call upon the United Methodist churches, charges, and cooperative parishes to:
   Intentionally develop ministries to meet four major needs that exist today in the rural U.S.A.
   1. Mend the brokenness of community life in rural U.S.A.
   2. Strengthen its ministry in rural U.S.A. In order to do this we suggest that the churches:
      a. Encourage seminaries to develop much stronger and more specific programs for equipping ministers to be pastors in rural settings.

     b. Encourage bishops and cabinets to greatly lengthen the tenure of ministers in rural areas, and to discover ways in which the local church can cooperate in such a process.

     c. Become adept at analyzing the needs of their own community, and in responding to them.

     d. Urge every local United Methodist church to study the plight of the racial/ethnic farmer.

     e. Encourage local churches and their pastors to offer counsel, support and emergency aid to farm families in trouble. . . .

     f. Support and become involved in cooperative and ecumenical ministry, sharing in specific geographic areas. . . .

  3. Call our nation to a stewardship of its natural resources. . . .

  4. Build bridges of understanding and partnership between rural and urban congregations and communities . . . [including exchanges].

B. We call upon districts to:

  1. Develop and or strengthen their missional stance in rural areas.

  2. Create cluster groups and other supportive networks . . . to facilitate spiritual formation.

  3. Encourage cooperative leadership through more creative use of available personnel and appropriate technology.

C. We call upon the annual conferences to:

  1. Analyze their [rural] crisis responses and provide [needed funding].

  2. Place personnel strategically in order to respond to rural needs. Insist that pastoral appointments be made with the . . . entire community in mind, and not just the needs of the congregation. . . .

  3. Become public policy advocates . . . bringing about positive change.

  4. Cooperate with other church and secular agencies in a rural response.

  5. Be in partnership with seminaries to develop programs, including "teaching" parishes and internships, to equip ministers to serve in rural areas.

  6. . . . invest conference foundation funds in rural economic development needs.

  7. Discover ways to enable the ethnic ownership of farmland.

  8. Model and support team ministry. . . .

  9. Develop [volunteer in mission] programs. . . .

D. We call upon the general church to:

  1. . . . prepare clergy to be more effective *pastors* in rural areas . . . [including sensitivity to] a new "language," a new lifestyle, and a new culture.

  2. Cooperate ecumenically. . . .

  3. Better learn the skills of personnel placement . . . [including establishing] a tenure that is long enough . . . to build trust/understanding . . . for becoming *pastors* to the *community*. . . .

  4. Recognize Rural Life Sunday. . . .

  5. [Help] U.S. and Third World farmers to share innovations and knowledge. . . .

  6. . . . monitor all church agency programs to ensure sensitivity to the present rural crisis.

  7. [Stress] . . . soil stewardship and ecology. . . .

  8. [Invest] in . . . local church based community development.

  9. . . . promote the cooperative style of ministry. . . .

  10. . . . research corporate ownership of agriculture and its effects upon . . . rural areas. . . .

  11. Develop and distribute a [global] educational curriculum. . . .

E. We call upon the Council of Bishops to:

  1. Develop . . . a pastoral letter . . . similar to "In Defense of Creation" on the [rural crisis].

  2. Encourage . . . longer term rural [cabinet] appointments. . . .

  3. Foster . . . cooperative . . . leadership by more creative use of . . . personnel and . . . technology.

Also see *Report on the Study on Strengthening the Church with Small Membership, 1989-92 Quadrennium* as forwarded to the 1992 General Conference of The United Methodist Church. For copies, call The United Methodist Church, Info-Serve, at 1-800-749-6007.

ISSUE FOR DISCUSSION

How do these statements affect or influence the identity of your rural congregation? Are local rural churches concerned with denominational legislation? How could this kind of advocacy be used to good effect?

Chapter 4

PROGRAM: THE CONGREGATION EXPRESSING ITSELF IN ACTION

Chapter 2 described the context of rural congregations and offered some ways of assisting pastors and people in thinking about their context and how that context shapes their particular congregation. Chapter 3 turned to the question of identity, which in some ways flows from the question of context. The resource units included in that chapter were designed to stimulate you to think about the identifying characteristics of your specific congregation.

Here in chapter 4 we turn to the third element of congregational studies: what it does. Exercises in the resources section at the end of the chapter will press you to think about the church's activities, structures, and plans, all of which are tangible. Clearly, the programs in which the rural congregation engages are a result of its sense of identity; its actions generally express its self-understanding. That self-understanding has been shaped by the rural context, the social situation of the parishioners, the history of the church, past clergy, economic factors, denominational actions, and so on.

Identity and program are joined at the hip in that they seem to represent the two poles of a congregation's functioning—within itself and within the community. Identity can be understood as how the congregation thinks of itself and is thought of in the community; program can

be understood as what the congregation *does* within itself and in the community. So identity is who the congregation is and program is what the congregation does. We have already seen that context influences both those poles, and we will see that process is the way decisions get made in the church as well as all those ways of doing things that are characteristic patterns of behavior. What has no doubt become evident to you is that these dimensions or elements are as tightly coiled together as a strand of DNA. They are not discrete aspects but constantly interactive components; they overlap with one another. For example, congregations structure their Christian education *programs* in ways that express their *identity* and their characteristic *processes* of relating. All these components are features of the same organic entity—the rural congregation—which has an essential integrity of its own. James Hopewell writes that a congregation is a discrete web of relationships unique unto itself.[1]

What the Congregation Does: Its Activities

Included in the program of a rural congregation are the following activities, plans, or structures:

● worship—including preaching, the sacraments, and music;

● Christian education—the education and formation of believers;

● nurture and fellowship—both pastoral care and community solidarity;

● evangelism—witness to Christ and inviting others to discipleship;

● mission and outreach—service to the community and beyond.

WORSHIP

There is no doubt about what the central activity of the rural congregation is: Sunday morning worship. This is the heart of all the activities, self-understanding, and distinctiveness of a Christian congregation. The church is most essentially itself during worship; it is in fact hard to imagine a congregation continuing to exist if it no longer worships together. In rural congregations, Sunday morning church is, for many, also the weekly public activity, far surpassing such touted events as town hall meetings, 4-H association meetings, or even stock car races. The primary function of worship, however, is to praise God, express our gratitude, and seek to discern God's presence in our lives and God's purposes for them.

Worship is the foundation; when we rural Christians want to say why we do what we do and what is distinctive about us, we point to our worship services. We worship God because it is God who created us and all that is, God in Jesus Christ who has redeemed us from our sinfulness and pointed us toward the life of faith and righteousness (and who continues to point us in that direction!), and because God sustains us continuously through the work of the Spirit. In worship the rural church responds to God's graciousness and sovereignty.

Craig Nessan, a theologian at Wartburg Theological Seminary, suggests in his "theology of the congregation" that during our Sunday morning worship we attempt to re-create or pro-create the kingdom of God.[2] If one is uncomfortable with the word *kingdom* (which we use because of its linkage to Scripture), other language that is also and differently helpful is "reign of God" or "community of God."

In worship we seek to gain at least a glimpse of "the feast to come," the full arrival of the society for which we pray "Your will be done, on earth as it is in heaven." We in the church know of course that the Kingdom is not yet completely here, that God's community has not arrived fully, but we also know that in Jesus Christ the Kingdom *has* arrived. We are caught in the tension between what is already here (see Jesus' saying in Luke 17:21 that "the kingdom of God is [already] among you"), and the not-yet-but-coming completion of God's community. We in the church know that tension well; we know that we are not yet what we shall be—at least we hope not! We are well aware of how far we continue to fall from what is ideal, what God's ways are. But in worship we respond to God and are reminded (and remind one another) that the future is in God's hands and that the community of God *has* in some ways already arrived. It is important to remember that. As we depart worship, the dissonance between the glimpse of God's kingdom that we caught in church and the life of the world impels us into the world to do evangelism and mission.

That is a very weighty view of worship, and it places an awesome responsibility and privilege on the pastor. The minister is called to help the congregation design and implement a worship service that, in fact, communicates the Kingdom, that does give people a glimpse or God's-eye view of life. That means that the rural minister is called to be just as competent and just as creative and just as strenuous in his or her efforts to plan, preside over, and conduct worship as any minister anywhere. The rural congregation is called to worship God and needs to worship God, just as surely as any congregation. It is through worship that grace is particularly communicated—through baptism, the Lord's Supper, the proclamation of the Word, and singing.

This fairly elevated view of what occurs in worship should not be taken as an endorsement of a highly ritualized or liturgical style (what people usually mean when they say "high church"). That may be entirely appropriate in some settings—even some rural settings. But more often, the rural congregation has its own way of "doing worship," which probably is more simple and less antiphonal. Tex Sample has emphasized in his book *Ministry in Oral Culture* the notion that rural congregations employ "the language of the heart," which is a vernacular peculiar to them. It is vital for the pastor to try to understand and speak this language of the people in ways that communicate the grace of God rather than assume that he or she knows how worship is "supposed to be done." How worship is "supposed to be done" may not communicate the grace of God at all but only imply the superiority of the minister and reinforce a supposed inferiority of rural culture. It is demeaning theologically to assume that God is not present in every culture; instead, God is best worshiped in ways that communicate to believers.[3] This is not meant to stifle the creativity of worship but to save it from bondage to a certain economic class or to cultural snobbery.

The resource units in this chapter deal with worship—especially preaching. Our main point here is that planning and conducting worship calls for the very best that the pastor and congregation can bring to it; worship is a source of hope and grace for people who very much need it. We want to, we need to worship God.

CHRISTIAN EDUCATION

Another important aspect of the rural congregation's program is its educational work. Usually we think of this as "Sunday school," and we may be too quick to discount it. In the rural community Sunday school programs can benefit from smaller sizes; they can link different classes and employ nontraditional teachers (e.g., older youth); and they can offer multigenerational experiences. There may be an opportunity in rural settings to offer "release time" from public school for classes in religion, Vacation Bible School, mission trips, ecumenical youth groups, and so on. All these fairly standard forms of Christian education can be employed in the smaller church. One of the most far-reaching relationships in the rural congregation can be the one established between the church school teacher and the students in his or her class. The congregation has a major role, formal or informal, in shaping the educational program of the church. One pastor in Belmont, Wisconsin, set up a computer Sunday school and established linkages around the country with other churches. The fifth- and sixth-graders in the class

loved it because it overcame barriers of distance and size.

Youth work is especially important in the rural setting in the wake of the deterioration of the family or at least due to the absence of parents from the home. Many rural families hold down three or four different jobs. Youth ministry is the mission field, an evangelism field for rural congregations. Not only does the church play a stabilizing role in rural young people's lives; it is also important for the strength of rural churches that youth begin to take shaping and decision-making roles in their congregations.

It should be clear that the rural congregation needs to educate and help in the continuing spiritual and moral formation of children and youth. It should assist in the education, formation, and nurture of adults as well. Nurture involves more than education; it includes coming to the assistance of those who are particularly in need in the congregation. It involves both a routine way of caring for and upbuilding others and a readiness to assist others when that is necessary. Sometimes we call this "pastoral care," but ideally it involves the care of the whole congregation.

FELLOWSHIP

Fellowship is a routine sense of being in relationship with other members of the congregation and sharing in a sense of mutual interrelation within the church. Certainly fellowship involves nurture, but it goes beyond that to include wanting to be together and play together as well as work together. Nurture and fellowship are vital functions of the church, because we all need a sense of community and trust if we are to think and talk about those parts of our lives that really concern us. There simply are not many safe places left in our world to do this. The rural congregation shapes who we are and who we become as well. It can be a place for moral deliberation and courageous action and planning, as well as a place for nurture and fellowship; the two are not contradictory. Corporate mission and action are only possible among people who trust one another.

EVANGELISM

Evangelism is tied into nurture and fellowship as well. Too often we rural congregations turn into closed fellowships where we are very friendly to one another but neglect those who are seeking to worship God and join our fellowship. We in the church sometimes find it difficult to invite others to join us in worship or even come with us to church activities. In the rural community the best kind of evangelism emphasizes inviting friends and relatives who live nearby as well as those who are new to the community to come to church or to church-sponsored events. *There are many unchurched people in every rural community these days.* Many of them are dying to be invited. If we in the church have good news to offer, if we are committed to our church home, then it is unneighborly not to invite others to join us. It is vital that we take the time and make the effort to think about how we can become open and welcoming to others. Many rural congregations plan events—dinners or parties or members hosting visitors for lunch—for precisely this purpose. It is what Christ asks his disciples to do.

MISSION

Mission is another aspect of the congregation's program—the outreach of the congregation into the community, region, state, or world. This aspect of program includes all the ways the congregation reaches out into the community in service. It includes the individual vocations of the church members as they go about their daily work in a Christian manner and incorporate Christian ideals and teachings into their daily routine and interaction. Mission may include projects of economic assistance, community development, relief aid, assistance to the indigent in the community, serving on boards and agencies, working with the Boy Scouts or Girl Scouts, providing a forum for political discussion, becoming involved in advocacy groups, and a host of other activities. Many rural congregations are engaged in countless acts of mission, often in informal ways that are so much incorporated into their church's style that they escape notice.

Jesus Christ carried on a ministry of compassion and justice; we have his example and his teaching that mission to neighbors is essential to the Christian faith. Recently it seems as though we have separated social ministry from the life of the congregation and made it merely an option for those who are so inclined. Rather than caring about what is happening to members of the congregation or to others in the community, social ministry committees are involved in ministry at a distance. It is true that Jesus clearly calls us to love distant as well as close neighbors; but too often, segregating global and local mission concerns has led us to overlook the needs of our local neighbors and neglect the root causes of the social evils influencing people in our backyard.[4] Rural congregations have always been particularly attuned to local concerns, but even they have suffered from this segregation. It is now time to attend to local (and global) mission as an act of the congregation. There may be poor people worshiping with you or living in your community; if those people are suffering, Christ asks his congregation to attend to them.

There are several other aspects of program that we could mention—stewardship, global missionary activity, and governance of the church come to mind. Surely these are worthy of attention, and when we discuss the component of process in congregational life in the next chapter we will be dealing with aspects of both governance (local polity) and stewardship. We have already touched on global missionary activity as an aspect of both evangelism and mission. However, our focus has been primarily on the program of the local congregation, and we have treated those activities that are central to the life of the rural church.

Relational, Programmatic, or Both?

A modest debate is ongoing among those who discuss the rural church. Some whom we respect very much, such as Doug Walrath and Carl Dudley, see the rural, smaller membership church as being very relational. This view suggests that there should be nothing quite as formal as a "program" in the church. Programming would be impersonal and would express a lack of sufficient care for the individual. Programming smacks too much of bureaucracy and planning and management by objective; it undercuts the warmth of a community where "everybody knows your name."

The contrast between relationally oriented and program-centered churches can be overemphasized. Programs can express the warmth of relationship. One of the surprising things we learned in interviewing rural congregations that were identified as "vital" was that most of them did some planning, and virtually all of them evaluated and paid deliberate attention to the activities that went on in the church.[5] It is true that too much emphasis on task, or the programs that result from activity-oriented planning, can undercut relationships and the warmth of community; it is also true that a lack of program sends the message that newcomers are not welcome. That is hardly relational. Indeed, many of the vital congregations we interviewed continually offered new programs as they were initiated, either by youth or by newcomers. An openness to expanding one's programs is important.

For too many rural congregations the expectation has been that they will mimic the larger church's program, no matter that those programs have been designed for larger, urban or suburban churches. Rural congregations knew all along that these programs did not fit. Over the years, rural congregations have customized large, urban congregations' programs to fit better. But we have tended to define our program too much over against the denominational norm, the target church that did not resemble ours at all. Sometimes we have failed to be creative about our own programs. There is nothing written in stone about the way the congregation does its work so long as the congregation understands that the function of its program is to carry on Jesus' mission to love God and our neighbors.

Following up on this, if "program" is the means "through which a congregation expresses its mission and ministry . . . to those outside the membership,"[6] then it becomes important to shape our program to meet not only our own members' needs but also the needs of those outside the church walls. For that reason we will turn our attention briefly to what has been happening to many rural families both inside and outside our congregations. How can our congregations' programs function to do ministry and

mission to families in crisis, whom we mistakenly assume all exist outside our walls? Resource unit 4.1 will stimulate thinking about designing programs to meet these needs.

Rural Family Life Endangered

The condition of rural family life is of concern to churches. More than in urban settings, the family was and is at the heart of traditional rural life. On the family farm in particular, there once was a cohesiveness of lifestyles seldom experienced in other settings. Economic pressures and the trend toward corporate styles of farming have threatened the family farm as that kind of basic rural community. (See resource unit 2.6.) Among those casualties are farmsteads that have been in the hands of a single extended family for generations.

The trauma of this economic upheaval is measured not only in dollars and cents, or bankruptcies and foreclosures. The loss of the farm is far more personal than that. It represents an emotional as well as physical homelessness every bit as devastating as that experienced by the urban poor. The resulting stress and loss of self-esteem and identity tear at the fabric of rural family life.

Traditional rural role relationships also may have hampered how rural families face such issues as economic tension and geographic isolation. Contemporary novels treat such themes as violence, abuse, and the alienation of men and women in rural families in that context. The thesis underlying such works is that shifting power structures in modern society have left men and women with no clear guidelines for redefining themselves in relation to their work or families. The result can be a spectrum of responses ranging from confusion to anger, and at worst, violence within the family or against the self.

Statistics relating to spousal and child abuse and domestic violence reflect the pain of anger misdirected outward; alcoholism and substance abuse, as well as other self-destructive behaviors, are among the expressions of such rage directed inward. The suicide figure is significantly higher for rural males than for the population as a whole. A study in Oklahoma for the period from 1983 to

1988 revealed that although farmers account for only 2.16 percent of the population in that state, they account for 6.12 percent of the suicides.[7]

More elusive are the increases in stress-related diseases and clinical depression. One woman rural activist who experienced the tragedy of losing the family farm reported, "The tendency in the rural community is to stuff it. Families bury their hurts until something either explodes or snaps. In our community, you often do not even know your next-door neighbor is on the verge of bankruptcy until someone finds the husband hanging from the rafters in the barn."

A prevalent factor contributing to such profound feelings of guilt, personal failure, and hopelessness is the secular doctrine of success. For some, this doctrine has become confused with Christian theology and the role God plays in creation. As that same rural farm wife expressed it, "If there is a drought or a crop fails, that's fate . . . or the way it is. Stuff happens. But if the farm fails, that failure is highly personal. God's back must be turned somehow in judgment." Under this viewpoint, experiencing a sense of grace and the presence of a loving God in the midst of crisis is almost impossible. A pressing consideration for rural churches as they reassess their mission to rural families is to express the grace rather than the wrath of God.

It is important for the church to know the stress indicators that operate in rural family life and to assist families in dealing with them. Fortunately there are talented people who are concerned about this. Sandy Simonson Thums, Assistant to the Bishop, Northwest Synod of Wisconsin, Evangelical Lutheran Church in America, has worked with individuals, families, and churches using her innovative Life Balance Wheel. Respondents are asked to rate the following eight health indicators on a ten-point scale, specifying which factors are perceived as positive and which are perceived as negative in their lives at the time of the survey:

mental health
financial health
physical health
spirituality
self-esteem
goals
work
family

Ms. Thums has found that responses fall into certain gender-related patterns. For rural men financial health is clearly the most significant factor in producing or reducing stress levels. If a man rates either financial health or self-esteem as four or lower on the scale—sees these aspects of his life as negative—the family life specialist asks if he has had thoughts of suicide. If men rate their financial health as being significantly negative, then the other health inicators tend to be problematic also.

The pattern for rural women is a little more diffuse. If the areas of spirituality and family are perceived very negatively, it is often indicative of either past or current abuse, including childhood episodes. In such cases, the family life worker raises questions about childhood and current family life. Although there is no single indicator for women that has the strength that financial health does for men, the two areas of financial health and self-esteem tend to color or influence the other areas of health as well.

Intervention can be difficult. When rural parents are forced to survive by working multiple part-time jobs, they may find themselves less and less able to respond to the emotional needs of their children. (Although urban families are experiencing similar stresses, the physical isolation of farm families can make intervention logistically more difficult.) With the decline in federal and state funds available for health and other services, and with rising medical costs, rural areas tend to be underserved both in physical and mental health care. Much of the burden for dealing with youth-related problems has been thrown upon the educational system. Yet declining tax resources make it harder to fund programs, and consolidation has undermined the role of the local school in many rural communities.

Problems of the family, in short, cannot be treated in purely economic or individualistic terms. The rural family in crisis both affects and is affected by the larger society in the local community.

Individual pressures, in turn, manifest themselves on a collective level. As chapter 2 outlines, the problems facing rural communities today are formidable:

● declining (and frequently aging) populations
● eroding retail and industrial systems

- dwindling job options and economic opportunities
- deteriorating infrastructure (roads, bridges, sewage and sanitary facilities, and similar physical concrete and steel underpinnings of community life)
- related dwindling of social services (health care, recreational options, local educational resources, to name but a few)
- environmental problems related to agricultural practices and waste disposal policies that threaten to make rural areas dumping grounds for urban America

Communities become caught in a kind of domino effect—a downward spiral in which it is hard to separate individual human problems (e.g., personal loss of identity and family structures in crisis) from the decline of a sense of community as a whole. The result is a letting-go of the traditional interpersonal anchors of rural life.

In many communities, the church may be the single public institution still intact and able to deal with the relentless pressure on the rural family and community. Unfortunately, the church may not be assuming that leadership role.

The Rural Church: Crossroads of Opportunity

Over the decades that followed the Johnson presidency and the Great Society, many communities—rural and urban—came to rely on governmental programs and official agencies to meet their health-care and other societal needs. The church, in effect, gave up its traditional roles as healer and caregiver and as minister to the physical as well as spiritual needs of members and the community at large. With the dismantling of such governmental programs and institutions over the past decade, a power vacuum has been created into which churches have only recently begun to step. Regaining a traditional sense of mission is no easy task.

The effectiveness of the church in dealing with interpersonal problems is influenced by the fact that the church itself is made up of the very individuals who may be experiencing great dislocation and personal pain. Along with this pain comes a wide range of emotions, including anger, which may be directed at the church itself, the pastor, or other congregational members. A handful of difficult parishioners can create what has been described by some as the "conflictive" or "antagonistic" church.

But there are alternatives. Voices from outside the pews—as well as from committed clergy and laity in rural congregations—argue that the church does not have to accept such a scenario.

It is especially in this area of awareness and response—working toward change on a relational plane—that the church could assume a strong leadership role. Although some of the problems that impede the church from rebuilding community, metaphorically and physically, are external ones, some of the barriers relate more to the spiritual life of congregations and the way the church defines itself, its spirituality, and its sense of mission.

From a congregational studies perspective, the resource units in the remainder of this chapter lay the groundwork for identifying those areas of church *program* that can address what is happening in the lives of church and community members.

RESOURCES FOR PEOPLE-CENTERED PROGRAMS

The resource units in this chapter deal with the programs of rural congregations. They challenge us to think about how worship, preaching, and other elements of the church's program could minister to the rural community.

4.1   A Cry from the Heartland

The following passage is adapted from a study by Roberta Hinman as part of her work in a rural empowerment program at Iowa State University. As you read it, imagine that "Tammy" addresses her plea to you as the pastor of a rural congregation. How could the congregation help her address the family difficulties and other problems she faces? Specifically, what activities (or programs) might be helpful to Tammy?

Although she is only thirty-nine, Tammy seems much older. Much of the time, Tammy's words come rapidly—in shotgun fashion—and she fidgets constantly in her chair, pushing a stray wisp of hair behind her ears or fumbling with the clasp of her worn leather purse. Although her skirt and blouse are neatly pressed, the seams are strained in places.

Tammy is talking about her life on an Iowa farm with her family, her fourteen-year marriage with Joe, and her relationship with her four children (Rob, twelve; Jennifer, nine; Susan, seven; and Adam, five). "It's scary to think I'll be turning forty in just a few months. Sometimes I think the ruts in my life are deeper than the ones the tractor leaves in our driveway. I can't seem to stop eating. . . . Like everything else, it's gotten to be a habit. Joe expects me to keep the house, our clothes—everything—so meticulous, yet I'm the only one who seems to care how it stays that way. Sometimes I think if I'd disappear, no one would even notice unless the next meal didn't appear on the table."

Ignoring the box of tissues placed on the edge of your desk, Tammy reaches in her purse for a worn, crumpled one. "Sorry about that," she mumbles, "I seem to be crying at the drop of a hat lately. Either that or eating."

When she picks up the thread of the conversation, her words come so quickly that several times you have to ask her to repeat herself. "Not that Joe doesn't have his troubles, too. We lost 60 percent of the corn and all of the hay last summer, and the bank is dragging its feet about loans for seed for spring planting. We've been buying hay meanwhile, but the quality is poor. Joe hasn't been sleeping well lately, and some mornings he really has to push himself to go out and do the chores."

You can detect a rising undercurrent of anger as Tammy continues. "Once Joe's outside, he sometimes disappears for hours on end. He expects the kids to help with the heavy chores, but he doesn't really seem to enjoy spending time with them. I try to be understanding, but I'm tired after substitute teaching all day, and kids are the last things I want to be dealing with. . . . "

Tammy's laugh is awkward, half apologetic, and she looks at you as if gauging your reaction. "Fourth-graders are awfully tough on substitutes."

You smile. "I taught, myself, for a couple of years."

But Tammy's gaze is fixed on the windows, and her voice has taken on a distant tone. "Adam has been acting up in kindergarten—they've called me in several times now to talk about it. . . . "

It is silent in the room for what seems like a long time. Tammy is looking down at her hands, her expression unreadable.

"Do you have other family in the area?" you ask, carefully gauging Tammy's reaction.

"Actually, we farm with Joe's folks," Tammy explains tonelessly. "We're buying the land from them, and the 480 acres and dairy herd are more than we could handle or afford alone. When Joe and I moved into the homestead, my in-laws moved into town—semi-retired, I guess you'd say, although Joe's dad still makes a lot of the decisions." Tammy hesitates, and as if out of habit, her voice lowers. "Joe's dad wasn't any too happy about the two of us getting married—in some ways, he's never forgotten that. So, when they have things to decide, Joe usually goes over to his folks' house. It's a lot . . . easier that way. Only lately . . . Joe . . . well, he's been complaining that his dad has been so rigid and unbending about everything."

The words are spilling out now, unchecked. "You see, with all that rain, the gardens and the basement were flooded most of the summer, and for a while I thought the health department might tell us to vacate. Lord knows where we'd go! We depend on those vegetables for year-round relief for our grocery budget with my canning and all, but I guess with the harvest so low, we're going to have to postpone those hot water heater repairs. . . ."

Despair hangs in the air like the humidity. Instinctively, you start searching your memory banks for anything that makes sense—anything you or the congregation could say or do that would make any kind of difference in this young woman's life.

But before you can respond, with an obvious force of will Tammy pulls herself erect in her seat. "Well, we can always heat what we need on the stove."

ISSUES FOR DISCUSSION

1. How could you as a pastor bring these concerns before your congregation?
2. How would you guide members to sensitively address the problems Tammy and her family are facing?
3. How might you preach following this session with Tammy?
4. Can you imagine a program of evangelism that could reach Tammy and others who have similar life circumstances?

4.2   Preaching in the Rural Congregation

One of the few resources for preaching in a rural congregation comes from Deborah Cronin. In a book entitled *Can Your Dog Hunt?* Cronin gives us a bit of theory that is illustrated by excerpts from the introduction of her book and from her title sermon.

From the introduction:

Statistics show that while most mainline churches are located in rural areas, many, and often the majority, of their pastors come from urban areas. Consequently, these pastors need guidance in preaching messages and stories which convey a sense of contextual reality to their congregations.

Experience indicates that the fine art of listening is central to understanding rural communities. Listening is best done on the front porch, over a cup of coffee at the town diner or feed mill, at Little League games, and all the other casual places where town and country folks tend to gather. It is in these shared conversations that the town's culture, history, and even its humor is shared.

The long tradition of rural story-telling comes out of this give-and-take of telling and listening, listening and telling some more. Stories which have been told for one or two generations (and sometimes longer) often explain why the present generation thinks, speaks, and acts as it does. This is why some of the most effective town and country theme sermons are grounded in story-telling. It is natural, and it fits. Many of the sermons found in this collection make fine use of story-telling. They also represent a variety of story-telling styles.

It is common for urban congregations to include people whose roots are in rural America; but for a variety of reasons, they have moved to the city and the suburbs. These people, likewise, respond positively to sermons which find their origins in the familiar setting of their own place of origin. For example, a few years ago I had the opportunity to preach at Boise First United Methodist Church, better known as "The Cathedral of the Rockies." On the way into the church my elderly mother, who happened to be with me that day, asked me about my sermon topic. I replied, "Dogs who can hunt." Her response, made while standing in the shadow of this large urban neo-Gothic church, was almost hysterical. "Whatever are you thinking!" she exclaimed. She proceeded to tell me that hunting dogs were hardly the right theme for a sermon preached in a state capital church.

The reader will find my sermon from that day, "Can Your Dog Hunt?" at the beginning of this collection.

Following the morning worship service I was delayed at the door greeting worshipers who, one by one, told me the story of the best hunting dog they had ever known. Some were in tears as they recalled the attributes of their canine best friend. Many of them told me how they had moved to Boise from the country. Several of them shared their faith with me, making the connection between this rural saying and the faithfulness of God. It was obvious that many of the folks there had found through the sermon a contact point with their rural roots.

Even people who have a totally urban background can derive spiritual meaning from sermons illuminating Jesus' teachings using rural symbols. It's helpful to remember that Jesus was a country boy, born in a cow barn in Bethlehem, and raised by a laborer in the small town of Nazareth. From the stories he told we know that he understood the language of seeds, barns, animals, and fishing. Our listeners better understand Jesus when we illuminate through our preaching the meaning of these stories. If some of these sermons also prophetically lift up the important rural issues of our day, such as poverty and good stewardship of the land, then so much the better.[8]

From the sermon "Can Your Dog Hunt?":

A man came to the country to hunt. He stayed at a private lodge which rented bird dogs to folks who didn't bring their own dogs with them. The dog he rented was named Preacher. Preacher was just a year old, so it only cost five dollars a day to rent him. But he was a good bird dog, and the hunter bagged the full limit of birds he was allowed to shoot.

The man enjoyed hunting with Preacher so much that when he came back the next year he specifically requested that he be able to rent Preacher for the duration of his stay. Preacher had become an even better bird dog, so the price to rent him that year was ten dollars a day. Year after year the hunter bagged his full limit of birds when hunting with Preacher. Year after year he requested Preacher, and year after year he paid a bit more. Twenty-five dollars one year, thirty dollars the next, and finally as much as forty dollars a day for this exceptionally good hunting dog who knew where to find the birds and just how to flush them out for the hunter.

And then, one year the hunter returned to the lodge, requested Preacher, and was told that the price for the dog would be only five dollars a day. The hunter couldn't believe his ears! Only five dollars a day? Why was the dog suddenly such a bargain? "Well," said the lodge owner, "After you were here last year another hunter rented Preacher for several days. However, instead of calling the dog Preacher, he called him Bishop. Ever since then, the darn dog hasn't been worth a plug nickel." . . .

Should we be surprised when Mark tells us that Jesus became famous and word about him began to spread throughout the surrounding region of Galilee? Jesus was like a dog who can hunt. He walked into the village of Capernaum, a fishing village beside the sea of Galilee. There Jesus called an unclean spirit out of the man, and set him free. The people were amazed and asked, "What is this? A dog who can hunt? He commands even the unclean spirits and they obey him."

But I want to ask you this morning,
are you a dog that can hunt?
Are you a person whose faith goes
beyond one hour on Sunday morning?
Do folks know you as a Christian in action,
or only as a Christian who talks a good game?
Could I ask you to pray
for a deep concern on my heart?
Could I be assured that you have
an open line of communication to God,
and that you'd be a prayer warrior on my behalf?
Are you a dog who can hunt?
Can I trust you to do your best
to respond to the hurts and needs
of your family,
your neighborhood,
your world?
Or are you so caught up in your own life

that no one else really matters?
Are you a dog who can hunt?
Are you a living disciple of Jesus Christ,
or are you a Christian in name only?[9]

ISSUES FOR DISCUSSION

1. What principles of rural preaching are evident in Cronin's sermon?
2. What rural images and stories connect with biblical images?

4.3   Worship in the Rural Congregation

Worship styles reflect the context within which worship is taking place. A liturgical style that is accepted in one church may be entirely out of place in another. Tex Sample suggests a technique that he terms "thick listening"—not only listening to the language of the people, but also paying attention to "the practices in which those words are embedded."[10] Pastors can use the tools of listening and observing to determine styles of worship that will be both participative and celebrative. Has the pastor in rural Minnesota quoted here employed "thick listening" with members of his congregation?

Style of worship is important. It has to be welcoming. You need to get people to come in the first place and then keep them.

One of the biggest problems with seminaries is the focus on "liturgical correctness" that doesn't mean anything or is inconsequential out here. It can, in fact, be a barrier to true worship. Liturgies need to be freed up. We need to use it, not have it use us. For that reason, every Sunday I vary things so that the service becomes an equalizer between newcomers and old-timers. Parishioners need to be a little off guard in the service. You don't want to scare them, but they need to know they don't know totally what's going on.

Bulletins, I tell them, are strictly advisory.

In a way, I suppose, that approach conditions them to be comfortable with change. But you need trust to get by with change. I didn't change a thing for a whole year and then went very slowly at first. Then great changes came. But they had to love me first.

A pastor can do a lot to help parishioners learn to make transitions. When I came to this congregation, the blue hymnal was a sacred cow here, but I refused to bring in the Lutheran Book of Worship with me as some parishioners hoped I would do. I said, "No—*you* need to do this. I will not bowl you over with this. *You* are responsible to do your own changing."

But then I used some prayers from the Book of Worship without telling them where I got them. I taught a sermon series on the liturgy—the one used for introducing the Book of Worship, but not in that context. It was just to help them understand the purpose of liturgy better. Then there were two funerals for pillars of the church. I'm good at doing funerals in a caring way and tend to use my own variation of service for this. One member of these families was a real fan of the old hymnbook, who thought (and still thinks) that the Book of Worship is a communist conspiracy. But now he was in a real bind, because he came to love me as a pastor and person, as much as he still disagrees about use of the Book of Worship.

Holiday services were another point of entry. They hadn't done much with these, and I tried to make them stellar. In this case, there were no traditions to step on. It was free turf. So I added a number of special services that people really liked . . . things that weren't in the hymnal. So people saw the value of change.

ISSUES FOR DISCUSSION

1. Should a pastor involve the congregation in planning worship services?
2. What might happen if the pastor did not plan any of the worship service?

3. What sorts of images or hymns or liturgies or practices express the language of the heart that speaks to rural believers?

4.4 Thinking About Evangelism in Your Church

Ah, the "e" word! We all tend to feel vaguely guilty about how our congregations are doing the work of evangelism, in part because we feel as though we should not put embarrassing pressure on others to join our church. Perhaps if we thought that we were inviting others to become followers of Christ and not just join a church organization—wonderful as it usually is—we would be less hesitant. There are a number of evangelism ideas that are especially suited to rural congregations. Most of them center around friendship groups and allowing people to gradually enter our fellowship before committing themselves. The downside of this is that sometimes we forget what is distinctive about the church as the Body of Christ and about Christian discipleship. In short, we may lack faith in the truth of the gospel. Given the importance of faith in Christ to membership in the church, it is nevertheless true that family-and-friendship evangelism is very appropriate to rural settings. The following case study comes from Hong Kong, perhaps the area of the world where people's privacy and individual beliefs are most respected and evangelism most likely to seem to church people to involve pressure.

After years of handing out tracts and going door-to-door in Hong Kong, the missionaries associated with International Missions there, a conservative U.S. independent missionary organization with missions in Asia and in Islamic countries, tried another tack. They had had some success with traditional methods of evangelism, but found that people who came once or twice to services, some of whom even converted to Christianity, often did not come back. One of the strengths of the Hong Kong mission is its integration of local evangelists, pastors, and laypeople from the inception of church planting.

So when a group from Mai Lum, the mother church, wanted to start a new church group in Seung Shui, the Chinese leaders decided to begin with six months of "friendship evangelism." For six months the group, named "Beautiful Life," invited people to eat together, sing, and play games every week, and "only then invite them to receive Christ." They invited friends, relatives, and coworkers during that period. Three working women rented a flat for their use and started a study center where students could come for tutoring and remedial school work for a fee. The flat served as the meeting place for the Beautiful Life Church.

For six months the church members did not initiate conversation about their Christian faith or pray or have devotions, a procedure that Randy Posslenzny said "about drove him nuts." However, after those six months, the membership of ten invited the fifteen regular visitors to become Christians and to participate in worship with them. Ten of the fifteen accepted, and the other five continued to be welcomed into the weekly meal and singing and games.[11]

We have heard similar stories about evangelism in rural U.S. churches, about fellowships where people are invited to become involved in one another's lives and activities before they are invited to become disciples and members of the congregation. Most of those activities have to do with eating and playing and relating to one another, and they have led many to discipleship in Christ.

ISSUES FOR DISCUSSION

1. What principles or guidelines do you see in the story of the Beautiful Life Church?
2. Can the members of your congregation invite friends, relatives, and coworkers to activities that the church sponsors (maybe not in the church but in someone's home)?
3. Can you imagine a new way of introducing others to the joy of the Christian life in rural congregations?

4.5   Thinking About Mission in Your Backyard

The following are some ideas to help congregations start thinking about how they can carry out the mission of the church in their communities.[12]

Ministry to the needy. One church discovered a family in the community in which the father was not able to work because of sickness and the mother only had a part-time job. There were three children, ages nine to fifteen. Initially, the Sunday school raised $200, which was not enough to meet the family's needs. The entire congregation stepped in to assist and raised $756. Although the family was very appreciative, the father had some difficulty accepting help because of pride. The pastor and a deacon visited the home, and this seemed to ease the situation.

Garden plots for families. Another church had a large plot of land on their property that was not being used. The pastor decided to ask the church if they could offer garden plots for persons in the community who had nowhere to plant a garden. Workers from the church were recruited to help till the ground, rope off the area into plots, advertise that the plots were available, and be there to help plant and work in the garden.

Clothing closet. The purpose of a clothing closet is to provide clothing to financially indigent persons free of charge. In one church, space was provided, and shelves were built by a summer mission group. (Discarded shelves from businesses may also be available.) Clothing was donated by churches, mission groups coming to the area, and the community at large. Two women donated their time by working in the clothing closet two days a month. During Advent they also had toys and were open one to two days per week.

English classes. A church located in a town where many of the residents were from Mexico and did not speak English began to offer free English classes for adults and children in grades one through six. A space was set up in the church and volunteers were recruited to teach English as a second language. Students were recruited through fliers and the local cable channel. (The public schools and local employers would also be good contacts.)

Tent ministry at the state fair. In a town where the state fair was held, three churches worked together to set up a tent at the fair where they offered visitors a cup of cold water and a place to rest. Also available were New Testaments, witnessing tracts, and fliers showing the locations of Southern Baptist churches in the Dakotas. All items for this project were donated.

Neighborhood awareness. A church that had bought their building from another denomination was still experiencing some resentment from the neighborhood nine years after moving into the neighborhood. At Christmas the church decided to bake one-pound fruit cakes and distribute them to about 125 homes in the neighborhood. Volunteers who distributed the cakes saw a lot of grateful smiles. They ran short of cakes and plan to finish the project by visiting the rest of the homes with cookies for Valentine's Day.

Sharing services with the community. A bivocational pastor who had twenty years of experience in construction found that over half the men in his congregation had experience in either building or mechanics. They organized work groups and went to work volunteering their expertise on various building projects in the community. One year their projects included a trip to Alaska (all the men paid their own expenses) to reroof a parsonage. As one participant expressed, "We worked twelve to fourteen hours a day and just loved it."

ISSUES FOR DISCUSSION

1. Notice that all these mission ministries match a congregation's resources with needs in the community. What resources can your congregation offer? What needs are in your community? Is there a match there?
2. There are clearly opportunities for evangelism in these mission projects. Could there be such opportunities in yours as well? How could your congregation witness to Jesus in the course of its mission outreach?

4.6   Thinking Programmatically About Your Church

There are hundreds of activities that go on at your church or in the lives of parishioners in the church. And yet sometimes rural congregations feel as if "nothing ever goes on here; we don't do anything except have coffee after church." The following questions are designed to counter that impression by encouraging the congregation to think about all the activities that do go on. Just listing those activities is a good start. These questions could be discussed in a variety of settings, including adult church school classes and youth group gatherings.

● What worship services do you have in your church? Special services?

● What Sunday school activities are there? Don't overlook vacation church school, or the Christmas pageant, or when a member of the church takes the kids in the church out to the lake or to the farm or to the park for a picnic. List all the events you can think of.

● What groups are there in the church? For women? For men? For the whole congregation?

● Does the congregation cooperate in a food bank? Does it distribute Thanksgiving or Christmas baskets? Does it donate to support the denomination's work in relief efforts (in response to hurricanes, droughts, bombings, tragic accidents)? Does it support overseas missions? In what other outreach activities does the congregation participate?

● How do church members invite others to join the church? Are there programs for new members? Is there an openness to visitors who might want to start a new group? Are there activities that encourage visitors to feel at home?

● Do people in the congregation donate their time to volunteer services, to the regional church camps, to service on civic boards, to their schools, to lead fund drives, to local charities, or to other charitable activities?

● How do people in the church earn a living? What kind of Christian witness do they have at work? Consider all the activities that members are involved in during their jobs and how they are carrying on the work of Christ in those settings. How are they carrying the program of the church into the community?

● Now, what have these questions missed? What other activities do we as a congregation participate in?

ISSUE FOR DISCUSSION

You might want to go back to resource units 3.1 and 3.2 at this point. How is the identity of the church carried out in its program? How clear is that identity in what the congregation does as a corporate body or as individuals?

Chapter 5

Understanding Process: Leadership and Style in the Rural Congregation

Having looked at context, identity, and program in the rural congregation, we come to the final component of congregational studies: process. People talk about process a lot, but the term is amazingly difficult to define. For our purposes here, we define process as a congregation's typical style of doing business—its way of acting. We could call it "administration." Process is most evident in the way decisions are made in a church. We were not too far from process when we discussed character as a part of congregational identity.

At the same time, it is the elusive style of a congregation that makes a congregation either attractive or uninviting. It matters a great deal whether the processes at work in a congregation build an optimistic and uplifting spirit or a negative and protective stance. We have thought about process in terms of *empowerment*—a good word, which fell into overuse for a while. What is it, we want to know, that makes a congregation empowering of its members or debilitating? What drains energy, and what gives energy? What is bracing and engaging, and what is demoralizing and depressing? We found that the area most in need of research in terms of congregational vitality, as well as one of the most significant contributors to vitality, was that of clergy-laity relationships. How can clergy and laypeople empower one another? What are the optimal conditions for this?[1]

We will be examining the question of empowerment in greater detail in the next chapter, but we are persuaded that empowerment depends a great deal on process. This makes sense; after all, content and identity and program all feed into or exhibit style and process. Let us start thinking about process by examining the ways that decisions can be made in rural congregations and then looking at how the size of the congregation affects leadership in it. Then we will look at the nature of rural spirituality and think about how rural myths debilitate laypeople and clergy alike. Then we will examine the roles of clergy and laity and also of men and women, and how these can affect congregational process.

Decision Making, Leadership, and the Influence of Church Size

In one of the few books to examine the process of clergy-laity relationships in terms of leadership theory, Alvin Lindgren and Norman Shawchuck focus on the issue of how decisions are made. They write that "a church that claims theologically to be the people of God and to function as a priesthood of believers must look carefully at who makes the crucial decisions about defining its ministries. Shared decision making by members will empower those members to action when those ministries get underway."[2] Their claim is that ownership and participation in decision making result in participation in implementing and carrying out ministry decisions.

They point to three broad categories of the process by which decisions are made and, within each, list three or four subtypes. We suspect that you can imagine or have experienced each of these styles in operation at a church council or session or church board or other meeting. Their categories are as follows:

A. Decision Making by No Decision (refusing to make a decision)
  1. The Plop (lack of listening and response)
  2. The Lost Question (getting off the track)
  3. The Terrible Question (inability to face the question)

B. Decision Making by Minority (a single person or small group)
  1. The Boss (decision by authority)
  2. The Railroad (minority decision by manipulation)

C. Decision Making by Majority
  1. The Vote (majority rule)
  2. Decision Making by Consensus
  3. 100 Percent Unanimous Consent[3]

Lindgren and Shawchuck see times at which several of these styles are appropriate, but it is clear that "Decision Making by Majority" processes should be the norm when significant decisions are before rural congregations. We suggest that "decision making by consensus" (or close to unanimous decision) should be the goal among church governing bodies in which the participation of all the decision makers is crucial. Relationships are the heart of rural congregations, thus fractured relationships and hurt feelings are too high a price to pay for 99 percent of the decisions that rural church bodies face.

It is far too easy to assume that clergy, laity, or both could simply adopt one of these styles or processes and henceforth enjoy an optimal process of leadership. These styles are formed over the years, and a cooperative style involves a great deal of trust and community. Our personalities in the United States tend to favor competitive and achievement-oriented processes over consensual or reciprocal interaction.

It is also important to consider how institutional structure enters into process, especially the clergy-laity relationship. Roy Oswald, drawing heavily on the work of Arlin Rothauge, considers the leadership structure of the church as a function of the size of the active membership of the church. Rothauge and Oswald's types include the patriarchal/matriarchal church, made up of under 50 active members; the pastoral church, composed of from 50 to 150 active members; the program church, consisting of 150 to 350 active members; and the corporate church, with over 350 active members.[4]

For our purposes the first two sizes of church are most relevant. The patriarchal/matriarchal church, with under 50 active members, is also often called the family church. Lay leadership, often issuing from one family or a few male or female leaders, has held this church together through the years as clergy have revolved in and out. It is not unusual for such a church to have a succession of as many as five pastors in ten years. The process that develops in this situation is one centered around the lay members, who will continue to be neighbors. Clergy in such churches are well advised to learn who the lay leaders are and to work with them closely. Church members will look to clergy to perform only traditional "official" roles until such time as the clergy indicate that they are planning to become part of the community and the congregation. Roy Oswald advises against assigning recent seminary graduates to these churches; bivocational lay leadership is preferable.

In the pastoral church, with 50 to 150 active members, clergy are at the center of leadership. Of process, Oswald writes, "The power and effectiveness of the leadership circle [pastor and lay leaders] depends upon good communication with the congregation and the ability of the pastor to delegate authority, assign responsibility, and recognize the accomplishments of others. Without such skill, the central pastoral function weakens the entire structure."[5] In the pastoral church, members have their spiritual needs met by the seminary-trained person. The church has a sense of itself as a family where everyone knows everyone else. This church exhibits a highly participative style and its characteristic process is one in which everyone has a voice and the clergyperson is the guide or key leader.

These first two sizes of churches probably account for 80 percent of Protestant rural congregations. The next type, with 150 to 350 active members, is the program church, in which programs of spiritual feeding begin to supplement members' need for a high quality relationship with the pastor. There are many cells of activity in this church, headed by lay leaders who take on some pastoral functions. Still at the center of church activities, pastors now spend much of their time planning with lay leaders to ensure high-quality programs. The pastor gives high priority to meeting the spiritual and pastoral needs of lay leaders.

The final type of church is the corporate church, with over 350 active members. In this church the minister becomes the head of staff, coordinates the activities of associates and assistants, and specializes in certain areas of ministry—usually preaching and worship leadership. The process at work in this church tends to be more businesslike (hence "corporate") and organizational.

While the size of the congregation suggests certain things about the process at work in the congregation, it is important for us to realize that size of church alone does not determine the process.

These resources from Lindgren, Shawchuck, Rothauge, and Oswald can help us identify features of the process or style that are operative in our congregations. More important than that, however, they point to the need to think seriously about the process that might best realize the potential of the rural congregation. The remainder of this chapter will do that first by focusing on the mission and spirituality of the rural congregation, and then by imagining how clergy and laity roles could contribute to a cooperative and energizing congregational process.[6]

Mission and Spirituality in the Rural Congregation

The early Christian church understood "mission" as something local. The need to share resources—to feed the hungry, clothe the naked, heal the sick, and empower the powerless—was central to Christ's ministry and that of the disciples in the early church. Underlying such simple acts of kindness in a hostile world was a radical political as well as theological statement. In the nineteenth century, "mission" often lost both a sense of meeting neighbors' *physical* necessities and also a sense of *local* immediacy. "Overseas mission" often entailed the unintentional exporting of a dose of cultural chauvinism along with the gospel. This subtle imperialism has been a temptation of the church since the days when Constantine declared Christianity to be the religion of the Roman state, in essence the established religion. Along with it came a hierarchicalism, sometimes expressed in the authority of clergy *over* laity. Certainly long-term trends toward professionalization tended to move in this direction.

Loren Mead has expressed the widespread opinion that this "Constantinian paradigm" of mission is rapidly fading out of relevance; replacing it is a paradigm that focuses far more on the work of the laity and also on local mission.[7] The emerging paradigm is one that is much more compatible with the rural congregation's affinity for lay leadership and also local mission.

In recent years the United States has come up against the hard reality that most of its citizens are becoming less prosperous than they have been. Only citizens at the upper end of the income scale are becoming richer, while the poor and the middle class are both becoming poorer.[8] This finding suggests that the mission of the church may be to people on its own doorstep as well as to people around the world, in its own congregation as well as in disaster-racked locales. This concept of a local, action-oriented role of the community of believers is informing a modest but very real revolution in the American rural church. As chapter 2 and the various models presented in resource unit 2.7 testify, congregations can become powerful agents for renewed mission in rural settings—where justice issues and rural spirituality merge.

However, sometimes it seems that rural spirituality is not high on the agenda of most rural parishioners. When the Center for Theology and Land sent seminary interns into rural communities that were involved in community development, they found at first that rural parishioners did not seem able or willing to talk about their spiritual lives. Even Sunday school leaders were reluctant to broach faith issues directly in interaction with fellow parishioners. As they spent more time in the rural setting, however, these interns found that what was missing was not *spiritual awareness* but a kind of *"God talk."* What appeared to be purely secular conduct was originating from very profound spiritual sensibilities. One seminarian, placed in a Neighborhood Housing Service office, found herself interpreting the agency's language to churches and faith language to the agency. At the end of the summer she told the staff, "You are all ministers acting out Christ's Great Commandment to love God and your neighbors as yourselves. Feel good about that ministry."

Based on similar experiences in other community settings, two factors at least seem to play a key role in bringing rural spirituality to the surface on a day-by-day basis: (1) mutual vulnerability, and (2) personal affirmation (see resource unit 6.3). Farmer Richard Thompson sums up how important this link between affirmation, spirituality, and mission is to the renewal process in rural communities: "The Bible says, 'Love your neighbor as yourself.' If you see yourself as scum of the earth, how much help can you be to someone else?"[9] Chapters 5 and 6 discuss specific strategies for unlocking this spirituality as a force for congregational and community empowerment.

There is much at stake these days in the rural congregation's developing a process that is participative, mission-oriented, and evangelistic. Gone are the days when the rural congregation could count on its being part of the culture; gone are the days when the church could assume that everyone was a Christian and a church member; gone are the days when social ministry was something that was done "for" others outside the congregation. Gone also are the days when everyone belonged to a church and we could

assume that they understood the language of the Bible. Finally, the old paradigm of respecting all authorities unquestioningly, including the pastor, is gone. Many people want an open, welcoming, participative process.

A process that suffuses the activities of the church is the result of many factors—including denominational polity, the character of the laity, the size of the congregation, and the clergy and how they relate to parishioners. One thing that seems to connect these many factors is a sense of power, overall well-being, and a clear sense of identity and purpose in the congregation. A number of rural congregations suffer from some false perceptions and misconceptions about power and leadership that filter into church process and result in protective and closed processes. Their spirituality seems cramped and restrictive rather than energizing and enriching. Rather than cultivating processes that are participative, mission-oriented, and evangelistic, these misconceptions tend to support processes that are closed, maintenance-oriented, and uninviting to newcomers. In order to facilitate a radical reorientation of church process it is important to understand some of these misconceptions, which block laity and clergy alike from using their power and exercising leadership.

The Myth of Powerlessness. One of the greatest obstacles to rural empowerment may be the inherent sense of powerlessness pervading the rural setting. Time and time again, despite the incredibly innovative and risky ventures of faith undertaken by the twelve model communities involved in our Empowering Community project, the common responses on the part of individuals and congregations were such statements as, "We really aren't doing much," or "All that isn't very important." They consistently discounted their accomplishments. Although this may be interpreted as humility or a fear of power, it became apparent in many cases that the real issue is a deep-seated need for both affirmation and a recognition of the power that is theirs.

As part of a stewardship project, Pastor Paul Skelley of Union Presbyterian Church in Lost Nation, Iowa, had congregational members summarize their gifts or talents anonymously and then offer them up to God on stewardship Sunday. Such simple affirmation reinforces the personal power one has to act and interact in the process of life in a congregation.

The Myth of Independence. Perhaps nowhere in American life does the frontier ideal of rugged self-reliance and self-sufficiency live on in purer form than in rural America. This anachronistic ideal is simply dysfunctional. It is extremely difficult for a contemporary rural family to admit its financial or emotional vulnerability and its need for neighbors and fellow Christians.[10]

Rather than cling to this individualism, rural Americans need to build on their longstanding reputation for helping and neighborliness. As these largely Christian values are being eroded, incorporating them into rural congregational process becomes imperative. If "power" comes to be associated with "change" or "loss of control" or even "networking" and is viewed with great suspicion by the self-reliant community and congregation, we have a sure recipe for stagnation. The congregation needs to acknowledge and lift up its interdependence with God, neighbor, and creation as a source of health and power for good.

The Myth of Maintaining the Golden Age. Anthony G. Pappas, in *Entering the World of the Small Church*, describes the differing attitudes toward change in small rural and larger urban churches. Whereas larger churches think in terms of linear movement or things progressing somewhat autonomously, small and rural churches often think in cyclical terms. Often that involves nostalgia.[11] So many of the changes rural congregations have experienced have been negative that change appears to be only a threat, not a promise for a renewed and vital life. Jesus showed great sensitivity to our desire to hold onto the known and certain rather than risk losing our lives in order to find them. Sometimes holding on to the myth of the golden age means that we fail to look for God's guidance in the new and changing, and fail to identify God's power and presence there.

Myths that argue against disturbing the status quo should not be interpreted to mean that change is impossible in the rural church and that processes that are closed and pessimistic cannot be transformed. Sometimes such change and transformation may need to be couched not in terms of advancement or innovation but rather in terms of maintaining or conserving the values that we Christians espouse. Empowerment or revitalization of the church must begin at the most intimate level of our faith and life as Christians: we need to know how we as rural people mediate the power of God.

In addition to fostering a new sense of collective mission and personal spirituality, rural congregations need to take a hard look at power relationships within congregations if they are to work successfully toward renewal. Two of the most important aspects of power relationships in congregations are (1) how people approach the whole issue of power, and (2) the roles that pastors and lay leaders play in fostering an empowering process.

Toward a Holistic View of Power

Among the most common definitions of power that are operational in modern society is that proposed by Max Weber, who argued that power is the ability to make things happen despite resistance. Power, by that definition, is a finite commodity over which individuals and institutions are in perpetual struggle. If one individual or institution gains power, another loses. The exercise of power, in effect, is an adversarial process—rooted in the control issue, the ability to act by imposing one's will on others.

That particular view of power is not a Christian one. Power, in a Christian context, is not finite; hence, ideally, it should not be a cause for contention. A Christian approach to power is holistic and relational. It presupposes an infinite source of power—the gift of grace accessible to all through human experience with God. Empowered action, in that context, is something relational, which affirms all parties involved. A Christian definition of power encompasses creative power, healing power, and power of the spirit.

● **Creative Power.** This kind of power is imbedded in the very essence of life. We are *all* a part of this power. We are created with unique gifts and talents and in turn are capable of being empowered to use those gifts to help others. The act of salvation, viewed in this context, can be seen as God re-creating us or bringing us back to be who we are intended to be.

● **Healing Power.** Salvation is the healing of our relationship with God, with Creation, and with ourselves. Broken lives cannot draw upon the power of wholeness. Christ offers restoration, thus reconnecting us to the powerful web of creation.

● **Power of the Spirit.** Tongues of fire show us the power of our innermost hearts. New languages of love and action are opened to us. Like the disciples at Pentecost, we are inspired to go out into our world, living our Christian ministry to the fullest.

This New Testament concept of power differs from Weber's in that *it does not operate on the basis of winners and losers.* In the Christian worldview, God's power is infinite and equally available to all, is to be exercised in a mutually supportive way, and is there to deal with life and the problems around us.

In short, *power needs to be seen collectively, not competitively, if community building in a Christian sense is to succeed.* Unfortunately, standing in the way of that concept of ministry is not only a win-lose dynamic among individual parishioners, but also a hierarchical mind-set that limits the contributions that "pastor" and "people" can make.

The Pastoral Role in the Rural Setting

As seminarians accept a call to a rural setting, they need to examine their personal concepts of leadership style. The roles of pastor and lay leaders in rural churches and communities are very different from those roles in larger or urban churches. Seminarians coming from urban backgrounds armed with urban-biased training may feel obliged to transfer some of that efficiency and businesslike structure to their rural congre-

gations, in a misguided desire to somehow bring them "up to speed" with the larger world of the church. Authors such as David R. Ray and Nancy Foltz contend that such thinking works against the very qualities that make small churches special.[12]

Ministry in small rural churches can be people-to-people, Ray argues, a model that closely emulates the early Christian community. Urban churches can learn and are learning a great deal from the people-to-people approach. The so-called cell congregation or church-within-a-church attempts to break down the large, impersonal congregation into more human, intimate institutions.

Among the stereotypes held by seminarians and first-time small church pastors is that rural congregations are all idyllic, friendly institutions where positive family values are still operational. In fact, powerful economic pressures and isolation can breed dysfunctional families, suspicion of outsiders, and other problems not unlike those engendered by the congestion and poverty of urban life.

Some go so far as to argue that the most decisive dynamic within the church is not the community setting, but the size.[13] Many rural churches are small. In such congregational settings the pastoral role is bound to be

● more relational and intimate than in large churches, where pastors often act as independent manager-leaders;
● far more visible and exposed than in large churches, where multiple clergy share responsibilities;
● much more diverse than in large churches, where multiple clergy specialize in particular kinds of ministry to specific subsets of the congregation—senior adult ministry, youth ministry, music ministry, preaching, and so on.

Some rural pastors enjoy the challenge of functioning as generalists. But the call to a single-pastor church can lead to burnout, brought about by a lack of privacy, deep-seated feelings of isolation, and a heavy load of responsibilities.

As one rural Iowa pastor pointed out, there are dangers in unquestioningly adopting the role of chaplain when assigned to small congregations (fifty or fewer members) even though congregations may be most comfortable with such a model.

> If we do not challenge parishioners to examine the status quo and empower transitions to a new, younger generation of leadership in the rural church, how are we different from those who write off the rural church or see community decline as inevitable? A passive priestly ministry will not come to grips with the kind of mind-set that says we can change—if that is what it takes to keep our church and community going.

In practice, pastoral ministry in rural settings combines a variety of roles and styles. A coalition of Iowa pastors that meets regularly to discuss pastoral and congregational roles lists the following characteristics that a successful rural pastor should incorporate into his or her ministry:

- helping parishioners understand relationships;
- helping them clarify their options; and
- helping them process change.

These pastors would argue that such functions go far beyond the passive chaplain model that tends to assume that existing congregational power structures and ways of doing things are "givens." Note, however, that this active pastoral role is couched in terms of *facilitating* rather than *leading*. In such a model, *process* becomes far more important than *goals*.

Especially for seminarians who come from urban backgrounds in which "bottom-line" oriented corporate values may be taken for granted, it may be hard to accept that "take-charge" approaches will meet with a cold reception in most rural churches. Besides risking circuit overload, the rural pastor who models an authoritarian, lone-ranger style of ministry—charging out ahead as a change agent or innovator—is going to severely limit his or her effectiveness. A pastor needs to remember that regardless of how long his or her tenure proves to be in a given church, that longevity pales when compared to the multigenerational experiences of many family members in a particular community. Any newcomer, pastor included, will not have the same clout as a community matriarch or patriarch. Hence, in the world of the small church, as Pap-

pas reminds us, the best ideas will be those that somehow percolate up from the individual and collective experience of parishioners. An effective rural pastor will learn how to use fortuitous "accidents" to empower a congregation to renew and revitalize itself.[14]

Longtime matriarchs and patriarchs of a congregation may not make it easy for pastors to sort out which of their expectations are important and which are not. Among the most valuable skills a rural pastor can cultivate are the following:

- *The capacity to listen*, combined with a broad, ongoing visitation policy with parishioners. This can reveal the individual needs and expectations of congregation members that may or may not ever be expressed in public congregational settings. Formal goal setting and survey procedures may be useful tools in that process, but only if they are conducted in ways that take into account a rural congregation's lack of familiarity with and possible suspicions of such tools.
- *The ability to take life at a different pace* than the seminarian typically has experienced in urban settings. If ever patience is a virtue, it is in dealing with the rural microcosm—yet patience must go hand-in-hand with a hectic workload and high stress. The built-in tension between incremental change and work-related pressures can itself be difficult to handle. (Especially in this context, it is significant that in the Roman Catholic tradition, first calls are deliberately urban; only when priests are experienced are they sent to rural settings.)
- *A strong sense of self* and an ability to seek appropriate support mechanisms to deal with the potential isolation and stress of being the sole pastor (including deliberately carving out time to feed one's own spiritual needs and cultivate inner resources).

"The temptation in encounters with parishioners," one rural Iowa pastor said, "may be to handle feelings immediately. But if you resist that approach, and work instead on process, it is amazing how the feelings will fall into place." As an example, he cites a fellow pastor who was successful in enabling the older generation in his parish to pass the torch of leadership to the younger generation—in part by concentrating his ministry on relational issues and processing change. What had been literally a dying congregation is now experiencing a dramatic renewal with a strong agenda of local ministry.

The rural pastorate demands a great deal of patience, sensitivity, and political acumen. Heading full tilt at reforming or changing church practices—however small—can cause major repercussions, including resentment and outright resistance.

As the sole ordained pastor is pulled in many different directions, in an environment where establishing a public identity is so important, the rural pastor needs to maintain a strong sense of who he or she is and then gradually unfold that identity in ways that the community can accept. Part of the challenge lies in reconciling (1) the holistic concept of divine power with (2) the human, hierarchical approach to roles, and (3) in the case of women pastors, the traditional patriarchal values at work in rural life as well. A final ingredient in the mix is (4) an individual's unique personality.

If the hierarchical model prevails, as one seminarian eloquently put it, a pastor starts out "with a certain amount of cash in the authority bank," given the high regard in which pastors are traditionally held in many rural communities. How well and long the pastor is able to use that authority depends on how circumstances and individual decisions "drain" or "increase" that capital. For instance, if the pastor needs to operate in a prophetic or challenging mode, he or she will continually need to rebuild a level of goodwill by some means (e.g., special favors to certain members of the congregation, making concessions in certain areas) if a healthy dynamic is to prevail.

How very differently the pastor would perceive his or her role if the goal were to establish a base of *mutual* ministry, rather than a hierarchical model! Congregation and pastor would be in a position to support each other and bolster each other's energy level as they work toward a common vision. Ministry, to borrow a political-economic term, would become a win-win (or positive-sum) game. In human terms, such give-and-take would also be a far more natural way to interact, especially in a setting where relationships are so important.

For ministry to become a mutual process, rural pastors, like the parishioners they serve, need to draw on grace as a means of empowering their work. Forgiving ourselves and one another is essential in permitting intimacy and allowing us to take risks. In short, it is essential to ministering to others. Pardon is the foundation that allows us to act on the basis of values other than reciprocity ("an eye for an eye"). As Scott Gustafson expresses it: the power of life—not just ministry—resides in forgiveness.[15]

Effective rural pastors will find unique ways to balance the ascribed and achieved power of their ministry—to bridge the gulf that can loom between pew and pulpit. One rural pastor (and one rural bishop as well) broke down the barriers to parishioners by wearing the traditional brimmed seed store cap that farmers often wear in the fields and slipping his clerical collar into a slot above the brim.

Irreverent? Anything but. The whimsical cap was a gentle reminder of the pastor's dual identity as both pastor and person. In a rural setting where everyone ostensibly knows everyone else—at least by role and past history—that kind of statement is very important.

Table 5.1: Skills for Rural Ministry

A study group of Iowa pastors compiled the following list of skills necessary for rural ministry (number 8 was contributed by Bishop April Larson of LaCrosse, Wisconsin):
1. Awareness that your approach must be people-centered (incarnational)—not program-based.
2. Sensitivity to the need to treat vision, mission, and history holistically. You need all three to move forward, not just a past-oriented approach.
3. Conviction that this is a place you want to be. The people to whom you are ministering, for the most part, *want to be here.* Rural life is desirable; rural communities are not just places where people happen to be "stuck."
4. Respect for the history and tradition of the community you are serving. That means sensing the dignity of the place. Life is good; you don't need to change it to fit your needs or views.

5. Recognition that it is hard to separate public and personal ministry. To some degree you are always "pastor"—always "on."

6. Inner resources to deal with isolation. Even if you cultivate a mutual ministry style, in many ways, you are alone—emotionally and geographically. It is hard to share with parishioners. Your spouse will feel this as well. Sometimes you miss the little things the most—you can't go home on holidays. Clergy families need to learn to care for one another.

7. Learning to make time to take care of yourself. That means communicating that need to your congregation. It means scheduling activities and time that allow you to feed yourself—your emotional, physical, and spiritual needs. (Goodness knows, the congregation will feed you a great deal physically!)

8. An appreciation for the ongoing struggle of your call to a rural setting. Rural life, with all its challenges, problems, and difficulties, is an active lifestyle.

9. Recognition that your rural church will have more things in common with an urban church than differences. The differences are significant, but not everything is different—although at times you might think so.

A trait these pastors did not list, but displayed throughout their association with one another, was a sense of humor. It is through humor and stories that we are most able to express ourselves—to grow, to relate, to share with others.

Each community has its own points of entry. Another rural pastor maintains that the community really began to accept him as "one of them" when he hit a home run at the annual church picnic. A Native American pastor working in an Alaskan tribal congregation different from his own background was first taken seriously in the community when he went out alone in a kayak on a successful hunt. Inexperienced pastors or those unfamiliar with rural life need to be especially sensitive to those connecting points as they go about their daily routine. Visitation, viewed in this context, becomes a powerful tool of listening and learning—as well as ministry in the fullest, most intimate sense of the word.

Finally, pastors who are comfortable with rural ministry have learned to find inner and outer support systems that sustain them through difficult times and in periods of discouragement or burnout. In cultivating a rich personal spiritual life, a rural pastor can draw on the ultimate partner in ministry on a daily basis, the Holy Spirit. A pastor in rural America without such support networks is most vulnerable indeed. Seminary training programs need to consider ways of incorporating theoretical and hands-on curriculum elements that promote positive spiritual, emotional, and physical habits that can sustain a pastor in his or her role over a lifetime.

Chapter 6 will discuss specific roles that a pastor may play in empowering certain kinds of ministry within a congregation, such as health care

and family support systems. (See the resource units in chapter 6 discussing the roles of the pastor and congregation as healer, prophet, and priest.) It should be stressed that none of these roles are mutually exclusive. At any given point, a pastor is likely to represent one or all of the roles discussed here to his or her congregation. Great skill and sensitivity are required to create balance among these specialized ministerial functions.

Although most seminaries reject the authoritarian model and subscribe to the concept of mutual ministry, it remains an ongoing challenge to foster skills that contribute to that kind of *ministering-with* approach.

Gender is still a significant component in the clergy-laity relationship. See resource unit 5.4 for a brief introduction to this issue.

The Power of the Laity

If the pastoral role is somewhat different in rural and urban settings, the same principle applies—only more so—to lay leadership. A passive, uninvolved laity is a luxury that small, rural congregations cannot afford.

In the large corporate church, parishioners can maintain some level of anonymity if they choose to do so without visibly undermining the institution. Within the rural or small church setting, that is virtually impossible. For starters, invisibly occupying a pew or getting lost in the crowd is impossible. This gives individual parishioners considerable power to make others feel either welcome or excluded and also to contribute to people's lives both within the church and in the larger community.

For very practical, personal reasons, rural and small church pastors themselves have a greater need to encourage an active laity than do their counterparts in urban settings. With more and more pastors serving "yoked" congregations covering larger geographic areas or riding the circuit to multiple calls, time and distance can become tangible barriers to effective ministry. Visiting the sick and infirm, concerning oneself with the health—mental and physical as well as spiritual—of parishioners is an alternative to the "pastor as the head of the church" model. Without the involvement of laity, the task of truly feeding the sheep of a given parish or parishes in any meaningful way becomes difficult, if not impossible. But it is important also for pastors to avoid the trap of equating only the laity's "church work" with "ministry." Ultimately, daily life and vocational witness are and must be central; work "at church" equips but should not overshadow daily life in the community and the home.

Laity can provide eyes and ears and hands and feet to do Christ's work. One barrier to broad-scale lay ministry, however, can lie in the generation gap within many rural churches and communities.

One young parishioner summed up the problem, based on her experiences when she returned with her husband to their farm community after nearly a decade away in a distant urban area: "The older women in the church want us to help. They say they're tired and that it's someone else's turn to take charge. But when you do, they quickly point out everything you are doing wrong—meaning it's different from what they used to do."

Charles Briem (Associate Conference Minister, United Church of Christ, Iowa Conference, Des Moines, Iowa) offers a similar point of view. He contends that among rural men, there is a generation gap—both philosophical and semantic—that makes it hard for male parishioners and male leaders to work together. The matrix in table 5.2 illustrates why these differences in language and worldview can be such formidable barriers to working together toward common goals within the church or the larger rural community. That is true for women as well as for men. Rural pastors themselves may contribute to the communication problems, since their personalities and personal styles of thinking and acting tend to be very different from those of their parishioners.

Briem's Matrix reflects the different languages, problem-solving techniques, and views of God employed by different generations. Using Myers-Briggs categories of personality types, researchers such as Gary L. Harbaugh find that clergy tend to be culturally left (i.e., intuitives), while rural women and men tend to cluster on the cultural right (i.e., sensates). The results, Briem points out, are radical differences in lifestyles as well as spirituality practices between sensates and intuitives. Parishioners are more "God-centered" than "Jesus-centered." Whenever pastors tend to focus on the light at the end of the tunnel, their sensate parishioners have trouble seeing it because they know that light is really a train!

Gary McIntosh elaborates on the generational pattern that Briem outlines, breaking the time span into three distinct periods; he also puts the trends in the specific context of religious attitudes and worship preferences for each of the generational groups.[16]

1. Pre-1945 (Builder/Pre-Boomer) Generation. This generation grew up in the 1920s, 1930s, and 1940s. They tend to have a high respect for authority, are private about their personal affairs, place a high value on thrift and saving, and are task-oriented.

Religious characteristics: (1) They are strongly devoted to their denomination and their church; (2) they emphasize formal programs and activities; (3) they have a strong sense of duty in mission giving, Bible study, and prayer.

Worship preferences: They prefer (1) a restrained atmosphere with minimal congregational participation (for example, formally introducing visitors); (2) hymn singing (note that some of their favorite hymns are not in the new denominational hymnbooks); (3) sermons that work through a scripture passage; (4) organ and piano accompaniment to congregational singing and special music.

2. 1945 to 1965 (Baby Boomer) Generation.

Part of the largest population bulge ever in the history of the United States, this generation's patterns include late marriages, few children (or none), high divorce rates and a low view of marriage as an institution (weak family structure; roles in flux), high levels of education, questioning of authority, and consumeristic or throw-away values. They tend to be more open-minded but less task-oriented than their parents.

Religious characteristics: (1) They are people-oriented (i.e., committed to relationships); (2) they direct their money toward people rather than causes; (3) they seek out practical Bible study, prayer, and sharing groups that focus more on people than on the program itself; (4) commitment to ministry out of a sense of personal fulfillment.

Worship preferences: They prefer (1) high congregational participation in prayers, speaking, music, and so forth; (2) "praise songs" and choruses rather than traditional hymns; (3) "anonymous" treatment of visitors to services; (4) how-to sermons; (5) use of guitars, drums, and contemporary musical styles.

3. Post-1965 (Baby Buster/Generation X) Generation.

Children of the 1980s and 1990s, these parishioners are now in their pre-teens through their mid-twenties. Although within the family, traditional roles are reasserting themselves somewhat, this generation tends to ignore authority in general. It is a cautious generation; it saves more, recycles, pursues practical education. It tends to be less task-oriented than either generation before it.

Religious characteristics: (1) They are concerned with causes and issues, especially at a local level (i.e., are committed to community); (2) they take an issue-oriented approach to stewardship, Bible study, and other church activities; (3) they see ministry as a way of tackling issues.

Worship preferences: They are much like their parents, the boomers, except that they prefer

(1) issue-oriented sermons; (2) less congregational participation and more anonymous treatment of visitors; (3) jazz groups in worship.[17]

Whether a pastor is trying to get to know the congregation, working at establishing worship or programmatic activities that fit the needs of various age groups, or bringing together different age groups to solve specific congregational or community problems, it is essential to take into account the generation gaps Briem and others have identified. A first priority might be to clarify language (or goals, styles, interests, and agendas) in order to work intergenerationally or with mixed groups of male and female congregation members; at other times, the most effective strategy might be to work with different constituencies in parallel but separate activities.

In addition to taking into account such built-in tensions within a congregation, bear in mind that the concept of "laity" or "lay leadership" itself is changing rapidly. Loren Mead and others maintain that with the redefinition of "family" and similar societal shifts, the church and its mission will need to undergo major transitions if congregations are to remain vital and relevant to significant portions of the population.[18] Those changes will have tremendous impact on the roles both clergy and laity play within the congregation and community at large.

It is safe to say that we are in the midst of a transition in the process at work in rural congregations. Overall the trend is toward a model where clergy and lay roles, though different, are clearly complementary and mutually reinforcing.

Finally, viewed in strategic terms, pastors need to be capable of discerning (1) where power lies in a given community and congregation, (2) the day-to-day concerns of their parishioners, and (3) how those concerns translate into priorities that will unite the congregation around a common mission. (See resource unit 6.3 [a] on visiting as one way of discovering such concerns.) How well one discerns these factors will determine how much energy the pastor and the congregation will have for revitalization and renewal. If pastor and congregation agree that a particular task or set of tasks is important, then perhaps they can agree that something else is going to have to give in order to accomplish that goal. Setting priorities becomes essential.

Table 5.2: Differences in Worldviews Table Among Male Rural Leaders

The observations adapted and summarized on this table are taken from Chuck Briem's lecture in April 1993 at the Rural Ministry Conference in Dubuque, Iowa. Briem's constructs (God Gestalts) are combined with materials from Douglas Walrath's book *Frameworks* (New York: Pilgrim Press, 1987). Briem draws on Dr. Gary McIntosh's article, "What's in a Name?" *McIntosh Church Growth Network* 3, no. 5; and Lyle Schaller's chapter on generations in *Reflections of a Contrarian* (Nashville: Abingdon Press, 1989).

BIRTH YEARS	(BRIEM) OR HISTORIC MILESTONES "AGES"	(BRIEM) GOD GESTALT	(WALRATH) BIRTH COHORTS	BIRTH YEARS FOR NEW GENERATION AS DEFINED BY FORMATIVE ADULT EXPERIENCES	PERSONALITY	CHARACTER
1900–1928	World War I	God is *discipline.*	Hard workers, strivers	"GI Generation" continuing through WWII—many with rural roots; low-teach era—college education not norm and less emphasis on teaching in general	Civic	Participative
1929–1935	Depression					
1936–1944	World War II	God is *love.*	System challengers: more assertive lifestyles	"Silent Generation"	Adaptive	Open-minded
1945–1959	Post-war era			"Boomers"—TV, jet travel, rapidly growing technology	Idealistic	Principled
1960–1967		God is *truth.*	Calculators and retreaters: less-assertive lifestyles			
1968–1975	Vietnam	God is *dead.*		Big Chill, Vietnam, assassinations: college educated economic boom times	Reactive	Practical
1976–1992	Global economic and technological revolution (Gulf War, Tienanmen)	God throws *dice.*		"Baby Busters"—High tech, cable TV	Ambivalent	Uncertain

Putting the Pieces Together

What then, makes rural empowerment successful? The answer lies in the relationship between pastor and lay leadership and between church and community. Is there a mutual will to act? People must be prepared to seek an evolving sense of mission—one that can balance new priorities against the need for preserving the best of what rural means in their particular community.

But ultimately, all will come to naught unless they can muster the energy and resources to work toward such goals. As one rural pastor expressed it, "In the end, all it takes to change is one person who believes in that vision for the church and who has enough credibility with peers to pull it off."

Simple? No, but with God's help, the rural church can grow and help the community around it to grow in love and service. At their roots, that is what congregational empowerment and rural ministry are all about.

RESOURCES FOR UNDERSTANDING PROCESS

The remainder of chapter 5 consists of resources that deal with rural issues in the context of the "players" at work in the rural community: the powerful and the powerless, families, laity, and clergy. The goal is to sharpen observational skills that feed into the processes at work in rural congregations. Important here are the opportunities for us to (1) weigh our own concept of ministry against those of clergy and laity in the rural setting; and (2) sensitize ourselves to the thoughts, hopes, and feelings of those for whom "rural" is a way of life.

5.1   Coming to Terms with Congregational Process
5.2   Why Dedicate Oneself to a Rural Congregation?
5.3   Lay Perceptions of the Pastor in Rural America
5.4   Women Clergy: The Patriarchal Setting
5.5   The Fine Art of Listening: Gathering the History of a Congregation

5.1   Coming to Terms with Congregational Process

How do things get done in your congregation? What process is at work in the local church you are involved in? This is a difficult question to answer since it involves intangibles such as personality, personal needs, historical structure, congregational size, and other factors we have listed. There are any number of other not-fully-noticed items that enter into the corporate culture of the rural congregation.

It would be a mistake to try to systematize all these factors; our sense is that congregational systems theory is not sufficiently developed to ensure that we would include all necessary elements. Nevertheless, process is too important to neglect. It includes such areas as decision making and leadership. The following exercise is designed to help governing boards and congregations as a whole come to terms with their process.

1. One aspect of process is simply the warmth of the congregation. What is the experience of members when they come to worship on Sunday morning? Does everyone in the church know everyone else's name? Are you sure?

What is the experience of visitors to the congregation? Are they welcomed and invited to coffee fellowship, or out to eat, or to be part of a small group? Is there any follow-up with visitors and friends of members?

What about young people? Is an effort made to involve them?

What about the children of members and visitors? Is a drink or refreshment provided for them during the adult coffee fellowship?

2. Another aspect of process is affirmation and celebration of gifts. Is there some way that the gifts of members are regularly lifted up and celebrated? Do people have a chance to express their appreciation of one another's gifts?

Are church activities, achievements of congregation members, testimonies from people in the church about their Christian vocation celebrated and affirmed?

3. Process also involves decision making. It seems clear today that ownership of and participation in congregational life is a vital aspect of rural congregational process.

Who makes the decisions in your church? Is it always the same three or four people? Does the board solicit opinions from a wide variety of people before making decisions?

As we discussed at the beginning of this chapter, Alvin J. Lindgren and Norman Shawchuck have identified three categories of decision making: decision making by no decision, decision making by majority, and decision making by minority.[19] Does one of these describe your congregational process? What are the liabilities and the assets of that?

4. Are there small groups in the church where people can enrich their spiritual lives and also share their worries and concerns? Are there places where people in the church can be vulnerable to one another? Can they challenge one another? Are they willing to get close to one another?

5. Where does the church engage the daily lives of its members? Does the church ever ask members where they encounter God in the world? Does it ask members to think about their lives in terms of the Christian faith and prayer? Does it ask members to pray and live in ways that manifest a Christian witness in the world? Can members talk about their faith with one another?

6. Do people have a sense of pride in their congregation? Are they feeling nurtured and uplifted in church to such an extent that they want to share that joy with others and invite others to be a part of it? Are there opportunities for new members to become part of the congregation—to really belong to the congregation? How are new members being assimilated into the life of the congregation? How long does it take before they become part of the leadership structure? Are all ages represented on the governing councils?

7. Mark the words in the columns below that best characterize the spirit of the congregation. (You may choose to mark a spot between the two columns.)

Informal . . . . Formal
Warm . . . . Cold
Able to disagree among selves . . . . Unable to disagree among selves
Caring. . . . . Impersonal
Open. . . . . Closed
Risk-Taking . . . . Protective
Innovative . . . . Traditional
Adventurous . . . . Stable
Add your own words

How would an outsider's evaluation of the congregation compare to yours? How do these characteristics grow out of church process? What are you doing right that you want to hang on to? What strengths were revealed by this exercise?

5.2   Why Dedicate Oneself to a Rural Congregation?

What follows is the response of a rural pastor in Illinois to the question, "Why should anyone dedicate oneself to rural ministry?"

One morning a few years ago appeared like any other summer morning. It was the best of times, because everything from the farm to the equipment sparkled in the bright summer sunshine. Memories of horses, of cattle, of fishing in the creek, gathering crawdads in the pond, smelling the odors of freshly mown hay—all of this flooded my senses. But before the morning was over, those pleasant thoughts turned into a nightmare.

I received a phone call midmorning from a neighbor of a family in the congregation I served; the neighbor told me that someone from the Federal Loan Bank was visiting the family's farm. The bank was foreclosing on their farm, and the bank officials were staking out the ground around the house to show the family how much they would be able to keep along with their home. I immediately jumped in my car and drove out to their farmhouse. Husband and wife greeted me at the door with open arms saying, "We're sure glad that you came. How did you know?"

I experienced with that farm family that day a deep sense of loss, a sense of grief almost like the grief that comes with the death of a loved one. We were able to talk. Before I left that day, some of the women from the church had arrived and were visiting with the farmwife. So the man and I took a walk down the lane by one of his fields. When I began to talk about where support could be found for him, we began to explore an even bigger question: Where do we find hope in such a sea of despair? I assured him that I, as his pastor, and the congregation, as his church, would be there for him to supply the kind of support and the kind of nurturing that he and his wife needed in their crisis. He said, "Well I thought that, but I just needed to hear it with my own ears."

Then there is another story about one of our church members, named Jim. Everything was going fine for Jim on the farm until his elderly father died. Jim and his father had been in partnership in agriculture for a number of years, and Jim found after his father's death that he could not go on with the farm. Jim became very depressed, even attempted suicide. He'd been seeing a professional counselor in Champaign and was seemingly getting nowhere in the counseling sessions. His wife turned to me one day and said, "Would you come out and talk with Jim?" And I said, "Margaret, I sure will. I was just waiting for the opportunity to come." We sat around the breakfast table one morning, drinking coffee, and Jim looked at me and said, "You know, I just don't think it's worth going on. I think I'm just going to end it all."

There comes a time in one's counseling experience when one begins to get a feel for what approach is needed for different individuals. That day I felt, "Well, I need to use tough love to get through his depression, to really make him stop and think about what he's doing and what he's saying." So I looked at Jim and I said, "Jim, if you do that to yourself there's going to be two things that are going to happen. Your family is going to grieve and hate your guts all at the same time for the rest of their lives. Secondly, I'll be so mad at you for doing that to yourself and your family that I'm going to have to find a different minister to do your service."

He looked across the table at me and said, "Do you really mean that?"

I said, "I wouldn't say it if I didn't mean it. Stop and think how what you're doing to yourself would affect all of us who love and care about you and value your friendship."

"Well," Jim said, "I don't think I'm going to be able to do the harvest this fall. I've got my crops planted, but I just don't see how I'm going to be able to farm this fall."

And I said, "Yes you will, Jim. Now let me make a little agreement with you. When you're in the middle of your harvest one day and you feel like you need someone to spend a few hours talking with you, have Margaret give me a call and I'll come out and spend some time with you on the combine."

Well, Margaret called me one afternoon and said, "Jim's ready to have you ride the combine with him tomorrow." I think Jim thought that I would only take a couple of rounds that morning in the field. I showed up with my blue jeans and my blue denim jacket and my farmer's cap on. I spent the entire day on the combine with Jim, and he really opened up about the stress points in his life's journey. His wife told me that our conversation over the breakfast table, which had taken place some two and a half months earlier, had been the real turning point in his recovery.

You ask me why I have dedicated my life to rural ministry. I think these two incidents show that being a pastor in a rural community is a sacred privilege, because you are allowed to walk with people in their deepest levels of pain as well as their highest levels of joy and celebration. You're allowed to get closer and deeper into their lives than you can in urban ministry. It's not unusual, if I know that a farmer is having a difficult time, to go out when they're doing their chores, to find out from one of their neighbors what time they do their chores, and just stop by at random, and say, "Hey—I want to walk with you this morning as you do your chores." And often that's the time when they really open up and bare their souls and their troubles to you.

Rural ministry is also very dear to me because it's an area where we're facing some of the greatest challenges in the church, and in our society as well. The challenges that face us are questions of identity: Who are we? Who calls the shots for us? Who is going to shape our future destiny? And who is going to shape what we're going to look like ten years down the road from now? The time is right for good leadership in the rural community, for people who are dedicated to those ministries instead of seeing them as stepping stones to an inner-city ministry or an urban ministry or a larger church or whatever. But for people who enjoy the challenges of helping churches catch a new vision for ministry where they are, they look at their resources and their needs and the needs of the community around them and the resources of the community around them and show them how to build bridges between those resources and needs and form partnerships. That can happen more easily in the rural community probably than anywhere else.

I also enjoy the rural community because it's a place where you can really be yourself. You don't have to put up any fronts. One person once said, "All people want in the rural church is to be loved, and to be able to love in return." How true that really is. They enjoy laughing with you, they appreciate your presence in their hours of crisis, they appreciate your presence in their hours of rejoicing, and they want to be there in yours as well.

A while back I did an interview for the university radio station on the fate of the rural church. I see the rural church as remaining strong into the next century. I also see the rural church being called upon to perhaps change some of the ways it does things, or at least the way it addresses the needs of the rural area.

The rural church needs to take the initiative sometimes; often it is the only viable institution left in a community. It needs to take the lead in economic, social, and spiritual nurturing and development in those communities.

ISSUE FOR DISCUSSION

What do you see as this pastor's motivation to ministry? What is discouraging to him?

5.3   Lay Perceptions of the Pastor in Rural America

Before a pastor can begin to address his or her role in a rural congregation, he or she must be sensitive to how the community at large may perceive the pastoral presence. The following excerpt from Jane Smiley's novel about rural life, *A Thousand Acres*, explains why a rural parishioner cannot bring herself to ask her pastor for help:

[He was] a fifty-year-old man rotated out of a big suburban church to our little town, and when he told us why [he didn't get along with the pastor, became impatient with some of the congregation, had doubts about how his earlier ambitions squared with his faith], he had spoken in a tone of voice that declared openly how moved he was by the crisis that resulted in his coming, but in fact, his confidences had resulted in embarrassment on all sides rather than something that felt like normal friendship.

... He was too much himself, too small for his position, too anxious to fit into our community, too sweaty and dirty and casual and unwise.[20]

The focus of this resource unit is to analyze the perception of Smiley's rural parishioner in the context of the following documents:

A. Parishioners Talk About Their Needs—a list of criteria one rural congregation laid out for their "ideal pastor," as well as reasons why such an individual would come to their community.

B. Growing into Rural Ministry—a series of journal entries from 1991 to 1993 written by an Iowa pastor wrestling with his "call" to the rural pastorate.

A. PARISHIONERS TALK ABOUT THEIR NEEDS

Pastor Don Dovre from the Manchester, Iowa, area unofficially asked his parishioners one Sunday, "What would you advise seminarians and seminaries about how to prepare for work in the rural church and what they are looking for in a pastor?" Here are some of the replies he received.

I often feel that small rural congregations are more willing to serve in the many duties of the church, the pastor is able to get to know all the parishioners well. They work more as a "church family." They are there for each other.

The rural area needs young ministers to help the young people to get them to come and join and attend church.

Usually a small congregation, usually friendly people, they usually do as much as they can to financially support themselves with money, time, and talents.

In a small rural congregation, everyone is connected somehow through relatives, work, or school, so it's like being in a family. This can be a plus or a challenge.

Needs to be able to work with people or congregations who have strong traditions within their church. Be willing to work with churches that face financial crises because of the local economy. Don't spend for spending's sake, more conservative with decisions. Can also face some very territorial battles that have also been a part of the church for years.

Facing declining population, decline in membership. Problem of churches consolidating.

A preacher's calling is simply to help, touch, listen, give loving kindness, teach the Bible and explain its passages. What you are you convey; spread the word by deeds.

To do God's will, answer the call to serve mankind. Instill good stewardship of land and resources, of youth and people.

This is an important time in the lives of rural congregations—make or break time so to speak. If you, as a pastor, have always wanted to make a difference, this could well be your opportunity. We need people who believe in our right to exist as a rural congregation. We need someone with the caring and zeal to help us continue what has been a long tradition of being the backbone of the church.

Smaller congregation than a city congregation and it would be easier to get to know his/her congregation on a more personal basis.

B. GROWING INTO RURAL MINISTRY: A PASTOR REFLECTS

The following are excerpts from the journal of Craig Bowyer, 1991 to 1995, during his pastorate at Bethlehem Lutheran Church, Lost Nation, Iowa.

Joan was frustrated. "Pastor," she said, "this is the fifth time in the last nine months that we have had a meeting to explain what a parish nurse would be doing. When will something happen?" But something did happen. Joan's leadership resulted in the three congregations in Lost Nation sponsoring a Parish Health Nurse. Remarkable? Yes, in many ways. Two years earlier Joan had not even chaired a committee. Two-thirds of the clergy involved were opposed to the idea. The project was led totally by laity. Congregations had to pledge monetary support. It was a new idea in a rural area. The way the project came together helped me realize something that is important in rural ministry.

RURAL IS DIFFERENT. It is a distinct and different culture.

Joan has become a leader. Leadership is so important—and leadership is location specific. Ordained leadership can "subvert the ideals being exhorted," says CTL director Shannon Jung. Leadership actions contradict what is being espoused when the culture is not considered.

When I was in seminary the usual warnings about some of the pitfalls of certain leadership styles were discussed. "The congregation knows more than the pastor about what is needed in the congregation. The members need to be the ones who have ownership of whatever is done, especially if there are changes considered." I already knew and agreed with these "warnings" because of what I had learned through my business experience. It was said, I listened and agreed, but I didn't understand. After the first two years here at Bethlehem I felt good about what was happening. Many very positive things could be pointed out to anyone who cared to listen. As they say on Wall Street, "the key indicators were up."

But two things became apparent. One was a *hard fact;* I was exhausted and not very easy to get along with. Secondly, through an instinctive evaluation, a *soft fact* emerged. I sensed that if I left tomorrow only one thing that was an "up indicator" would be kept going by the congregation. That one thing would be the Parish Health Nurse. It would continue because it was lay-led and developed. My contribution was only to plant the idea. Joan's leadership success taught me something. I needed to make some changes. In searching to better understand my leadership it dawned on me that I was very goal-oriented. People who knew me were aware of how goal-driven I was, but I hadn't realized how much it had affected my leadership. Goal-emphasized leadership wasn't working. I decided to emphasize process instead of goals. I started working on the how and why of what was being done instead of working for a specific end. When Joan was frustrated with the progress of the parish nurse project, I would encourage her by talking about what to expect in the process, and by affirming her leadership. There were several biblical and theological reasons for changing from goal-orientation to process leadership. One of the biblical understandings that helped me shape a different leadership style is the parable of Lazarus and the Rich Man. I understand the parable to be saying that the Rich Man's sin was not neglect, but lack of taking Lazarus seriously as a child of God. The sacred right of each of God's children is to receive respect. We are created in God's image, and God allows us to make foolish decisions, even those that hurt us. No matter how foolish our decisions God never ceases loving us, never treats us any less than as an important person, always treats us with complete respect. In light of that biblical understanding and others, I began seriously wrestling with my leadership approach. Why wasn't it working when it had worked so well when I was in business? I began to realize that even though I like the rural area and I grew up in the rural area, I am urbanized like any of the rural sons and daughters who have gone to college and/or have lived in large cities. I have a different understanding of how the world works than I used to have when growing up in a rural community. I considered that now I may not be able to see what was really going on because of cultural bias.

Recently Tex Sample was recommended to me. He seems to agree that it is difficult at best to minister in one culture when we subscribe to the values of another. In *U.S. Lifestyles and Mainline Churches* Tex uses cultural parameters to define his categories, Left, Right, and Middle. He leans heavily on financial criteria to define the categories. The Cultural Right shares with the Rural culture many means of understanding the world. My interest in Tex's work is in his ability to put into words what happens when a leader of one culture tries to lead persons from a different culture. . . .

Tex has put into words what I have sensed, [but] I would modify what he says a little. My statement would be, "I am becoming convinced that those of us trained in the universities and the seminaries are socialized into a way of relating to the world that makes it very difficult to understand the world view of people in the rural culture, but there are a few common models that we can use as a beginning of understanding." I have found that the people in the rural culture are very used to having clergy who are differently socialized, and they tend to have tremendous patience, to a point.

Rural congregations worry about their future. The first two years as a pastor I was asking the question,

"What does the congregation need to do in order to expand their vision of the future in terms of ministry and mission?" I now ask the question, "What is the congregation already doing as ministry and how do they want me to assist in that ministry?" Changing wasn't easy. When looking back at my journal notations I see that as recently as March of 1990 I felt very rudderless. I no longer had the sense of direction that goals give one, and I was in waters unfamiliar to me. . . . For the past two years I have "backed off" on goal-oriented leadership. There have been surprisingly dramatic results, especially since it has been a relatively short time since I quit imposing my goals on the congregation and the congregational council. I notice in myself less anxiety, more energy, more enjoyment of the people, an increase in the ability to preach good news rather than law, less disappointment and anger, fewer instances of taking things personally.

A dozen young individuals have stepped forward and have begun to provide leadership. One expanded her calling ministry when she realized it was ministry. Another developed a significant service for the community by helping people see the need and then guiding the three denominations in town to sponsor the Parish Nurse. Another has taken on leadership of an organization that will become a powerful influence in this part of the state. The congregation has responded with less arguing, fewer comments about the pastor having his own way, fewer confrontations about practice of sacraments, funerals and weddings, fewer mutterings about conflict, and increase in acceptance of Bethlehem as a congregation "that is above average, where the women are strong and the children are good looking."

You ask, "What empowers a congregation to do the will of God?" In a rural congregation it isn't the pastor. The first requirement in the rural congregation, what has to happen first, is healing. A congregation that is beginning to heal will begin to show empowerment. A congregation can only heal when it knows that it is taken seriously and treated with respect. What empowers us is hope, hope that something will make a difference, hope that God is in charge and not something else; and what empowers us is belonging to a group of people who have the same source of hope as we do.

I try to remember. Pastor, step back and let God work. Be there with his people as God works his marvels. Name the bogeyman, sing praises to the Lord, name the ministry the flock are already doing, bless the one who makes it possible. The Grace of God passes all understanding.

1993

1/20/93 It has been nearly two years since I have begun writing this letter. The Spirit reveals more and more as I struggle with ordained ministry. The biggest personal agony was why God had called us to rural ministry when so much of our interests, world view, approach to relationships, understanding of conflict, etc. were not rural. Why did God call a strong personality, a person who doesn't understand the meaning of the word *subtle,* a person who never knew there was a back door much less be good at using it, why call a duck out of water? I shared my concern and frustration with the congregation in the sermon the day of the annual meeting. God answered. The annual meeting had some conflict. . . . The people involved have been powerful . . . mainly because they have had very sharp tongues that they were willing to use. Their power came from intimidation. Finally, it was as if a ton of rocks was lifted off my shoulders. I know why God has called me to rural ministry. There are situations where a strong pastor is needed. . . . The pastor in the rural setting can use the parent-child model to good use. A person who has abilities that are not "rural" can fit into rural ministry by carefully changing what needs to be changed, and also by knowing the congregation well enough to know what is needed in leadership. The pastor has one foot in the congregation/community and one foot out of the community. It is that foot out of the community that may be the most useful.

3/2/93 The stress . . . seems to have dissipated, in fact I can't remember when I have felt less stress. The difference as far as I can tell, seems to be contact with Mark Olson and his writings, *The Evangelical Pastor.* He affirms so many things that I have believed and developed in the seven years at Bethlehem.
 We are at odds with the culture.
 It is a post Christendom age, we need mission now.
 Nothing will happen without vision.
 Mission statements are where we have been, goals are what we want to do.
 A vision statement is what we want to become.
 Let's encourage and teach small business by local people.
 Let's encourage local people into the ordained ministry by providing seminary training off campus so they don't have to quit a job and uproot a family.

Let's get serious about investigating ways for young farmers to get a start.
Let's develop methods to farm smaller acreages and make a living.

1995

6/3/95 Recently I have become even more sure that process and not goals is what needs to be the focus of the pastor in the rural setting, [so much so] that I have found myself regretting the leadership approach that I began with. . . . Then I realized that because of the Spirit I came into this call with a leadership approach that was strong, goal oriented, and flamboyant, because that was . . . the best thing at the time. Then I began wondering if there were other congregations where the pastor needed one approach . . . when they arrive and another a few years later. I strongly advocate longer stays out in rural calls, but does that mean that we will have to be aware and make changes . . . as the congregation grows and changes in their faith expression?

. . . There is [also] the time and situation where leadership needs to be more directive. Moses was a reluctant leader. The Hebrews didn't call him, or vote on what he told them had to be done. If they would have had the opportunity to have input to the Exodus, they would still be in Egypt as slaves. There are times the pastor needs to take charge, but they need to be carefully considered and evaluated.

ISSUES FOR DISCUSSION

1. Based on these impressions from pastors and parishioners, what issues, skills, attitudes, and strategies would seem most important to you in being an effective pastor in a rural setting?
2. What connections do you see between the needs of parishioners outlined in document A and the focus on "process" that emerges in document B? Suggest ways a pastor could resolve the apparent contradictions between such a process ministry, the biblical image of Moses, and the criticisms of the pastor in Jane Smiley's novel.

5.4   Women Clergy: The Patriarchal Setting

The following is an excerpt from an independent study by United Methodist Pastor Lorraine Roth, entitled *Rural Ministry and Longevity of Clergywomen in Local Parish Ministry.*

Women are currently being ordained at record rates; at the same time, women are leaving parish ministry at a faster rate than men. Of United Methodist clergywomen ordained as elders from 1974 to 1983, 34.4 percent left parish ministry within ten years, while 25.5 percent of clergymen had gone in other directions. Most striking is the statistic for those ordained at ages thirty-one to forty, with 39.6 percent attrition for women, compared to 26.1 percent for men.* Gender is clearly associated with longevity in the local parish. Longevity is also influenced by age upon ordination, and other factors. Many denominations have not yet studied longevity. They do, however, report that women wait up to two years for their first call. When that call comes, it is from a church to which the woman has applied, a church which invites her to come, and wants her to succeed. Is this exodus then strictly a United Methodist phenomenon? What other dynamics might be at work? Might it relate to rural settings, where most seminarians will begin ministry?

Rural and small churches provide special challenges, often intensified for women. Most seminarians come from large churches, and begin ministry in much smaller settings. United Methodist "entry level" churches tend to be small; small churches in other denominations often extend calls to women, who typically accept less pay. Women thus enter struggling churches, and the perception of their ministry as less valuable is perpetuated. Few seminaries offer courses related to rural ministry, so new clergy are unprepared for the contrasts. Seminaries tend to offer social, intellectual, and spiritual stimulation. Rural environments offer stimulation in different ways, which may not be immediately obvious. Most seminarians learn to emphasize programming, while rural ministry's more usual priorities are visitation and preaching. Family churches are likely to see little need for outreach, and to view newcomers as outsiders. Congregations aware of their position as stepping stones perceive the clergyperson as outsider; and often suffer from low morale and/or conflict. Too few seminaries challenge negative stereotypes of smaller, rural churches and their association with women clergy.

The stresses of life and ministry in rural America are often intensified for clergywomen. Rural pastors live in a "fishbowl," and small towns tend to have conservative images of pastors, especially women pastors. Support may be difficult to find in rural areas, where there may be great distances between colleagues, especially female colleagues. Coupled with outsider status, this leads to isolation, felt most severely by single women with no support in the household, and miles away from family or close friends. For single clergy, a new appointment requires leaving one's entire support system behind.

Isolation may be extreme, as single clergy are most likely to be viewed as outsiders in a family church, especially the anomaly of a single woman pastor. Single parents, male or female, face special child care issues in rural settings. Singles without children may be assumed to be always available, with no interests or responsibilities outside the church.

For married clergy, family pressures may affect parish longevity, since times of high church demands, such as holidays, coincide with high family demands. Spouses' careers may make the United Methodist itinerancy especially difficult for clergywomen, and small communities are unsure about the role of the pastor's husband. Each new appointment necessitates uprooting the family, and settling them into a new environment as the pastor undertakes a new parish. Women clergy with children may find themselves caught between the congregation's high time demands for the pastor, and their high expectations for mothers. Women of clergy couples may struggle with special identity issues, being more easily seen as the pastor's wife, and in a secondary pastoral role.

Complicating the issue is the possibility that more women enter ministry in response to personal crisis, and the support they receive from local churches and seminary communities during those crises. In the parish, support networks are left behind, and the pastor is the one expected to continually give support. Women enter the parish hoping to bring their experiences, their view of ministry and the world, to their work; and often find these gifts unmatched to small churches. Added to this is women's tendency to view life as a journey, and thus more likely to experiment and appreciate the freedom to risk. Most women leaving the parish enter other forms of ministry, while most male counterparts go into entirely new careers.

Being free to minister remains a struggle for women. Many laity and clergy are unfamiliar with, or remain unconvinced of the appropriateness of clergywomen. A recent United Church of Christ survey reported that 38 percent of ordained women had at some point been unemployed, compared to 24 percent of men. Discrimination was cited as the most common reason for unemployment among UCC clergywomen.† Few role models are found "in the trenches," and women have to constantly clarify their role and establish their identity. The "stained-glass ceiling" is well documented, with women tending to "top out" sooner. Men are strongly preferred as head pastors. Women are more accepted in specialized ministry, or in church planting, among new Christians who don't yet know what pastors look like. Female associate pastors often find their ministry not taken seriously, and their contributions minimized. Another harsh reality for clergywomen is sexual harassment, which leads some to retreat into "safer" ministerial settings. A 1990 survey reported that 77 percent of UM clergywomen had experienced harassment, most frequently at church social functions. Colleagues and pastors were the offenders 41 percent of the time.‡

With this overabundance of factors at work, what is to be done, and by whom? Seminaries? Parish pastors? Church hierarchies? With no definitive description of the problem as yet, there can be no definitive solutions. Yet there is clearly a problem, when 30-40 percent of our ordained clergywomen leave parish ministry. How can seminaries equip pastors to deal with rural ministry, and prepare women for the realities of life in the parish? Surely they need to avoid "sugar-coating" the stresses, and to encourage male students and faculty to affirm women in leadership positions. Guidance might be given for all clergy in building support systems, and maintaining spiritual health. Seminarians need to be aware of the realities of life in rural and small churches, and have opportunities to discuss the problems as well as the joys. Women might be helped in being more assertive as leaders, and as those seeking appointments and calls in local churches. Above all, women in rural ministry should move heaven and earth to establish and find support groups!

Once in the pulpit, or in church hierarchy positions, how might pastors educate and prepare congregations for clergywomen? Pastors, especially clergywomen, need to be very intentional in helping themselves, planning time for outside relationships and activities, and establishing vital support networks. Women need to be more assertive in making their needs known, and UM bishops and cabinets, and their counterparts across denominations, should be urged to listen. They might be more intentional about seeing that women are in closer proximity to one another, so that support might be more easily found. Every pastor, especially those in rural and small churches, should always be preparing their congregations for the next pastor—including the possibility of a woman as the church's preacher and administrator.

Many problems of clergywomen are not unique to ministry; but they are our problems to address. Some of the problems in rural and small church settings are not unique to women; but they are often intensified for women, and such settings do pose unique problems for clergywomen. As believers in the gospel of Jesus Christ, and the priesthood of all believers, we need to be raising the questions and addressing the issues; until the time comes when we can worship and work together side by side, as equal disciples of Jesus Christ, involved in God's mission to the world.

* DOM/Minning Longitudinal Study of UM Clergy.
† "New Study on Unemployed Clergy," *United Church News* 11, nos. 1-2 (April 1995).
‡ "UMC Sexual Harassment," *The Christian Century* 107 (12 December 1990): 1160.

Three excellent books that further the discussion of women clergy roles are Celia Hahn, *Growing in Authority, Relinquishing Control* (Washington, D.C.: Alban Institute, 1995); Nancy Foltz, *Caring for the Small Church: Insights from Women in Ministry* (Valley Forge: Judson Press, 1994); and Carol Becker, *Leading Women: How Church Women Can Avoid Leadership Traps and Negotiate the Gender Maze* (Nashville: Abingdon Press, 1995).

ISSUES FOR DISCUSSION

1. How do gender issues enter into church process?
2. What can be done to unleash the gifts women bring to ministry? By denominational officials? By lay leaders in rural congregations?

5.5   The Fine Art of Listening: Gathering the History of a Congregation

Tony Parker and the other authors discussed in this resource unit are trained sociologists and astute commentators on the rural scene. They literally make a business of understanding and capturing the voices and nuances of rural America. A pastor new to a particular rural congregation needs to cultivate the same capacity to listen in order to develop a sense of the context in which he or she is working.

The resource included here can help in refining those listening skills. The instrument was developed in 1993 by Barbara Borth, a seminarian at Wartburg Theological Seminary in Dubuque, who studied and spent internship time in the field with different agencies in the Midwest that are working with empowering rural churches, including the Iowa-based PrairieFire and the Center for Theology and Land. Borth offers concrete suggestions on how to approach the task of gathering the information listed. However, consider also the comment of a rural Iowan: "If I want to know what's going on in my town, I hang out mornings for coffee a couple times a week in the local diner."

A GUIDE TO GATHERING THE HISTORY OF A CONGREGATION

At a recent retreat, someone quoted Roy Oswald as saying that a pastor needs to be a "historian and a lover" in a congregation. The partial result of hearing that phrase is the following outline for gathering the history and other pertinent facts about a congregation and its neighborhood within the first four months of beginning a pastorate there. It is one way to get to know some people and to begin to know one's congregation. Explore as many of these areas as possible with the help of people rather than books from the library. As the new pastor, one can ask a few leading questions and *listen*. It is through listening that one comes to know the story and the storyteller.

I. Founding Fathers and Mothers
   A. Visit the person who knows the story of the founding. (Consider tape recording the story if written histories do not already exist.)
      1. Year, ethnic origins of founders
      2. Type and place of building
      3. Are there any pictures in existence?
      4. Have any significant anniversaries been celebrated? Were histories written at those times?
   B. Are any descendants of the founders still living? Are they members or living somewhere else?
      1. Obtain a list if they are nearby. Go to interview/visit each of them. Make a specific request for stories of their lives which will help them come alive as real people.
      2. While there, get to know some personal story of the family one is visiting.

II. The Congregation Through the Decades
   A. Prepare a sign-up sheet asking for two people—if possible—from every decade. Begin with the current one and then work back as far as people can go.
   B. Arrange to meet the two people. Find out everything possible about life in the congregation and community during their particular decade. Encourage the inclusion of change and loss along with the joys and progress. Again, tape record these interviews, if possible. Ask about seeing pictures.

III. How Does the Congregation Get Things Done? How Do They Feel About Themselves?
   A. Ask questions of the church council president at agenda planning sessions.
      1. Do meetings begin by sharing the leading of opening devotions?
      2. When is the annual meeting?
      3. What has Council or the stewardship committee done in the past?
   B. Observe how decisions are made at the council meetings. Is it by consensus or are Robert's Rules of Order used? Do the people seem to have high self-esteem?
   C. What committees exist and when do they meet?
      1. Parish Education/Sunday School (Ask someone to lead you through curriculum and supplies. Can you visit each Sunday School class?)
      2. Women's/men's groups
      3. Altar guild
      4. Property/grounds/cleaning committees
      5. Other

IV. Sunday Morning Worship
   A. Times
   B. How are lay people involved?
   C. Holy Eucharist (How often, who bakes the bread? What lay people are involved in serving?)

V. How Does the Congregation Observe the Church Year?
   A. Ask for a different volunteer to share about each season of the church year. Take them in order beginning with Advent, doing one each week (this assumes a starting date in summer). Add special holiday/memorial services to the rotation where appropriate.
      1. Advent. Color of paraments, special services?
      2. Christmas Eve
      3. Christmas Day
      4. (New Year's Eve)
      5. (New Year's Day)
      6. Epiphany
      7. Ash Wednesday

8. Lent
9. Good Friday
10. Easter (Sunrise service/midnight Holy Fire; breakfast; lilies or other flower traditions; Easter egg hunt?)
11. Pentecost
12. Trinity Sunday
13. Season of Pentecost
    a.) Summer church school?
    b.) Vacation church school?
14. Also ask about Memorial Day, July 4, Thanksgiving

B. Get to know each volunteer, and what their special interest is in the particular season for which they volunteered to share. Encourage them to be thinking about it for the coming year. How might the traditions faithfully and creatively be observed? How would they be willing to lead with your help?

V. Funeral Practices
A. Are there particular customs observed at the time of death?
   1. Do the women of the church have a bereavement committee to serve meals after funerals? Who are the contact people? Are there any particular customs about types of food, or who furnishes what?
B. Is the burial service from a standard Book of Worship used? Is Holy Eucharist ever included as part of the celebration of life eternal?
C. Ask for a guide to take you on a tour of the local cemetery. Where are graves of founders of the church? Where are graves of the last person to die from the congregation and the others who have died in the past year? Are there family members left behind who need to have pastoral visits?

VI. Birth and Baptismal Traditions
A. Is a birth announced to the congregation in any special ways—such as with a rosebud? Whose responsibility is it to buy the rose? How does the family get it after the service?
B. Are there any special traditions of this congregation having to do with baptism? Have there been any booklets or other teaching tools used in the past? Does the congregation celebrate in any special way?

VII. Discovering the State and County
A. When going to the county seat to change over licenses and/or addresses, learn when the state joined the union, state mottoes, etc. Also learn about the county, history of its name, when it was incorporated, significant facts about the county courthouse.
B. Does a county museum exist? What are the chief economic and natural resources of the county? Are county maps available? Are there county parks?
C. If a county map has been obtained, ask the help of someone to place a marker at the point where each parishioner lives.

VIII. Discovering the Small City or Town
A. Gently and gradually arrange a series of visits to various institutions and the people working there. In each place try to arrange a tour, meet staff, learn a little history, identify if possible any parishioners working there.
   1. Schools
   2. City Hall
   3. Recreational facilities
   4. Local newspaper office (take in your subscription)
   5. Local hospital or health clinic (learn about pastoral call policies/patterns)
   6. Local funeral home
   7. Area mental health/county health offices

8. Area nursing homes (ask someone with a family member there to take you the first time; are there shared ecumenical chaplain duties?)
9. Other churches (Is there a ministerial association?)
10. Library

B. Learn about businesses, other factors in the economy. What brought people to this area—originally and in recent years? Were there any American Indian/Alaskan natives living in the area when the Europeans came? What is the ethnic makeup of the town now? Is there a Chamber of Commerce?
   1. Local restaurants, grocery store
   2. Grain elevator, feed store, implement store
   3. What is the range of other businesses?

After all this listening and gathering of history has been finished, perhaps a celebration could be held to honor the past, enjoy the present, dream about the future. Perhaps the new pastor would be invited to say what his/her visions of the future would be. Whenever it is done, any comments by the pastor would surely have to begin with affirmation of all that God has done in the community before this time. Any ideas for the future would surely emphasize working together with the people to continue to build on what has been done.

For further discussion of listening skills, see excellent books by John Savage, *Listening and Caring Skills in Ministry*, which describes nine essential and learnable listening skills (Nashville: Abingdon Press, 1996); and by Lyle E. Schaller, *The Interventionist* (Nashville: Abingdon Press, 1997), which offers hundreds of questions that any pastor should ask when coming into a new parish that merits planned change.

Chapter 6

BUILDING COMMUNITY: STRATEGIES FOR EMPOWERING RURAL CONGREGATIONS

Clearly, this workbook has been written out of a deep concern that congregations learn to study and analyze themselves as a way of working toward increased vitality. That may involve growth in numbers, in spiritual maturity, in mission outreach, and in fellowship. Whatever kind of growth and vitality we are considering will almost certainly involve a growth in community.

Our interest in congregational studies is as an instrument for building up the community of God within each congregation. In this chapter we are interested in collecting the different parts of congregational studies and integrating them in a way that will contribute to the revitalization of the rural congregation you are or will be involved with. See resource unit 6.1 for one way of integrating the four components discussed in the previous four chapters. We organize this integration around the project of building community in full recognition that the community Jesus asked his disciples to build extends to the whole world. Despite that commission to be ever widening the bounds of the Christian community, the effort toward building that community begins with the local congregation (hence the relevance of congregational studies) and the local community. We begin with a case study, drawn from a personal interview with the lay leader of a rural congregation in North Dakota.

"We could gradually bury each other . . . Or we could get involved again . . . minister to one another . . . "

The Dakota farmer was lean and tall, oversized for the carved oak pew on which he was sitting as he talked to me about his tiny rural congregation. From time to time he gestured broadly around the empty sanctuary, punctuating his words.

"One Sunday as I looked up and down the pews I realized it—everywhere I looked there was only gray hair—like mine. There aren't a lot of young people here anymore, only three kids in one of the congregations we're yoked with. We can't really use bringing youth into the church as a way of turning ourselves around like some rural communities can. A lot of older folks had gotten out of the habit of working in the church—it was like they'd served their time—and now there wasn't a younger generation to take over."

A couple of council members and the young new pastor talked about it, the farmer explained. But it was the parishioners who finally came to the conclusion. "As we saw it, we had two choices. We could gradually bury each other until nobody was left. Or we could get involved again—minister to one another."

He paused, and for a moment I had a feeling he was reliving those choices his church had made some five years ago. "We picked life," he said simply. "Instead of complaining we didn't have enough kids to put on a Christmas pageant for us, we adults did our own for the shut-ins at the retirement home—and the kids were angels mostly. It was hard for a lot of parishioners to travel, isolated as we are, so we hired a bus to take a bunch of folks on an inner-city mission church cleanup project halfway across the state. Even those who couldn't go, the homebound folks, could do sewing and stuff for it."

A year later, when a welfare mom found herself stranded back in the tiny rural town, the parishioners were ready to respond. "We had five days before she was going to be evicted," the farmer explained. "So we didn't have a lot of time to debate about it. Our pastor pitched in seven hundred dollars; a bunch of us matched or bettered it. Within four days we had a favorable council vote to put a down payment on a house in town. We rented it out at cost, basically, with an option to buy."

I guess the surprise must have shown in my expression.

"Oh, it was controversial all right," he chuckled, not waiting for me to ask. "With some anyway. But people didn't have to pitch in money if they didn't want to, and we didn't use budget funds to do it. She's married now to a guy from a town about ten miles away. Her kids go to the local school, and all of them are active in our congregation . . ."

His narrative trailed off as he struggled to put what had happened in some perspective. "Only four new people and all," he said finally. "I suppose it wasn't much in terms of growing a congregation . . ."

Personally, I think it was—and I told him so.

Accepting the Call to Ministry: A Five-Step Approach

Given the broad scope of problems facing rural churches and their communities, it may seem difficult to know where to begin. One group of rural Iowa pastors and laypeople have outlined the key steps to rural revitalization as follows:

1. Sustain hope.
2. Build awareness.
3. Weigh the price.
4. Do it!
5. Evaluate.

Their plan reminds us that the best starting point is to focus not on the negative but on the positive aspects of a rural congregation's mission, ministry, and resources.[1]

As Pastor Bill Peters of St. John's Evangelical Lutheran Church in Olin, Iowa, expressed it, "It all has to begin with hope—a belief that change can happen. You cannot go anywhere without it. Hope is so basic that it isn't even a first step. It has to be an underlying condition or state of mind."

Christian spirituality and values are hopeful. The "good news" tells us that within every problem there is an opportunity; for every identified need there is a potential resource. Doors may close, but when they do, God is there, opening windows for us if only we can see that power in our lives.

Instinctively, farmers understand this kind of risk-taking and the inevitability of change. They are always planning ahead with the rhythm of the changing seasons—but also with the clear understanding that a thousand and one external forces can make all of their careful planning moot in a matter of seconds. Perhaps that underlying edge of uncertainty is one explanation for the tendency that Chuck Briem and others have observed in many rural settings (especially among males) to see situations in terms of problems and not opportunities. Farming is an ongoing struggle against forces one cannot predict, much less control. In an hour, weather can destroy a year's hard work and planning. Reacting becomes an ingrained tool in the survival kit of rural Americans from childhood.

Awareness: Seeing Problems As Opportunities

This conditioned pessimism (or realism, when seen in the context of the elements that rural folk battle most of their lives) can be combated. Affirmation is a powerful antidote. Problems can and must be processed in the context of options and opportunities. As one rural Illinois pastor expressed it, "Naming the problem has to be coupled with knowing the alternatives." One pastor used a "personal gift box" to help parishioners identify their abilities. He was responding to the need to affirm potential before moving forward to actual problem solving. Formal tools such as the congregation and community context assessments and surveys provided in the resource units in this chapter can be used successfully in identifying and prioritizing challenges—cutting them down to manageable size. However, pastors in rural settings need to be careful not to assume that parishioners or community members will use such techniques in the same formal way as highly urbanized corporate congregations often do. Far better is a less formal survey instrument administered personally, by either the pastor or the lay leadership on people's own turf. Informal visiting around the parish by the pastor is another way of achieving the same thing.

Priorities that build on existing traditions, strong points, or "points of pride" (identity) of a rural congregation are also likely to be favorably received. Urban emphasis on mobility and innovation are not valued as highly in rural society as they are in urban society. Such considerations also affect timetables for projects, as well as the goals a rural congregation may set. Given the strong undercurrent of spirituality in rural life discussed in chapter 3, it is important not to underestimate the power of the Spirit both in stimulating and sustaining renewal. Revitalization depends upon it!

Weigh the Price: Coming to Grips with Change

Until one is prepared to count the cost, revitalization remains no more than an academic exercise. If change is going to happen, both pastors and congregations need to be prepared to put price tags on their decisions—personal and professional, individual and collective. However, it is important in weighing those costs to remember that retaining the status quo—doing nothing—exacts heavy costs for communities and the people living in them (see resource units 1.2 and 2.5).

Rural ambivalence toward change is a potential source of either strength or weakness. Stability and traditional values are powerful forces binding rural people together; however, living with an eye perpetually on the rearview mirror can blind one to the possibilities ahead. Process, or how one deals with change, becomes all-important. In a fast-paced and mobility-oriented suburban church, innovation and variety may be seen as signs of a dynamic, vital ministry. In that culture, goals may become more important than process. Such an approach in a rural setting might be disastrous. To a rural congregation, progress and innovation may be perceived not as motivators but rather as threats. Every congregation, one rural pastor maintains, has its unique "pride points"—in one case hymn singing, in another the quality of the potluck. To tamper with these pride points is likely to cause unproductive conflict and to undermine whatever good intentions the pastor might have.

How, then, does a pastor or lay leader work toward altering unproductive behavior patterns and promoting more positive ones? Pappas and others offer very practical suggestions for facilitating change:

1. Framing change as *maintenance*. At times change may be important in its own right (i.e., a break with the past), but at other times it can be interpreted as a means of preserving traditional values.
2. Interpreting change in the context of *historical patterns*. Very often disasters draw a community together. In the purposeful, collective coping that follows a disaster can be found the seeds for meeting the challenges of contemporary rural life.
3. Presenting change as *endemic*. The most likely ventures to succeed will grow out of *a particular setting*—out of very local concerns.
4. Reinforcing the change as a desire that *must come from within*—from the individual and the community. A pastor is in a unique position by virtue of his or her role—at once insider and outsider—to facilitate this process.[2]

These and similar strategies can empower change where more confrontational approaches fail, because they dovetail and are in tune with the realities of rural life and values.

An overriding issue is the importance of sensitivity to the rural context in which the strategies are being used. Pastors and lay leaders alike need at all times to remember that the church is in part a reflection of its rural community, both in its mission and in its theology. Not only the *how* but also the *who* of rural ministry is significant when looking at the role of the clergy and of the lay leadership. In short, style can be as crucial as substance in successfully serving the rural church.

The Power of the Spirit at Work: The Will to Act

Ultimately, for all the optimism and awareness of both problems and potential, there must come a time to act—simply to "Do it!" Armed with the belief that rural people *can* do something to effect change, and cognizant of the prices that change will demand, one must have the will to act or take the leap of faith that overcomes fear and inertia. Ecclesiastes speaks to this:

When clouds are full,
they empty rain on the earth;
whether a tree falls to the south or to the north,
in the place where the tree falls, there it will lie.
Whoever observes the wind will not sow;
and whoever regards the clouds will not reap.
(Eccles. 11:3-4)

In other words, to wait for the right moment is human nature, but in fact that moment never comes. Just do it, the prophet assures us: "In the morning sow your seed, and at evening do not let your hands be idle; for you do not know which will prosper, this or that, or whether both alike will be good" (Eccles. 11:6).

In God's hands, our efforts will be blessed. The hope and promise of the power of the Spirit working among us is one of the most powerful energy sources empowering individuals and congregations in their efforts to revitalize their churches and communities.[3]

Many paths lead to the goal of unlocking or nurturing that kind of spirituality. Traditional Bible study may be one of them. The Des Moines–based PrairieFire program begins with Bible study as a focus of community building. A PrairieFire staff member is assigned to the field to develop and nurture leadership cadres. Carrying this approach one step further, Center for Theology and Land staff working with the Empowerment for Community Development research (on which this book is based) developed a fifty-two-week lay curriculum, *Planting the Seeds of Community*, is a scripture-based guide for rural Christians and congregations as they reassess their sense of identity and mission in the community (see chapter 3, table 3.1).

Although such a biblical focus can be successful, other approaches have value as well. Prayer and the sacraments have their roles. Whether the denomination is formally liturgical (worship that is oriented to the cycles of the Christian year) or not, the impact of ritual—both in good times and bad—can be affirming and empowering. The collective power of the family of believers coming together to celebrate or mourn can lead to the kind of affirmation and catharsis, respectively, that make growth possible.

Sometimes the impetus for growth may arise out of partnership or dialogue with purely secular agencies. Several of the twelve models involved in the Empowerment for Community Development project linked congregations and schools, banks or other businesses, public agencies, and so on in an effort to meet a commonly perceived community need.

In short, church leadership needs to be flexible enough to tackle the task of community building in ways that make sense in a particular context. What may work in urban, corporate congregations may not work at all in a rural setting. What works in one rural church may not work in another. As Cornelia Flora and colleagues remind us, "Today, rural communities probably differ more among themselves than they do, on average, from urban areas."[4]

Evaluation: Looking Back to Look Forward

Although it is important not to become bogged down by patterns of the past, evaluation nonetheless plays an important role in the revitalization process. How that process is carried out is crucial. The goal dare not be to allow those outside the process to snipe from the sidelines. Instead, the approach should be a nonjudgmental assessment process in which the participants strive to learn from their experiences and strengthen partnerships as well as the specific activities underway.

Regardless of what tasks a congregation or community is tackling, although consensus may be possible, unanimity is highly unlikely. Action cannot depend upon 100 percent agreement. But if projects (1) arise out of some commonly perceived need, (2) invite grassroots participation, and (3) incorporate ongoing input from as many community members as possible, chances of support are much greater. When one rural Iowa congregation (Bethlehem Evangelical Lutheran Church in Lost Nation, Iowa) conducted needs assessment in the form of a grassroots visitation with seventy parishioners, common themes identified were the need for youth programming and the problems of affordable housing. With this common interest base established, forty survey respondents (over half of those who perceived the issue as important) also indicated willingness to help tackle youth programming issues!

In addition to the strategies proposed above—living in hope, building awareness, counting the cost, taking action, and evaluating the results—several other development techniques deserve special attention here. The remainder of the chapter will focus on potential partnerships that draw church and community closer, as well as ways of sustaining ministry in the face of challenges and obstacles.

Potential for Partnerships

Particularly in very small churches and communities, it is important not to become trapped in the mind-set that the work of the church is limited to the resources available within the church building's four walls. In the microcosm of rural life, distinctions between secular and religious, church and community, and so on tend to blur. Pastors themselves may find it difficult to separate their roles as *pastors* and *citizens* of the community. As the case presented in resource unit 6.6 B illustrates, some parishioners will see any attempts on a pastor's part to function as a private citizen as illegitimate. A pastor needs much maturity and a deep sense of selfhood to deal with such a perception. The Bible itself offers many examples of how Christ challenges the disciples to co-ministry, and these passages can be used as resources for the pastor in educating his or her flock to a broader definition of carrying on the mission of the church.

Rural communities, on the other hand, are less likely to harden the lines between what constitutes secular and what constitutes religious realms. For example, traditional values may mean less opposition to prayer or religious music at public meetings. Resource unit 6.3 B presents the experiences of one community as it worked to promote partnerships between secular (governmentally funded) agencies and the established church. Where resources are limited, rural communities need to be encouraged to develop creative networking with nearby towns and villages in order to carry out specific kinds of ministries. In still other areas, ecumenical coalitions can open up rich possibilities for the entire community. (For a more in-depth look at some possibilities, see the various cases and community models presented in resources 2.7 and 4.5.)

In addition, the work of activists in rural Appalachia and the work described in some of the cases in this book also point to the possibility of innovative partnerships that can result when rural and urban areas work together. Among the possibilities are

- work groups from urban (or rural) settings helping other communities with lesser resources (e.g., with housing rehabilitation or church restoration projects);
- urban congregations acting as outlets for crafts and other products developed by rural parishioners who lack easy access to distribution systems, advertising, and mass markets;
- youth or other parishioner exchanges to promote greater awareness of urban and rural lifestyles.

Denominational policies could also be considered here. The prevailing pattern in Protestant denominations of reserving rural congregations for newly ordained clergy can contribute to problems such as burnout and stress. Inexperience and isolation can take a terrible toll, especially in the absence of formal judicatory support for pastoral networking or mentoring in most rural areas. The call policy of the Roman Catholic tradition is based on a very different kind of system. First calls are almost exclusively to associateships in large urban settings; following that experience, priests may have opportunities to serve their own midsize parishes. Calls to small, rural parishes are most likely to come late in a priest's career. As one Iowa priest suggests, this pattern assumes that older priests are less likely than younger ones to be impatient, to pass judgment, or to ride roughshod over the local congregational culture; hence, they are more likely to survive in very traditional communities. Critics argue that such a pastoral approach may mean that congregations will not be challenged to tackle the customs or issues that could be contributing to their gradual decline. Regardless of the relative strengths and weaknesses of the Roman Catholic model, change is unlikely in the Protestant pattern of assigning or calling the least-experienced pastors to rural or small congregations.

Nonetheless, both seminaries and national church governing bodies can do a great deal to facilitate the seminary-to-parish transition. Seminaries can model networking by mandating weekly roundtables that stress both spiritual and social interaction as underpinnings of a viable pastoral lifestyle. Judicatory bodies can offer benefits, such as travel stipends, regular in-service workshops, and spouse/pastor gatherings, that reduce isolation for rural clergy. On an ecumenical level, participation in groups such as regional ministerial associations can provide further support for pastors as they go about their ministry.

The Conflictive Church

A final problem facing recent seminary graduates—or any pastor for that matter—is coping with conflict in the church. In small, rural congregations where long-standing, intimate relationships are so very important, unresolved conflicts can be especially painful and destructive. Kenneth Haugk's book *Antagonists in the Church* is an enlightening study of how parishioners who cannot deal effectively with conflict in their lives often turn their anger and frustration outward within a congregation, inflicting great harm in the process.

A parishioner may feel deep-seated anger or resentment toward a fellow churchgoer, but to express that anger may be difficult, since the two need to get along as neighbors in a closed community. The pastor (an outsider to the conflict) may find himself or herself the target of those negative emotions. Unless the pastor can help the parishioners in such a situation learn to cope with conflict, his or her ministry may well be in jeopardy.

Haugk's advice to clergy struggling with such a call includes some practical suggestions for "hanging in there." It helps to remember that (1) it is unlikely that any leader is going to experience 100 percent support in a church; (2) conflict is as common in the church as in any other institution in our society; (3) finding an idyllic, stress-free congregational setting is nearly impossible; and (4) getting rid of the "antagonist" may be a frustrating tack to take, since "success" may merely lead to a power vacuum in which new antagonists emerge.[5]

If conflicts are systemic within a congregation, it does not pay to take the issues or the situation itself personally, but rather to objectively weigh the possible solutions. Too many pastors, Haugk contends, resign under pressure, when what they *really* need to do is learn to use conflict mediation strategies (see resource unit 6.6[c]). As a pastor in such a setting it is also very important to have the capacity to suspend judgment, to exercise and model forgiveness, to love whether or not you feel loved, to work at protecting your church as a whole rather than focusing all your energies on the dysfunctional member, and to recognize support when and where you find it. Finally, it is essential to maintain a sense of overriding optimism that effective ministry can occur even in the face of great challenges and difficulties.

Here our assessment of strategies for rural ministry comes full circle. We reinforce the advice offered by the group of rural Iowa pastors at the beginning of this chapter, as they summarized the driving force behind their own ministry:

- Build awareness (affirming one's self and others in the process)
- Weigh the costs
- Act!
- Evaluate
  and above all,
- **Never lose hope**

Ann Morrison discovered as she went about the task of developing a personal vision that work with rural congregations can become a compelling life's work, in which the smallness of scale can result in a sense of ministry and mission that is immediate and intensely personal. As one rural woman summed up her conception of what "ruralness" is all about:

Rural is a way of life [that offers unique possibilities] for friendship, compassion, and cooperation. When my second husband was ill, the community planted and picked crops for us; the service station filled the tractors with gas; the bill at the restaurant was paid. This is community.

In a human and theological context, knowing one's neighbor and being a neighbor become inseparable.

In talking about their congregations, rural clergy speak of the same kind of connectedness, even in the face of geographic isolation and the lack of some of the amenities that rural counterparts may take for granted. As one pastor sums up ministry to an Iowa congregation:

Being a rural pastor means being able to see and understanding the sense of community behind a lot of hidden pain and feelings of loneliness. As pastor, I feel my parishioners are partners in ministry. There aren't a lot of pastors who can talk to people in the pews about their own needs, but they are out there in rural America.

The hours are long and the problems may seem overwhelming at times. However, pastorates in rural congregations can challenge clergy to new levels of growth, both personally and professionally.

Maintaining the energy for that kind of highly charged congregational service demands learning to let go and learning to give.

Faced with the immensity of the challenges, pastors can become victims of their perceived need for strength and independence as they go about the task of ministry in their rural congregations. But when clergy and lay leadership alike learn to minister to one another—to know when to bind up one another's wounds and when to let others wash one's feet in loving service—true congregational ministry becomes possible.[6]

Ann Morrison: A Case Revisited

God Smiles on Strawberry Fest," read the headline. Thus began the rural weekly's account of the Hayden Community Celebration and first annual Celebrity Cow Milking Contest. Among the community leaders participating in the latter was the Reverend Ann Morrison, now in her third year at Hayden Christian Community Church. The newspaper article ended with a description of Ann's performance: "Unable to jump-start her cow into production, Rev. Morrison vainly pulled on the teats until a member of the audience yelled, 'start praying, Ann.' Immediately a stream of milk went into the bucket."

That clipping, along with a quotation about the rural church from Carl Dudley, is one of the prized mementos displayed over the battered desk in Ann's tiny office:

In a big world, the small church has remained intimate.
In a fast world, the small church has been steady.
In an expensive world, the small church has remained plain.
In a complex world, the small church has remained simple.
In a rational world, the small church has kept feelings.
In a mobile world, the small church has been an anchor.
In an anonymous world, the small church calls us by name and by nickname![7]

Those two documents express, in a nutshell, the heart of Ann's vocation as pastor.

A large, prominent urban church had offered her a position straight out of seminary, and initially Ann took that offer. But within six months of making that decision, she was back in Hayden—this tiny community tucked away in a forgotten corner of rural America, where she had done her internship. Has she ever regretted her decision? Ann's diary entry on her one-year anniversary in Hayden speaks of great joy:

Lord, you have led me on a tremendous journey. I never would have believed or imagined such a path. I'm sure my seminary classmates would hardly believe it if they could see me now! I've traded in my concerns for fashion and here I sit in blue jeans, running shoes and T-shirt, driving a pickup truck (traded in for my sports-type car), riding my bike to make calls when weather allows it. People from my past who have come out to worship here with me all seem to say the same thing. "You look so happy! There's just something so different about you now." I look happy because I AM happy!! Your Amazing Grace, Lord, has brought me this far.

But for all that, "It was a tough calling," Ann admitted as we sat together watching the hummingbirds dart around the bright red feeder suspended outside her office window. "When I took the position as youth pastor in that two thousand–member congregation, I either was listening for my call with a closed mind or God knew there was a lesson for me to grow through, and the path led through this huge church. At any rate, I soon discovered that the ministry that was in me was not possible in this kind of bureaucratic church environment. Instead of making use of the gifts God gave me, the church was narrowing my ministry. It was like going through a funnel with a long spout at the end. My spirit was withering; my spirituality was being stifled. Worse, as a woman, I experienced some terrible sexual harassment in that anything assessed as good or as a gift from God was taken from me and given to one of the male associates. The prayer circle I started was shut down because I was told it shouldn't take that long to pray! Without a doctorate, I was told I was not educated enough to conduct Bible study. I was suffocating, and I didn't know how to get out."

But the Lord, Ann says, answered her prayers in a "most awesome way!" One day as she sat in her office, the senior pastor walked into her office laughing—a piece of mail in his hand.

He said, "Take a look at this if you want a good laugh. This is the worst newsletter I have ever seen. Those farmers can't even spell!"

When he tossed the newsletter on her desk and walked out, Ann gasped with shock. There in front of her was the church newsletter for the congregation in Hayden whose pulpit she had filled while interning at the seminary.

"That day as I took my once-a-month turn preaching to that enormous congregation, I heard the Lord say to me, 'Ann, this is not your home.' I remember so clearly what I heard," she explains, "because for a moment I stumbled in my carefully crafted sermon (edited by the senior pastor, of course)."

Ann felt a calmness and feeling of peace that she describes as inexplicable. The headline on the front page of that newsletter said that the search committee thus far had two candidates for the position of pastor. She ran to her office after the service and closed the door. Hands shaking, she grabbed the phone and dialed the relocation office. Within twenty minutes she had her answer: the church in Hayden would consider her as a candidate.

A week later she and her daughter and new husband all visited Hayden for an interview. "When the questioning was over," Ann says, "the three of us strolled and prayed, but it didn't seem long before they came looking for us. They had taken a vote, and it was unanimous. My tears were not the only ones falling that day—this time I knew that here is where I was meant to be, praise God!"

Although the large congregation was not thrilled about her decision, they let her out of her contract early. Her first Sunday in Hayden, fittingly enough, was Easter—a day of hope and promise and life renewing itself.

At the end of her first year, the church sanctuary is dotted with homemade banners put together by young hands in preparation for their baptism. "I hung the first seven there the Sunday the first group was baptized. The congregation was awed by the beauty of these youthful creations. Now there are fifteen banners hanging there—living testimony to the spiritual growth of the congregation."

Despite Hayden's size, nearly thirty children come forward now for the children's sermon. The youth group of third- to sixth-graders is so big it is going to have to split in the fall.

"You see people living out the gospel in joy, and they are inviting others to join them. Only the Lord knows where all these new families are coming from! But when they come, they are received with warmth, are fed with the gospel and the table set by the Lord Jesus Christ. And they stay to be a part of the excitement of a church that is on fire with the Spirit!

"Success in ministry," Ann concludes, "isn't measured in numbers or dollars, it's in the spiritual growth, which brings its own rewards. It's measured in the work that is life. It is measured in the joy of the journey."

Her most recent letter was signed, as always, "Rejoicing in the Lord, Ann."

RESOURCES FOR BUILDING COMMUNITY

As documented throughout this text, one of the most crucial elements of rural ministry is that of process in ministering to community in rural settings. The resource units in this chapter consist of materials that integrate the components of congregational studies and challenge clergy to reassess their roles as a crucial step in learning how to develop healthy clergy/congregation relationships, and in the process, empower the work of community.

6.1 Integrating the Components of Congregational Studies
6.2 Integrating the Pastoral Role
6.3 Affirmation As a Tool of Ministry
6.4 Health Ministry in the Rural Community
6.5 The Role of Pastor As Priest: Sustaining the Rural Community
6.6 Awakening the Prophetic Voice: Dealing with Change and Conflict
6.7 Technology and Community: Getting Online

6.1 Integrating the Components of Congregational Studies

In the previous chapters we have considered the components of congregational studies: context, identity, program, and process. The resource units have provided ways of thinking about your congregation. Our intent is that by stimulating your imagination and memories you have drawn a picture of your congregation's context at the conclusion of chapter 2; of its identity at the conclusion of chapter 3; of its program at the conclusion of chapter 4; and its process at the conclusion of chapter 5.

At this point it may be helpful to try to put these pieces together, to integrate them, at least somewhat. More important is the task of building community. So this resource will begin by paying some attention to integrating the components, but then it will offer a "Congregational Assessment Wheel" to assist you in locating those areas of strength that your congregation could continue to enjoy, and also areas that need some concentrated attention.

A. PUTTING THE PIECES TOGETHER

It may be helpful for each individual to work through the following questions by himself or herself first, then share the results of her or his thinking with one other person and then in smaller groups.

Overall, it might be best to work with different groups in the congregation first, and then bring all the various groups together so that each can hear the possibly quite different answers to the question of who this particular congregation is for them. You could make the exciting discovery that this congregation is made up of groups who each appreciate different aspects of the same whole.

Think back to the exercises we did in the resource units that summarized each of the elements (2.8 on context, 3.1 on identity, 4.6 on program, and 5.1 on process).

● Which of the four units was most suggestive to you in thinking about the nature of your congregation?

● How do the various units fit together?

● What exercise opened up new ways of thinking about your congregation?

● If you had to pick one program, aspect of identity, process, or contextual factor that was most determinative of your congregation, which would it be?

● What surprised you in what you or others said about the congregation?

B. ASSESSING YOUR CONGREGATION'S WELL-BEING: A CONGREGATIONAL ASSESSMENT WHEEL

Our friend Sandy Simonson Thums developed, over a period of years, an individual well-being wheel, which she used in various workshops to get people to identify and assess their overall well-being. Her areas for people's self-assessment were in the sectors of mind, body, spirit, self-esteem, work, goals, and family health. Here we are introducing a similar instrument in the hope that it will build on the questions and integration you achieved in the exercise above and also help you locate areas of strength and areas for improvement.

Please rate the extent to which the statement on the left is true for your congregation on a scale of 1 to 10, with 1 meaning "not at all true of our congregation" and 10 meaning "couldn't possibly be any more true of us."

Members of our congregation are very open with one another (will share almost anything).
1 . . . 2 . . . 3 . . . 4 . . . 5 . . . 6 . . . 7 . . . 8 . . . 9 . . . 10

Our worship services show a good mix of traditional and creative, new elements.
1 . . . 2 . . . 3 . . . 4 . . . 5 . . . 6 . . . 7 . . . 8 . . . 9 . . . 10

Our congregation has a clear sense of mission in the community. (It can identify its mission to the town or country.)
1 . . . 2 . . . 3 . . . 4 . . . 5 . . . 6 . . . 7 . . . 8 . . . 9 . . . 10

Members and visitors can sense the love of God in the warmth and friendliness of the congregation.
1 . . . 2 . . . 3 . . . 4 . . . 5 . . . 6 . . . 7 . . . 8 . . . 9 . . . 10

When someone in our congregation is sick, that is announced and we pray for them.
1 . . . 2 . . . 3 . . . 4 . . . 5 . . . 6 . . . 7 . . . 8 . . . 9 . . . 10

Our congregation celebrates its history and context and also the community's history.
1 . . . 2 . . . 3 . . . 4 . . . 5 . . . 6 . . . 7 . . . 8 . . . 9 . . . 10

We think about the needs of people in church and community and shape our activities to people's needs.
1...2...3...4...5...6...7...8...9...10

People in the congregation can identify the strengths of the church and feel good about the church.
1...2...3...4...5...6...7...8...9...10

The minister is able to share leadership in a way that builds up members of the church.
1...2...3...4...5...6...7...8...9...10

People can disagree in our church and work out those disagreements or simply agree to disagree.
1...2...3...4...5...6...7...8...9...10

We have certain goals in our congregation, we know what they are, and we work toward them.
1...2...3...4...5...6...7...8...9...10

Our congregation knows how its members are employed and emphasizes that their daily work is God's work.
1...2...3...4...5...6...7...8...9...10

The minister is competent in performing the traditional ministerial roles (preacher, visitor, teacher, administrator).
1...2...3...4...5...6...7...8...9...10

Our congregation has no financial difficulties because everyone practices stewardship.
1...2...3...4...5...6...7...8...9...10

The educational program of the church shows a concern to nurture every age group.
1...2...3...4...5...6...7...8...9...10

The pastor feels comfortable with his or her identity enough to appreciate the church's identity.
1...2...3...4...5...6...7...8...9...10

Families feel supported in our congregation.
1...2...3...4...5...6...7...8...9...10

People usually feel good about worship and other church programs (are glad they came).
1...2...3...4...5...6...7...8...9...10

Our congregation does enough planning and thinking about the future that we do not fear it.
1...2...3...4...5...6...7...8...9...10

The pastor really cares about people in the congregation and shapes his or her ministry to their concerns and life situation.
1...2...3...4...5...6...7...8...9...10

What goes on at church really addresses people in the community; our activities are appropriate to this context.
1...2...3...4...5...6...7...8...9...10

This congregation has a sense that it reaches out to others to invite them to discipleship.
1...2...3...4...5...6...7...8...9...10

The congregation feels like it is God's people; we try to discern God's will for our life.
1...2...3...4...5...6...7...8...9...10

The members of our congregation are comfortable praying with one another and participating in Bible study.
1...2...3...4...5...6...7...8...9...10

This congregation has a lot of people involved in making decisions.
1...2...3...4...5...6...7...8...9...10

When individuals have completed their own assessments, they can share them with one other person. Then groups can discuss their overall assessment. What will probably happen is this: A pattern will emerge, and you will find many people in the congregation rating some items very highly. (If you so desire, you can add up the numbers to determine which items were rated highest and which lowest. Those having the highest scores are the congregation's strengths; the ones with the lowest scores are those that may need improvement.) Concentrate on ways of celebrating and continuing the congregation's strengths; also, think about ways that certain areas of congregational life can be improved.

When you have completed this exercise, you will have used congregational studies to think about how to build community—God's community. May God bless you in that work!

6.2   Integrating the Pastoral Role

Solo pastorates in rural communities can be lonely ventures. Geographic distances often make networking with other colleagues difficult, and the intimacy of the small community means that one can seldom leave one's role as pastor. To avoid burnout and to pursue empowering ministry, clergy need to cultivate a ministerial style that balances their own needs, their parishioners' expectations, and the broader community's needs.

In the following statements, seminary students working with the Center for Theology and Land in Dubuque, Iowa, discuss the role of the pastor based on field experiences in a variety of settings. Their comments shed light on the issue of how pastors can balance the many demands on their time in a rural congregation, and still play a positive role in community development.

David (after serving in a rural nursing home involved with churches in establishing ministry to the elderly): People in the nursing home had a lot to give despite many misconceptions by the congregations. They don't like being put into a box that's the end of their life. They still feel like they have things to give. I learned, also, that rural congregations need to be aware of trying to incorporate those people in their life as much as possible. Too often when people get to a nursing home or become shut-in, a process of ministry begins that is just *to* them. The pastor goes once a month to deliver communion or just to visit, and otherwise there's not much interaction.

Mark (after helping a church and community nonprofit agency convert an abandoned school to a community center): But in a way weren't we all doing community development work? I found myself spending a little more time than expected establishing relationships in order to reach my goals. I got interested in the old converted school project when I heard the dreams and visions for it, so I was just a little anxious to get in there and do something. Yet I was unable to until people were ready to join me in doing that. The only way that interaction was going to come about was sitting around the cafe. I enjoyed that—for a long time. But felt I should be doing more. Finally, when I just kind of resigned myself to the fact that maybe I'd be doing that a lot, all of sudden there was a turn-around, and by the second week people were pushing me to do things. I guess by that time they trusted me.

Donna (placed with a rural area developing a People-to-People ecumenical volunteer network): I think the community development I saw happening here was the ecumenical body and also the various towns working together as a big community, the whole county. The people didn't care which church they were from.

So a Roman Catholic contractor's going to provide the supplies and do the job for a person from the Assemblies of God church. Then we have the Lutheran group fixing a house of a Roman Catholic. There's no questions asked. Here's the money, the supplies, and the people. We'll do it.

Gary (a Protestant working to support a parish nurse working in a Roman Catholic congregation): I guess several things struck me. First of all it was how much spirituality permeates rural people's entire life. They don't ever say that. They don't talk about that, but as you visit with them you realize that much of what they do and much of what they say is grounded in their own understanding of what it means to be spiritual or connected to God. And maybe it's because a lot of them are farmers and I've found that farmers by and large have a connectedness to creation just because of the nature of their work. The other thing that sort of struck me was that I knew that people liked to tell their stories, but I didn't realize they had a desperate need to tell them. We'd go to visit and we'd think we were only going to be there for twenty or forty minutes and that we were going to make four visits in the afternoon, and we'd make one. Three hours later we'd say, "Now, we really have to go this time."

Those two things struck me. And personally, in terms of my own growth and being supervised, I discovered that it was good for me to be challenged. And I think all too often as pastors, especially solo pastors, we aren't. We aren't always challenged and we don't always challenge ourselves. So having a supervisor who said, "Well, what does that mean to you or what do you see in that?" and kind of be pushed was real important for me.

Jan (working in a conflictive congregation trying to convert an old school to a retail and community center): I'd say that here community development would also be building bridges. Rather than meeting an immediate need it would be to look at the relationships within the community itself. I was surprised to discover that the community still had not visualized how they saw their mission with the school project. They had many different ideas and strategies, but they really still did not have a vision as a community in how they were going to realize this goal—the conversion of the school into a community center.

I think the other thing, too, was in understanding what great respect and confidence they can invest in the pastor. That was reinforced to me. I don't know if you'd call it a burden of being a pastor, but you really need to take that into consideration. Your parishioners are going to expect a lot from you, but also hold you up as well. That was fulfilling for me, I guess, in realizing what a call would mean: the possibility of being reaffirmed in my ministry by a congregation.

Development—pastoral or secular—is not done in its own vacuum. It's done because you're bridging with other sources and other individuals, other groups that promote some sort of forward movement. If you have to name the role to strive for, it would be a bridge builder.

Gary: I asked two older women at a care facility what their expectation for a pastor was. They said, "Well, we really don't have much except that they keep it simple, and they're simple, and they're just here." The clergy comes and visits. I labeled it a ministry of *being*. That's all they expected. And the pastors said that what they received from ministry in a rural setting was that often the expectations weren't all that high except that they keep it simple and that they were there. But they really felt supported, especially by the elderly.

Jan: I think my understanding of what is rural has changed . . . sometimes what we consider our urban problems (like poverty) are in the rural setting. Environment doesn't necessarily mean that it's different community at all. And I guess I would mention again that what rural ministry would mean, then, is this mission concept, this mission understanding. That we take into account the setting.

Gary: I want to echo first what Dave said, and that's that rural has to do with an attitude. It's more a mentality than a size or population. Also I think what Jan said about mission is true. I listened to a speaker one time who said the church goes into areas and establishes missions; but that, really, that process is backwards. People establish missions in hopes they will become a church, when we really should go in and establish a church in hopes it will become a mission. I think there's a subtle difference, but I think it's a critical difference. Rural or urban—anywhere is a mission field, and we have to approach it as missionaries.

There's also a prevalent attitude, among some people at least, that people in rural areas are by and large uneducated. That's a fallacy. You cannot go into a rural area and talk down to them. I think people who are not used to being in a rural area do that. It comes across and people know that and they won't respond to people like that. Parishioners will challenge us. They want sermons that have content. They don't want fluff, because they are very articulate. They're very knowledgeable people. They're very wise, and we can't underestimate them.

Mark: There are some unique things in a small town setting. You can let your kid go out the door and know that every house that kid passes people know where the kid is going and the kid is relatively safe. I saw kids on the street. Parents trusted completely everyone in the town cared for those kids, which is unique to a small town. You see some of those things, and I think you see the closeness of some relationships, and some are closer than others. I kind of like those things. I think I could do it. I think I wouldn't even mind trying it sometime and then judging whether I would want it permanently, which is a change from where I started out.

I would prefer the title community developer. Community development goes hand-in-hand with pastoral ministry whether you like the title or not.

ISSUE FOR DISCUSSION

If you were asked the same question that triggered this student dialogue—How do you describe the role of clergy in a rural setting?—what would your answer be? How do themes such as intergenerational relationships, secular and church links, the vocation of neighbor, affirmation, and mutual ministry fit into a potential job description for the rural pastor?

6.3   Affirmation As a Tool of Ministry

One of the seminarians in resource unit 6.2 hit upon a powerful factor in rural culture when he said, "I knew that [rural] people liked to tell their stories, but I didn't realize they had a desperate need to tell them." Time and time again elsewhere in this text, *affirmation* and *listening* emerge as powerful tools of community building in the rural setting.

A. VISITING

The following reflections are from Pastor Craig Bowyer, formerly of Bethlehem Lutheran Church in Lost Nation, Iowa.

"Visiting" can develop the relationships that become the glue that holds rural homogeneous congregations together and molds them into alive, Christ-centered, evangelical congregations with a strong active sense of mission.

What is visiting? A conversation, initiated by a trained visitor, with one other person, that is intentional in purpose. *Visiting* is a word that is well known to rural people. Virtually everybody visits. But the custom has undergone some change because people can travel to other places, away from those they can normally visit. Visiting has changed because people watch an average of forty hours of TV per week, and it is impossible to visit while watching TV. In spite of the changes, most people probably would understand *visiting* to mean approximately what their grandparents would have understood it to mean.

God took *covenant* and redefined it to convey a different meaning. The term *covenant* had been secular and was redefined to be a religious term that had a deeper and more significant meaning. Similarly, *visiting* is a secular term that we have redefined. It has become "an intentional conversation that helps one person get to know another person." The object is to set up a situation where the person being visited can share part of who he or she is as God has made him or her. It is baptismal in its action.

What is the purpose of visiting? To develop a relationship based on knowledge received and given. This is important in several ways:

1. Most of us in rural areas know "everyone," or more accurately, we know about everyone. Many times I have gotten to know someone and realized that what I thought I had known was inaccurate. Often I would come to an understanding of why that person did certain things that I had found objectionable, and those actions then became less objectionable.
2. The person that is visited is not asked to do anything at the time of the visit. The purpose of just getting to know the person is to be kept very clear.
3. Everyone is unique in God's creation. Everyone has been given certain gifts and interests. That makes them interesting. The purpose is to find out why they are an interesting child of God.

What do we hope to accomplish? The visitors will be changed, as well as those who are visited. They will have a relationship they did not have before. All involved will come to a better understanding and work together in the future for the coming of the kingdom.

Many programs in the church seem to start from a pathological base (they look for sickness or weakness). For instance, the calling and caring ministries are good, but they are looking primarily for the caller to minister to the person who is being called on. It is assumed that the person receiving the call is in need. My observation is that caring calling and pastoral care, as important as they are, do not become the glue that holds a congregation together as an active faith community.

The visiting process comes from a different assumption. It is assumed that each person is unique and has God-given gifts and interests—gifts and interests with which the visitor wants to connect. Relationships based on shared gifts and interests (strengths) can pull a congregation together and hold it together.

It seems that in God's relationship to us, God is very careful not to take away any of our dignity. God comes to us as an equal, not as a caregiver. When we visit others we tend to be the power person if we have what the other person needs. We are equal when we both have something to offer the relationship.

If the calling and caring or pastoral care person comes to the visit knowing that there is something the visited person needs, is it possible for the caller to be a true brother or sister with the care receiver? We have a problem if we want to "do for." The preposition *for* does not make an equal equation. The receiver of the care is not on a par with the giver. In our culture, rich people develop and administer programs *for* the less-advantaged. I refer to the parable of Lazarus to indicate Jesus saw a real problem with caregivers who did not touch and know and recognize as unique individuals the ones they were helping. Calling and caring are valid, but with extreme caution, and with different purposes than visiting.

How is visiting a congregational process? The beginning setting for visiting is worship. The visitors are to be strengthened, commissioned, and sent out from Sunday morning worship. The congregation is told in advance why the visitors are coming. The visitors meet back in a worship setting to share the treasures that have been revealed. Visitors also will share pertinent (nonconfidential) information, especially stories they have heard, in a group setting with other visitors so that both needs and skills can be identified. The congregation then will know who has an interest in a specific task or goal. The stories are reflected upon biblically and theologically.

Does visiting work? Only if used regularly, intentionally, and prayerfully.

B. LEARNING THE LANGUAGE OF CHANGE

The following observations are from a summer seminary intern, "Carolyn," who was placed with a rural regional neighborhood housing authority. The goal of the placement was to involve churches more significantly in the mission of improving housing conditions in that rural area. Among Carolyn's personal goals were understanding the rural culture and reconciling and defining her role as a future pastor working in a secular setting. At the outset, she sensed that people in the agency did not see working on community housing as ministry. They assumed that this kind of public service work is secular, and hence found it hard to understand why a seminarian would be placed in this setting.

I wished at first that I had more information about the community—as if somehow that would speed up the adjustment process. Now I'm not so sure that is possible. A person working for the church in a rural setting needs to be strong, to avoid being chewed up. It is a constant balancing act—between caring and listening, functioning as a catalyst or charismatically, the role of visionary and conflict resolver.

One day the town newspaper editor challenged me, "Why would the church or seminary get involved working with the housing authority? Isn't the church competing with other service groups or agencies by assuming such responsibilities?" It forced me to articulate my views about my ministry. "In working here, I see that the church is really fulfilling its tradition to be *in community*. As a pastor, I need to know how to model that." The editor seemed pleased with that and could understand what I was doing there.

As a result, I am looking at the distinction between church and secular in a different way. If a church is going to act in the arena of human life and experience, conflict does not have to be a result—even though it has been a while since the church took responsibility for the community. In this community, the food pantry was an inroad. People seem to want the government to pay for everything, although they are working themselves away from this. The church has a real role to play in this change in community life.

You need to learn to live with a rhythm of work life that is sometimes "hurry up and do" and then one of waiting. The upside of that is that even under constraints, you do sometimes have time for reflection. It's human to want orientation to that kind of experience, but sometimes you can only experience the kind of learning you need to do in "disorientation."

Don't be thrown by the fact that rural "god talk" is not "seminarian talk." It's there—just not as systematic. Laughing together sometimes can be as prayerful as prayer. Unchurched people on the staff suddenly began to talk "church talk" and seemed to be seeing what I am doing as credible. It seems especially healthy for women on the staff to see me in this role, and some are sharing more of themselves and their problems with me. They are pretty open about their stereotypes of what seminarians are supposed to be like. I worry sometimes about being isolated because of being different. As a pastor, am I going to be able to function as a regular person, not just in some role that people ascribe to clergy? Maybe a pastor shouldn't be so concerned about being a leader, but just work at living humbly, yet in ways that somehow make a difference.

I feel very affirmed in my calling. One day someone left a bouquet of flowers on my desk with the simple note, "Thanks for listening." Theology and pastoral care training are helpful, but in the end, it is the Holy Spirit who works the miracles.

Networking with other interns helped. We supported each other in the learning process. You need that in order to hang in there. Rural pastors need that kind of network as well. [It would have helped] to have had a mentor within the ministerial group in town]. It would have been valuable, too, to participate more in community worship life. Above all, I felt a growing sense of the importance of being a human being first and a pastor second.

ISSUES FOR DISCUSSION

1. Integrate Pastor Craig Bowyer's views of visiting with Carolyn's analysis of her internship experience with community building.
2. Carolyn's experiences have ramifications for rural pastors choosing the path of "tent-making" min-

istry, in which a career outside the church is essential for making the position of clergy financially viable. Note also the implications of affirmation for pastors as well as individuals in the church and community. How can clergy live like ordinary people yet be set apart? What do you see in Carolyn's approach that is helping her set the stage for mutual ministry shared by the secular community and clergy?

3. What kind of training could help teach the kinds of listening and affirming skills advocated here—in the seminary and in the community itself? What liturgical formats could be used to affirm people's stories, gifts, and spiritual growth?

4. Suggest strategies for transforming a traditional lay "calling" ministry into an effective "visiting" program.

5. Suggest strategies for transforming a "set apart" traditional clergy leader role into a "community developer" role.

6.4   Health Ministry in the Rural Community

As congregations and pastors define the work of ministry in their communities, it is important to use Scripture as a resource to identify the focus of that outreach. Roughly 20 percent of the Gospels are devoted to healing encounters of various kinds. For example, among the passages that deal with Christ as healer in the Gospel of Mark are the stories of the hemorrhaging woman (5:25-34), the possessed boy (9:14-29), and the deaf-mute (7:31-37). This unit suggests the seriousness of the rural health care problem, along with ways churches can use a *healing* ministry to witness to their faith.

The parish nurse model described in the documents in this resource unit is a way for congregations to address the lack of accessible medical services in rural areas. In the Iowa model, described in document A, a denominational hospital provides supervision and training for nurses serving individual parishes and ecumenical coalitions of congregations. In the Illinois model, described in document B, nine Lutheran congregations work with a combination of secular and public regional hospitals. Of special focus in the ministry are the elderly and uninsured families with young children who may find themselves without access to care.

A. The Parish Nurse

NURSES PROMOTE WELLNESS
by Finn Bullers
(Dubuque) Telegraph-Herald
August 29, 1996

Volunteer Ethel Burmeister-Sterk, a 70-year-old retired nurse, spends up to 20 hours a week ministering to her brothers and sisters. She's what's known as a [nondenominational] parish health minister. She might pick up the phone and gently remind a member of the Catholic Church to take her medication. She might give a member of the Lutheran Church a ride to a Dubuque doctor's appointment. Or she might make sure a stubborn elderly man from the Presbyterian Church does what the doctor says. Other activities might include a cholesterol screening or a blood-pressure check. It's all part of her role as wellness advocate, educator, listener and friend.

Burmeister-Sterk, and other nurses in 28 tri-state communities, meet bimonthly at Mercy [a Roman Catholic affiliated hospital in Dubuque] for continuing education. . . . The nurses, many of whom volunteer their time, are not substitutes for health agencies. They act as a bridge in the medical gap that leaves an increasing number of rural folks without health care.

Granger Westberg of Oak Park, Ill., started the idea of a parish health ministry seven years ago at Lutheran General Hospital in Park Ridge, Ill.

B. TOWARD A HEALING COMMUNITY

The following are excerpts from the final evaluation session with the seminary intern Brent, his supervising pastor, and a group of parish nurses with whom he worked in rural Illinois—all of them working out of Lutheran congregations.

Brent: The parish nurse program seems to be especially compatible with the traditional Christian focus derived from Matthew on proclaiming the Word, teaching, and healing. Among the important things I learned is to what a great degree healing and proclaiming must go together. How you define ministry is essential; in other words, the paradigm will determine what we prioritize as a denomination, congregation, or individual Christian. Reinforcing this particular mission in rural communities is the strong tradition that "we take care of our own." A note of caution is that "our own" does not necessarily mean or include everyone. Inclusivity is among the greatest single problems that needs to be addressed in such ministry in rural areas, including seriously cultivating the extended definition of family or community that Luke talks about.

Education is another neglected area. For example, there is a lot of concern about drug and alcohol abuse, but not necessarily from a prevention perspective. People who will help fund benevolence projects do not often see the need for education that could keep problems from occurring in the first place; in other words, they are often reactive rather than proactive. We need to look through Jesus' eyes to find the interrelatedness and deal with the brokenness.

The medical community doesn't think this way either, even in spite of scientific evidence showing that the more holistic a system is, the more healing takes place, including the spiritual dimensions in health. A challenge is to learn how to help people see the relevance of and connections between faith and health. There tends to be a fix-it mind-set rather than a long-term lifestyle orientation. The long-term chronically ill probably see the need the most.

Nurse P: Pastors can do a great deal to help rural congregations begin to address these issues. It starts one-on-one, with people assuming personal responsibility for their own health care. The church needs to teach what caring is all about. Then sometimes it is hard for families to care for their own—they know too much. It may be easier for strangers to analyze and help. Again, the church can help find ways to make that possible. There can be disadvantages to "knowing."

Nurse J: Even medical personnel need to learn to cultivate partnership models. Most medical personnel admit they don't have the background they need in some cases for providing emotional support—not just pills.

Nurse M: Sometimes doctors are too locked into scientific models to give the body a chance. Baby boomers themselves tend to buy into this—that science can cure everything. There is a lot science cannot do. Mental and emotional factors are important; dying happens to all of us. Life support can be a trap—not a blessing. The older generation understands that, and people in their middle years are questioning things some. It's a slow process. I did some farm chemical research and know that it's slow going. It's hard to convince people that land is capable of regenerating itself and that land and personal health are tied together.

Nurse R: Laypeople can do a lot in support groups, helping one another deal with grief, parenting, stress, and so on. But you need to be careful how you use laity because of the difficulty with confidentiality in rural areas . . . something true even of professional volunteers like emergency medical technicians. So many people are related that privacy becomes a real problem. But genuine concern bridges confidentiality.

ISSUES FOR DISCUSSION

1. Denominational and community traditions can affect how parishioners and clergy approach rural mission. Unequal distribution of resources can also play a role. What are some barriers and cautions you see in implementing a single- or multicongregational health ministry? How could preaching and teaching sensitize parishioners in these settings to the potential for such mission or partnerships?

2. Imagine that you are a pastor, called to serve a rural community of 1,500. The local health clinic—a satellite of a neighboring town some fifty miles away—just closed a year ago, and the town's only doctor died in January at age eighty-nine. How could you work with a team of clergy, laity, community leaders, and a regional hospital to meet the following challenges:

   a. Assess who is hardest hit by the lack of adequate local medical care. To what extent are needs physical and to what extent are they emotional or spiritual; in other words, is the issue illness or loneliness?

   b. Assess the need for technical medical services or for a loving support network that would provide personal care such as help with taking medication properly; rides to checkups, visits, and phone reassurance for the elderly; checkups for school children of parents who have no insurance; or child care for children during illnesses when both parents are working outside the home.

   c. Decide whether your community would benefit from a parish health ministry similar to the one described in the newspaper article above. How might you act as a catalyst to start parishioners thinking about such a program? How might such a program be organized? What are the barriers to such a ministry? What are the resources and opportunities for such a ministry? How would you preach to such concerns?[8]

6.5 The Role of Pastor As Priest: Sustaining the Rural Community

Along with the healing and prophetic ministries of a congregation, rural churches play important roles in sustaining community. Especially important are the rituals surrounding life and death that make community not only possible, but strong and supportive in the face of pain, suffering, and disaster.

Below is a transcript of a class session in a seminary course in how exegesis and preaching can contribute to building Christian community. The format of the course was to analyze specific scripture passages about barriers to Christian community and strategies for overcoming them. The focus of the semester-long, three-credit class was a set of ten different passages in 1 Corinthians. For each passage, an outside specialist in a particular field was brought in to stimulate discussion. The class itself was team-taught by professors in preaching and New Testament.

The opening lecture, entitled "A Rural Activist Speaks Out," was given by Judy Shelly, co-director of the Town and Country Alliance for Ministry, Eastern Iowa, and Associate for Community Development, Center for Theology and Land, Dubuque, Iowa.

You've heard of the Bermuda Triangle? Well, I live in the Rural Triangle, because I get lost . . . no one can find me because my address is Charlotte, my phone is Preston, my kids go to Goose Lake, and I live smack dab in the middle of all of them. My job with T-CAM is working with congregations and empowering leaders to do God's work, to build the Kingdom. In the last ten to fifteen years our communities have really had a big change.

Picture a beautiful church: brick facade, high steeple, nicely trimmed lawn. Steps lead up to doors that are open. You walk inside and see rows of nicely polished pews with cushions. There's a sunbeam gleaming in a beautiful stained-glass window. Membership is about 700, and there's about 120 kids in the Sunday school. The town itself sits almost like a picture in a calendar, surrounded by corn and bean fields. It's a community of diversity. It's diverse in age, education, occupation, gender, and vision.

Pretty inviting for a first call? Well, since the farm crisis of the eighties, this is a community that pits neighbor against neighbor, friend against friend. It's a community of pain, grief, and hopelessness. As families lost their farms . . . people were judging them, and they were no longer seen as an asset to the community. Tension mounted between individuals, businesses, families, and church bodies.

Is it still intriguing? Good, I'm glad there are still a few nods. This is a community that's seeing its young people leave. They cannot get jobs, and if they can, it's at minimum wage. This is a community where alcohol and drug use is up, and a kid of any age can get anything they want. Our churches are seeing a decline in attendance and in giving. So let's think about this beautiful church that we talked about in the beginning. It still sits there just as beautiful as ever, but the lives outside of that church are very, very stressful. So let's talk about what's going on within the four walls of the church.

A congregational meeting has been called because there are some major decisions to be made. People come in through those big beautiful doors. Joe, a businessman with a "Going Out of Business" sign in his window, sits in the back of the room. Ron is a farmer who has lost his farm, but now he's an insurance man. He sits clear to the right side of the room. Then we have John, an agribusinessman who knows Ron, who sits on the left side of the room. Then we have Jane, whose husband died accidentally with a gun; she stands by the kitchen door. You've got the picture. There are even a couple of youth, but only because it's required for their confirmation. So all together there are about sixty people, and the average voting age is sixty-one.

When someone asks, "Where is a copy of *Robert's Rules?*" you get the point; you know how hot the room is. One young man in the confirmation class stands up and recites the rule word for word, because he had to learn it in 4-H. When the meeting is over, a couple of the leaders get together with the pastor and say, "Let's analyze this."

What they discovered was scary. Of a congregation of seven hundred people, only sixty cared enough to come. That's less than a tenth. The average age was sixty-one. Every person in that room could go out that night and have a steak dinner.

Any reactions?

W: Other than a rural community, you described my home church.

L: But that's not a rural church.

W: Not a rural church. That is a suburban, upper middle-class church.

L: So there are nonrural churches experiencing the same thing. That's interesting. You closed your statement with a reference to this steak dinner; that means that the people who couldn't afford a steak dinner were not there. That was your way of kind of measuring their financial status in the community.

M: You think the people whose farms failed felt that they were frozen out. They felt that.

Judy: Well, that's a question I have for everyone. Why aren't these people there? These marginalized people are not coming to our church services. They are not coming to the decision-making board. What's going on with them that they're not coming, that they are not feeling that they're important enough to be there?

M2: I was going to make a reference, before you did, to the steak dinner. I think you're right, that it would be those that felt the pain or those that can't afford it that wouldn't be there. They also feel the humility that they cannot support the church, and so it's because it's an economic/financial decision that they stay away, the majority of them, because if they can't afford a steak dinner, they can't afford to give to the church. I think when that happens in a community, that is one of the most humbling experiences that anyone can feel and that the best thing to do is stay away—it's the most comfortable, probably not the best, but it's the most comfortable.

W: Another way of asking this is, "What reasons do they have to go to church?" We've talked about reasons they stay away, but what reasons do they have to go?

M: That's an ugly question: Is there anything worth going for?

M2: I think part has to be taken as the church's responsibility. What I'm hearing people talk about is the individual's response. Their friends condemn them or whatever, but what's the church's response? Go to any church the Sunday after someone has experienced a death in their family, and will you find that family in church? More than likely not. In fact, you might not find them in church for the next two or three weeks. How come? Because there's an attitude towards them in church that we cannot talk about the real pain that we have in the setting of the church. We have to put on a face, we have to be positive. In our Sunday school we will listen to someone, if they're hurting, just long enough to find an opening so we can get back to the agenda for the Sunday school class. We really don't deal with pain well in the church.

W: Since the church is the Body of Christ, if people are not able to bring their shame into the church, I'm wondering how we are embodying Christ or embodying God? We have this wonderful tendency to always want to blame the victim—whether the victim isn't answering the door or not coming to church or whatever they're doing—rather than to ask the question of ourselves. What have we been doing in the past that they can't answer the door? What kind of community has been going on here that they can't experience fellowship now; that when they are in need they can't receive our coming to them? Are they going to perceive our coming to them as that we're better than they are because we still have it all together and they've lost it all and they're no longer equal? On what basis were they equal in the first place?

R: I had a chance to spend the summer in rural ministry. I have not grown up on a farm; I grew up in a city, and one thing I found that was really helpful when talking with people is going out of those four walls to where the people were, to where their farms were. I even asked if I could help slop the hogs, but they wouldn't let me do it. I was amazed because I spent about three or four hours with a couple of guys—we just talked out there—and they really opened up. They explained things to me that I had never thought of. I couldn't understand why they weren't open, why they weren't more vulnerable. In fact, I was to preach that Sunday in their church, and what I was hoping to do was share some vulnerability of my own to encourage them to be vulnerable. They told me something I never realized; the reason they don't open up is because you give one inkling of openness in that community and it's going to be spread all over that county by the next day. So you have no sense of privacy in that community. If you have no sense of privacy to suffer with your own pain, how are you going to be able to open up to share publicly? I just think that it's really important to be able to go outside of those four walls, and it's too bad that the pastor and the other people look at the problem of what happened at the meeting in the four walls instead of going outside those four walls to find out what happened at the meeting that wasn't going on.

M: I'd almost stake my life on the fact that there are the resources in that town to solve the community's problems. There's enough money in that town right now to solve that community's problems. I grew up in a rural community, and it's out of vogue to shop in your community, to deal with people in your community. Everybody goes out of their community. Some of the problems that exist are because they go to the larger cities to buy everything they get, to buy their groceries in the supermarket chains when small retailers are sitting in town starving to death. No one seems to care. They are prophets in their own country; in a lot of respects they don't lead their lives in ways that support their own communities.

There's a little town called Sioux Center in Iowa, up north, that's an integrated town. Everything goes inward, and they are flourishing in times of trouble and tribulation for the rest of them. Their churches are united, their farms all work basically in that community, and I'll bet they've got the resources to solve every problem financially if people would do it. But because we've become an isolated situation, we don't particularly care if the guy down the road loses his farm. Somebody else will come down and take it over, and I'll do business with that individual.

L: We, as pastors, are powerful people, and we can effect change. Think of the difference between a pastor who urges a community and does so in a constructive way and a pastor who brings division and strife to a church. One can build up and make a church grow and reach out to a community. One can destroy a church. We're powerful people, folks. There is power associated with our training and with our position. When I met with the farmers this summer, I heard that said again. They respect that position; there's status there. In some ways they fear it and dislike it as well, as we've heard said, but there's real power there.

ISSUE FOR DISCUSSION

As you analyze the lecture and the discussion, imagine that your rural community of 750 is experiencing conditions similar to the ones Judy described when you assume your new role as pastor at one of the local congregations. How would you deal with the following facets of your work?

- pulpit response
- special grief or other support group development
- visitation strategies
- other: explain what and why

Seminarians and rural clergy need to rethink constantly how they would approach the multifaceted role of pastor in order to be successful as prophet, priest, and healer in a particular community. It is also essential for a rural pastor to find ways to empower those same skills among parishioners for the work of community to succeed.

6.6   Awakening the Prophetic Voice: Dealing with Change and Conflict

Although it is important to see the potential for community and the church in rural America, it is essential not to trivialize or minimize the potential challenges that community building involves. For every church ready to take a leap of faith to new and exciting mission, there are others that for generations have been torn by internal strife and political chaos.

For the pastor, one of the most controversial and challenging aspects of rural life is the issue of how people deal with change, particularly in a society where tradition is highly valued. Some specialists in the field of community development maintain that the surest way for institutions to maintain the status quo is to change. A conundrum? Not necessarily.

For example, on a secular level, anthropologist Conrad Phillip Kottak applies the views of paleontologist A. S. Romer to contemporary cultural change and economic development. His provocative analysis suggests that for traditional rural societies the goal of maintaining stability against threats is the main impetus for change.[9] Changes happen when community values are threatened. The application of Romer's Rule to rural community development suggests that people are unlikely to cooperate with projects that require major changes in their daily lives. The beneficiaries of any development usually wish to change just enough to maintain what they have. Although people do want certain changes, they are motivated by their traditional culture and the concerns of everyday existence. Top-down models for change that do not take into account unique aspects of rural or other community culture are not likely to succeed.

Change and tradition are not incompatible. But a sense of safety and certain spiritual behaviors and attitudes need to be in place if parishioners are to successfully adapt to changing conditions in their communities and congregations. Pastors can do a great deal—through sermons, worship, Bible study, and the qualities and attitudes they personally model—to create a climate in which change is not only possible, but probable. Key to successful change is also the capacity of the pastor to build a sense of ownership within the congregation for a particular idea and to disengage his or her own ego and identity from the project. The pastor can raise the question of what changes the community wants or needs and help people articulate their own desires.

Yet a major fault of too many pastors in rural settings, one North Dakota farmer maintains, is that they come charging in with agendas of their own that may in no way reflect the grassroots concerns or priorities of their communities. Without key parishioner ownership and support for an idea, the results can be devastating: "If they insist on trying to push through their approach anyway, pastors need to remember that it is *us*, not *them*, who have to live with the consequences. *They* can leave, but this is my home. Long after they are gone, I am going to have to live with what they did or how they did it."

In cases where conflict itself is embedded into the congregation's history, the task of community building can become formidable. What forces and factors create a self-destructive climate in a congregation? Consider the following documents that discuss conflict within the congregation and also a process for working through and resolving conflict.

A. AN INTERN EXPERIENCES CONGREGATIONAL CONFLICT

The following observations come from "Wendy," a seminary intern who spent a summer working in a conflictive congregation.

In my visits with people in the community I came away with several impressions. Salvation/redemption seems like a hassle. For many people in the community who have weights of various kinds—family, job, history, personal pain—the struggle of making things better is too much to muster.

Of course, if the alternatives are to die or to act, only the most desperate refuse to act. But if the option of not acting brings anything less than death, action is very hard to produce. For some here this seems to be the situation: redeeming action (community development, personal spiritual growth, new ways of being) is too much trouble. It is easier to remain as is. I also detect a hint of fear; they fear that if they give it their all, all the hope and energy they can muster, it might fail. How many, I wonder, have made the silent but conscious choice not to risk it. For some, living with bearable depression is better than all-out loss.

I am also perplexed by how people living in the very same community can perceive that community in such different ways. In all the conversations it seemed that a person's general disposition shaped their perceptions more than any outward circumstances did. Two people at the same event saw entirely different things happen. A person who felt the community to be a warm and safe place saw the church's ministry as Christian caregiving; one who saw the community as back-biting saw the church's programs as gossipy and exclusive.

The theological implications of this may have great bearing on how a community shapes its vision of health and redemption. If each person's individual idea of redemption shapes how they see God at work in their common life, how does a village or faith community arrive at a common vision [or] live out God in their midst? Community salvation/redemption must involve . . . a place reserved for things held in common . . . where individual goals are subordinated to common goals.

I would hear about people and have them described for me always in the same way. I came to see how certain people played prescribed roles for everyone. I don't know how long it took for these people to be assigned their roles, but once they got them, everyone else made sure they kept them. Even if the person didn't act the part right, people still saw them through the same lens. Is this common vision gone bad?

Part of the definition of health must include the environment necessary for a person to develop and become who God calls them to be. A healthy community removes the constraints that keep people from realizing [that] vision. It allows people to change, take risks and grow. And, especially in a small community, if one person changes and grows, each person is asked to change, as they modify the way they see the person and act toward them.

Of course, on the flip side, a community must act to provide supportive constraints that guard against isolation, abandonment, and self-destruction. Israel struggled with this balance throughout her history. They had to maintain their unique identity as the people of Yahweh, but as the shell of their life stiffened, they had to open up and make room for the greater things God would do among them. [Part of a pastor's job seems to be to] teach a new language, the language of the Spirit. I don't think anyone is devoid of Spirit, but some seem to be quite asleep to the Spirit among them. It brings up interesting questions about how a pastor works with and for people.

We are supposed to be bearers of good news to the outcast—but we are afraid of them. We make it seem as though they have to prove themselves to us, rather than we to them. Opening the doors wide to those not within, even if they are intimidating, making them feel welcome and accepted, is the task of the church. Is this especially difficult for the rural church?

In [a small community], the actions of each individual add to the village's identity, its life, and its health. We can't say, "don't worry about what people think." They are connected to each other and it matters how people think, act, and what they say to each other.

When I shared with them about my going away, they were overwhelmed with the thoughts of leaving home, leaving the connections of memories, lives, and roots. I look at them and marvel at the security of basic common ground. True, it can be stifling; but it is also very grounding, and a source of stability. To help those basic connections be life-giving would go a long way in making this a healthy place.

I think any pastor in a rural setting would have to recognize the depth and power of those long-term connections.

B. A CONGREGATION COPES WITH CHANGE: A CASE STUDY

Use the following case to focus your thinking about how a pastor or layperson can function in a "prophetic mode"—challenging a church (such as the one described in 6.6[a]) to action or change without destroying or splitting the congregation in the process.

Context: The congregation is located in a small rural community that has experienced the loss of all Main Street businesses and its local school. The church retains a full-time pastor only through an inter-denominational yoking agreement with a free-standing town congregation. The pastor begins to work with the village board and the church to explore community redevelopment possibilities using the abandoned school as a community center.

When ethical issues arise over how funds from the sale of the school are to be used, the pastor takes his concerns to the church board. Some members fail to see any issue; others worry that people in the community will get mad at the church if anything is said. A few board members share the pastor's concern. When the pastor informs the board that as a private citizen, he intends to confront the situation publicly, board members do not respond, positively or negatively. Using personal funds, the pastor presents the school board with a written offer to purchase the school—an offer that triggers intense controversy in the community.

Dynamics within the church: Initially, the yoking agreement seems like a positive one for all concerned. However, when the two churches join in shared ministry, requirements of the two denominations call for separate boards in addition to a unified governing body—an ambivalence that leads to conflict. The pastor chooses to confront the parties directly and at first receives support for doing so. But the sale of the school becomes a catalyst for some parishioners who had not been comfortable with either the yoking agreement or the pastor's efforts to promote closer inner-congregational working arrangements. These parishioners now begin to network with nonchurch community residents who objected to the pastor's conduct in the controversy over the school. "He's an outsider," they argue, "and has no business being involved in community issues. His only job is to save souls."

Denominational relationships come into play as members from the two congregations discuss their concerns with judicatory representatives. One of these officials—of a different denomination from the pastor—is drawn into the situation. As town church versus country church issues and denominational favoritism concerns surface, parishioners begin to hold secret meetings and speak in terms of "us" and "them." A public forum chaired by denominational officials has the effect of deepening divisions and validating the conflict. The pastor is not allowed to attend the meeting, and thus becomes the focus of the "problem." Nonparishioners attend, bringing the public issues regarding the school into the discussion.

A proposal to bring in outside conflict negotiators to work with small groups over a set period of time is rejected. When the pastor is removed from the pulpit by the judicatory official of the town church, the country church affirms the pastor's call, and that denominational body agrees to underwrite a bank loan to buy the school. Committees are established to begin restoring the facility for use as a multipurpose community center.

Within a matter of months, however, factions begin to form within the country church. Less than six months later, the pastor resigns. With the church struggling to meet school mortgage payments, parishioners begin to convert the facility to apartments and an in-house convenience store. An intern pastor resigns after several months' service.

C. THE CONFLICT RESOLUTION PROCESS

Consider the following model for dealing with conflict and change (suggested by Professor Thomas R. Albin, University of Dubuque Theological Seminary).

1. Define the problem or conflict. Be sure to consult with all parties—individually, at first, and then collectively. The goal is to understand one another's perspective. Who is involved? Who is affected? How did the conflict occur (root causes) and how often? What was the cost in terms of time, people, money and other resources, environment, attitude, and spirit?

2. Define the obstacles standing in the way of resolving the conflict; then list possible ways of overcoming them.

3. Analyze the nature of each obstacle. Does it primarily involve a person, an attitude, time or scheduling, money, facilities, communication, leadership style, decision-making processes, approaches to conflict, conflict avoidance, or other factors?

4. Suggest several possible solutions (at least three, preferably five or more). Include action steps to diminish or resolve the problem. *Do not* evaluate possibilities as you brainstorm them. (Steps 5 and 6 begin that evaluation process.)

5. Develop the criteria for achieving the ideal solution.

6. Discuss the advantages and disadvantages of each possible solution. (Use a rating system: e.g., + + + + = very advantageous, − − − − = very disadvantageous.) Remember to factor in the impact on people, facilities, and finances, as well as the practicality and political costs.

7. Choose the best solution based on the criteria developed in step 5.

8. Develop consensus on the best possible solution and the means of implementing it. Secure commitment to support the solution, the implementation plan, and evaluation.

9. Implement the agreed-upon solution and monitor its progress for effectiveness and efficiency. If the evaluation is positive, continue the process.

10. If the evaluation is negative, return to step 6 and choose another solution. Proceed with steps 6 through 9 until an effective solution is found. (Sometimes minor adjustments in the implementation plan are appropriate instead of a new solution.)

ISSUES FOR DISCUSSION

Use the conflict resolution process outlined in section C to guide your response to the case study in section B.

1. If you were a pastor facing similar challenges, how would you (a) build consensus, (b) deal with the factions within the church; and (c) deal with those *outside* your church who can affect your church's involvement in the community. Suggest a specific time line over a period of six months for such things as sermons, pastoral visits, public information campaigns inside and outside your congregation, meetings, and so on. What do you feel are the bare-bones internal and external resources and support mechanisms you would need in order to handle the situation?
2. At what point—if ever—should a pastor be prepared to go out on a limb to enforce change in the prophetic mode modeled in the Old Testament? Can a pastor in a rural setting function in the capacity of "private citizen"? Present compelling reasons both for and against this role. How would you define *your* responsibilities as an individual Christian and as a pastor in a setting like the one described? Facing such choices, what would you do?
3. Note that the church in the case was growing beyond Rothauge's fifty-member "chaplain model." Discuss unique problems and approaches to ministry in such a "transitional" congregation.

For an in-depth look at church conflict, read Kenneth C. Haugk's *Antagonists in the Church: How to Identify and Deal with Destructive Conflict* (Minneapolis: Augsburg, 1988).

6.7   Technology and Community: Getting Online

WHAT IS THIS TOOL?

Ecunet is an electronic communication network representing well over ten thousand congregations from more than fifteen denominations and groups. Ecunet links clergy, seminarians, laypeople, congregations, synods, and regions—urban and rural. The system is international in scope, makes direct communication with any other subscriber a snap and offers a vast amount of resources. For example, Ecunet's discussion groups vary widely and include topics ranging from "Sermonshop"—a freewheeling, content-rich discussion of next week's sermon text—to "New Wine News"—news of the outpouring of the Holy Spirit. The World Wide Web and the Internet may incorporate and extend Ecunet's reach soon.

To both rural pastors and their congregations, distance can become a formidable barrier to spiritual growth and development. Witness the pastoral consortiums in North Dakota, Pennsylvania, and elsewhere of concerned rural clergy seeking innovative ways of bridging the enormous constraints of geography that can impede valuable networking among congregations and isolate pastors from essential peer support networks. Denominations supplement rural salaries to make up for the higher costs inherent in networking and professional development for rural pastors.

RURAL MINISTRY ONLINE

The advent of computer and distance learning technologies represents an enormous potential boon to both clergy and congregations—provided the resources are available to purchase the necessary equipment in rural congregations. Following are excerpts from one meeting over the Internet between rural pastors from all over the United States initiated by the Center for Theology and Land (Internet address: theology_and_land.parti@pcusa.org) in 1993—a dialogue that continues as this text goes to press.

September 25, 1995: I like the idea of forming a small group of "experts" to provide some sensible solutions to the problems in the small and rural church. I think the meetings should be semi-private. That is, a small group that actually is discussing and working on the issue with the ability to write notes, but allow others to follow along by reading the notes, or at least post regular reports back to this meeting.

August 8, 1995: I heard of a community that set up a video camera in the library, got volunteers to man it, and then had people come in and tell their stories. Often families would come in and ask for grandpa or grandma's tape to show the children!

August 8, 1995: You will be in my thoughts and prayers for the next few weeks as you end your ministry in this setting.

August 8, 1995: Your closing thought makes me wonder if the reason so many recent seminary graduates get into trouble early on is that they forget to listen and realize how unique any community is, and few realize how no congregation is the model they studied in seminary. Throughout the Net, I see new pastors struggling with issues of listening, patience, understanding what battles to fight, and not to fight them all.

December 17, 1994: [IA] - We [ELCA] are considering creating a listening network for rural and small-town folks, especially in light of a possibly tighter financial market in the spring. I'd be grateful for any experience, materials, suggestions, etc. in the area of peer listening groups/relationships in rural and small-town settings.

Note the themes coming through this dialogue: sharing of materials and resources; cooperative ministry models; celebration of ministry in rural areas; innovative and original clergy tools (the arts, scriptural resources) for affirming and challenging rural culture; the need for human, face-to-face interaction; pastoral concern for the financial problems of their communities; to name but a few. There are many rural ministry networks.

HOW DO WE GET ON?

Rural communities are finding it easier every day to connect to the Internet. The first place to start learning how to get connected is your local library. Most rural states have programs to connect all public libraries to the Internet. Many public libraries that are so connected offer low-cost E-mail accounts for your use. The next place to look is the local school system. Schools have been leading users of the Internet in the United States. They have found many uses of the Internet to expand the walls of their classrooms. The computer resource person at your nearest school may be able to share new ways to gain access. Many rural communities are also served by an Internet service provider (ISP). ISPs can be anyone from the local phone company to an independent businessperson selling Internet access.

Another place to look for your online connection is your national church. Many denominations have programs to connect their pastors to some kind of electronic messaging system. One example is Luther-WEB, a program of the Evangelical Lutheran Church in America to connect all Lutheran pastors and lay leaders to the Internet. The last places to look for your Internet connection are the national services such as America Online or CompuServe. Prices do vary, but these are usually the most expensive services.[10]

For information on Ecunet or Presbynet contact:

Online Service Company
P.O. Box 2130
Lawrenceville, GA 30246
800-733-2863 or 404-682-8888

For information on the Lutherlink segment of Ecunet contact:

ELCA Resource Information Service
8765 West Higgins Road
Chicago, IL 60631
800-638-3522

Also available is Cokesbury Online, which caters to United Methodist leaders as a forum within the CompuServe network. Call 1-800-672-1789.

All of the electronic services to reduce barriers of distance for rural pastors are temporary and will change, often rapidly, as the Internet evolves.

ISSUE FOR DISCUSSION

Brainstorm ways denominational bodies and seminaries can encourage use of these tools as part of a larger concept of rural ministry.

A Compendium of Resources for Ministry with Rural Communities

Books

Agria, Mary. *Building Healthy Communities: The Stories of 12 Communities in the Midwest.* Dubuque, Iowa: Center for Theology and Land, 1995 (phone 319-589-3117).

Austin, Richard Cartright. *Hope for the Land.* Atlanta: John Knox Press, 1988.

Becker, Carol. *Leading Women: How Women Can Avoid Leadership Traps and Negotiate the Gender Maze.* Nashville: Abingdon Press, 1995.

Berry, Wendell. *Home Economics.* New York: Farrar, Straus and Giroux, 1987.

_____. *What Are People For.* New York: Farrar, Straus and Giroux, 1990.

Bertels, Sister Thomas More. *In Pursuit of Agri-Power: The One Thing North American Farmers and Ranchers Can't Produce.* Manitowoc, Wisc.: Silver Lake College Press, 1988.

Bhagat, Shantilal. *The Family Farm: Can It Be Saved?* Elgin, Ill.: Brethren Press, 1985.

Biles, Daniel V. *Pursuing Excellence in Ministry.* Washington, D.C.: The Alban Institute, 1988.

Brown, Lester, et al. *State of the World 1995: A Worldwatch Institute Report on Progress Toward a Sustainable Society.* New York: W. W. Norton and Company, 1995.

Browne, William P., et al. *Sacred Cows and Hot Potatoes: Agrarian Myths in Agricultural Policy.* Boulder: Westview Press, 1992.

Brueggemann, Walter. *The Land: Place As Gift, Promise, and Challenge in Biblical Faith.* Minneapolis: Augsburg Fortress, 1977.

Burt, Steven E., and Hazel A. Roper. *Raising Small Church Esteem.* New York: The Alban Institute, 1992.

Carroll, Jackson W., Carl S. Dudley, and William McKinney, eds. *Handbook of Congregational Studies.* Nashville: Abingdon Press, 1986, 1997.

Ceynar, Marvin E. *Healing the Heartland: Nonviolent Social Change and the American Rural Crisis of the 1980's and 1990's.* Columbus: Brentwood Communications Group, 1989.

Christianson, James A., and Jerry W. Robinson. *Community Development in Perspective*. Ames: Iowa State University Press, 1989.

Chromey, Rick. *Youth Ministry in Small Churches*. Loveland, Colo.: Group Books, 1990.

The Church: Responding to Rural America. Louisville, Ky.: Presbyterian Church (USA), 1991.

Cornman, John M., and Barbara Kincaid. *Lessons from Rural America: A Case History*. Washington, D.C.: National Rural Center, 1984.

Cronin, Deborah. *Can Your Dog Hunt?* Lima, Ohio: Fairway Press, 1995.

Cushman, James E. *Evangelism in the Small Church*. Decatur, Ga.: CTS Press, 1988.

Danborn, David B. *The Resisted Revolution: Urban America and the Industrialization of Agriculture, 1900–1930*. Ames: Iowa State University Press, 1979.

Davidson, Osha Gray. *Broken Heartland: The Rise of America's Rural Ghetto*. New York: Doubleday, 1990.

Dawes, Gil, and Alexander Rhoads. *Plenty in the Land: A Church Curriculum on Corporate Agriculture*. Des Moines, Iowa: PrairieFire Rural Action, 1992.

Dozier, Verna J. *The Authority of the Laity*. Washington, D.C.: The Alban Institute, 1990.

Dudley, Carl S. *Basic Steps Toward Community Ministry*. Washington, D.C.: The Alban Institute, 1991.

Dudley, Carl S., and Douglas A. Walrath. *Developing Your Small Church's Potential*. Valley Forge: Judson Press, 1988.

Evans, Bernard F., and Gregory D. Cusack, eds. *Theology of the Land*. Collegeville, Minn.: Liturgical Press, 1987.

Fish, Charles. *In Good Hands: The Keeping of a Family Farm*. New York: Farrar, Straus and Giroux, 1995.

Flanagan, Joan. *Successful Fundraising: A Complete Handbook for Volunteers and Professionals*. Chicago, Ill.: Contemporary Books, 1991.

Flora, Cornelia Butler, et al. *Rural Communities: Legacy and Change*. Boulder: Westview Press, 1992.

Flora, Jan, et al. *From the Grassroots: Profiles of 103 Rural Self-Development Projects*. Boulder: Westview Press, 1992.

Foltz, Nancy. *Caring for the Small Church: Insights from Women in Ministry*. Valley Forge: Judson Press, 1994.

_____. *Religious Education in the Small Membership Church*. Birmingham, Ala.: Religious Education Press, 1990.

Freudenberger, C. Dean. *Food for Tomorrow?* Minneapolis: Augsburg, 1987.

Friedman, Edwin H. *Generation to Generation: Family Process in Church and Synagogue*. New York: Guilford Press, 1985.

Garreau, Joel. *The Nine Nations of North America*. New York: Avon Books, 1992.

George, Susan. *Ill Fares the Land: Essays on Food, Hunger, and Power*. London: Writers and Readers Publishing Cooperative, 1984.

Gore, Al. *Earth in the Balance: Ecology and the Human Spirit*. New York: Houghton Mifflin Company, 1992.

Goreham, Gary A. *The Rural Church in America: A Century of Writings: A Bibliography.* New York: Garland Publishing, 1990.

Griggs, Donald L., and Judy McKay Walther. *Christian Education in the Small Church.* Valley Forge: Judson Press, 1988.

Guenthner, Dan. *To Till It and Keep It: New Models for Congregational Involvement with the Land.* Chicago: Evangelical Lutheran Church in America, The Department of Environmental Stewardship, 1994.

Gustafson, Scott. *Ministry with the Power of Jesus.* Lawrenceville, Va.: Brunswick Publishing, 1991.

Hahn, Celia. *Growing in Authority, Relinquishing Control.* Washington, D.C.: The Alban Institute, 1995.

Halverstadt, Hugh F. *Managing Church Conflict.* Louisville, Ky.: Westminster/John Knox Press, 1991.

Harbaugh, Gary. *God's Gifted People.* Minneapolis: Augsburg Fortress, 1990.

Harrington, Donald. *Let Us Build a City: Eleven Lost Towns.* San Diego: Harcourt Brace Jovanovich, 1986.

Hart, John. *The Spirit of the Earth.* New York: Paulist Press, 1984.

Haugk, Kenneth. *Antagonists in the Church: How to Identify and Deal with Destructive Conflict.* Minneapolis: Augsburg Publishing, 1988.

Heartland Center for Leadership Development, *The Entrepreneurial Community: A Strategic Leadership Approach to Community Survival.* Lincoln, Nebr., 1989.

Hildebrand, John. *Mapping the Farm: The Chronicle of a Family.* New York: Alfred A. Knopf, 1995.

Hopewell, James F. *Congregation: Stories and Structures.* Philadelphia: Fortress Press, 1987.

Hultgren, Arland J., ed. "The Land," *Word and World: Theology for Christian Ministry,* vol. 6. St. Paul, Minn.: Luther Northwestern Seminary, 1986.

Hunter, Kent R. *The Lord's Harvest and the Rural Church.* Kansas City, Mo.: Beacon Hill Press of Kansas City, 1993.

Innovative Grassroots Financing: A Small Town Guide to Raising Funds and Cutting Costs. Washington, D.C.: National Association of Towns and Townships, 1990.

Isachsen, Olaf, and Linda Berens. *Working Together: A Personality-Centered Approach to Management.* Coronado, Calif.: Institute for Management Development, 1991.

Jackson, Wes. *New Roots for Agriculture.* Linclon: University of Nebraska Press, 1985.

Jackson, Wes, Wendell Berry, and Bruce Colman, eds. *Meeting the Expectations of the Land.* San Francisco: North Point Press, 1984.

Johnson, Douglas. *Empowering Lay Volunteers.* Nashville: Abingdon Press, 1991.

Jung, L. Shannon. *We Are Home: A Spirituality of the Environment.* Mahwah, N.J.: Paulist Press, 1993.

Jung, L. Shannon, and Kris Kirst. *Revitalization in the Rural Congregation: What We Know, What We Need to Know.* Dubuque, Iowa: Center for Theology and Land, 1995 (phone 319-589-3117).

Jung, L. Shannon, et al. *Rural Ministry: The Shape of Renewal to Come.* Nashville: Abingdon Press, 1997.

Keenan, Maryanne P., ed. *The Chronically Mentally Ill in Rural Areas: Model Curricula for Social Work Education.* Rockville, Md.: U.S. Department of Health and Human Services, 1987.

Kemmis, Dennis. *Community and the Politics of Place.* Norman: University of Oklahoma Press, 1990.

Kramer, Mark. *Three Farms: Making Milk, Meat and Money from the American Soil.* Toronto: Bantam Books, 1981.

Krause, Tina B., ed. *Care of the Earth: An Environmental Manual for Church Leaders.* Chicago: Lutheran School of Theology at Chicago, 1994.

Krebs, A. V. *The Corporate Reapers.* Washington D.C.: Essential Books, 1992.

Leas, Speed. *Moving Your Church Through Conflict.* Washington, D.C.: The Alban Institute, 1985.

Lilburne, Geoffrey R. *A Sense of Place: A Christian Theology of the Land.* Nashville: Abingdon Press, 1989.

Lindgren, Alvin J., and Norman Shawchuck. *Let My People Go: Empowering Laity for Ministry.* Schaumburg, Ill.: Organization Resources Press, 1988.

Lingenfelter, Sherwood G., and Marvin K. Meyers. *Ministering Cross Culturally.* Grand Rapids: Baker Books, 1986.

McDaniel, Jay B., and Charles Pinches, eds. *Good News for Animals? Christian Approaches to Animal Well-Being.* Maryknoll, N.Y.: Orbis Books, 1993.

Masumoto, David. *Epitaph for a Peach: Four Seasons on My Family Farm.* San Francisco: Harper Collins, 1995.

Matheny, Judy C. *Resources on Small Membership Churches: A Bibliography.* Berea, Ky.: Appalachian Ministries Educational Resource Center, 1989.

May, Roy H., Jr. *The Poor of the Land: A Christian Case for Land Reform.* New York: Orbis Books, 1991.

Mead, Loren. *The Once and Future Church.* Washington, D.C.: The Alban Institute, 1991.

Morgan, Dan. *Merchants of Grain.* New York: Penguin Books, 1980.

National Research Council. *Alternative Agriculture.* Washington, D.C.: National Academy Press, 1989.

New Times—New Call: A Manual of Pastoral Options for Small Churches. Louisville, Ky.: Presbyterian Church (USA), 1991.

No Place to Be, Farm and Rural Poverty in America. Des Moines: PrairieFire Rural Action, 1988.

Norris, Kathleen. *Dakota: A Spiritual Geography.* New York: Ticknor and Fields, 1993.

_____. *The Cloister Walk.* New York: Riverhead Books, 1996.

Oswald, Roy. *Clergy Self-Care: Finding Balance for Effective Ministry.* Washington, D.C.: The Alban Institute, 1991.

Oswald, Roy, and Otto Krueger. *Personality Type and Religious Leadership.* Washington, D.C.: The Alban Institute, 1988.

Paddock, Joe, Nancy Paddock, and Carol Bly. *Soil and Survival: Land Stewardship and the Future of American Agriculture.* San Francisco: Sierra Club Books, 1986.

Pappas, Anthony G. *Entering the World of the Small Church: A Guide for Leaders.* Washington, D.C.: The Alban Institute, 1988.

_____. *Mustard Seeds: Devotions for Small Church People.* Columbus, Ga.: Brentwood Christian Press, 1994.

Pappas, Anthony, and Scott Planting. *Mission: The Small Church Reaches Out.* Valley Forge: Judson Press, 1993.

Parker, Tony. *Bird, Kansas.* New York: Alfred A. Knopf, 1989.

Peterson, Eugene. *Under the Unpredictable Plant: An Exploration in Vocational Holiness.* Grand Rapids: Eerdmans, 1992.

Phillips, Kevin. *The Politics of Rich and Poor.* New York: Random House, 1990.

Ray, David. *The Big Small Church Book.* Cleveland: Pilgrim Press, 1992.

_____. *Small Churches Are the Right Size.* New York: Pilgrim Press, 1982.

Rolvaag, O. E. *Giants in the Earth* (1927). New York: Harper Collins, 1955.

Rothauge, Arlin. *Sizing Up a Congregation.* New York: The Episcopal Church Center, n.d.

Sample, Tex. *Blue-Collar Ministry: Facing Economic and Social Realities of Working People.* Valley Forge: Judson Press, 1984.

_____. *Ministry in an Oral Culture: Living with Will Rogers, Uncle Remus, and Minnie Pearl.* Louisville, Ky.: Westminster John Knox Press, 1994.

_____. *U.S. Lifestyles and Mainline Churches.* Louisville, Ky.: Westminster John Knox Press, 1990.

Santmire, H. Paul. *The Travail of Nature: The Ambiguous Ecological Promise of Christian Theology.* Philadelphia: Fortress Press, 1985.

Schaller, Lyle. *The Small Church Is Different.* Nashville: Abingdon Press, 1982.

Slattery, Patrick, ed. *Caretakers of Creation.* Minneapolis: Augsburg, 1991.

Smiley, Jane. *A Thousand Acres.* New York: Alfred A. Knopf, 1991.

Smith, Rockwell, et al. *The Role of Rural Social Science in Theological Education: With Particular Application to the Town and Country Ministry in the Methodist Church.* Evanston, Ill.: Bureau of Social and Religious Research, Garrett Theological Seminary, 1969.

Steinke, Peter L. *How Your Church Family Works: Understanding Congregations As Emotional Systems.* Washington, D.C.: The Alban Institute, 1993.

Strange, Marty. *Family Farming: A New Economic Vision.* Lincoln: University of Nebraska Press, 1988.

Tufano, Victoria M., ed. *Rural Life Prayers: Blessings and Liturgies.* Des Moines: The National Catholic Rural Life Conference, 1989.

Walrath, Douglas. *Leading Churches Through Change.* Nashville: Abingdon Press, 1979.

_____. *New Possibilities for Small Churches.* New York: Pilgrim Press, 1983.

Walrath, Douglas, ed. *Activating Leadership in the Small Church.* Valley Forge: Judson Press, 1988.

Westberg, Granger. *The Parish Nurse.* Minneapolis: Augsburg, 1990.

Williams, Roger T. *Empowering Your Rural Community: How to Create a Brighter Future for Your Small Town.* Madison: University of Wisconsin Press, 1990.

Articles

The Christian Century. During 1992–1995 the magazine printed a number of follow-up articles on historic churches that they had highlighted two decades earlier.

Finck, D. "Farmers Are Still Killing Themselves." *Farm Journal* (October 1990): 36-39.

"New Study on Unemployed Clergy," *United Church News* 11, nos. 1-2 (April 1995).

Oswald, Roy. "How to Minister Effectively in Family, Pastoral, Program, and Corporate Sized Churches," *Action Information* 17, no. 2 (March/April 1991): 1-7.

_____. "When Membership Declines," *Action Information* 17, no. 3 (May/June 1991): 5-7.

Palma, Dolores. "The Top 10 Ways to Revitalize Your Downtown." *American City and County*, November 1992, 52.

Rains, Patrick. "Flight or Fight: The Town that Took on Wal-Mart—and Won." *American City and County*, November 1992, 50.

Smallwood, Carla. "A Matter of Pride." *American City and County*, February 1993, 80.

"UMC Sexual Harassment." *The Christian Century* 107 (December 12, 1990): 1160.

Welles, Edward O. "When Wal-Mart Comes to Town," *Inc.*, July 1993, 76-88.

Wind, James P., ed. *Second Opinion*. Publication of the Park Ridge Center, no. 6. Chicago, Ill.: Park Ridge Center, 1987. Issue on rural health care.

Educational Events

Annual Conference on Rural Health. National Rural Health Association, One West Armour Boulevard, Suite 301, Kansas City, MO 64111 (phone: 816-756-3140).

Annual Meeting of the Center for Rural Affairs. The Center for Rural Affairs, P.O. Box 406, Walthill, NE 68067-5428.

Annual National Institute on Social Work and Human Services in Rural Area. Rural Clearinghouse for Lifelong Education and Development, 111 College Court Building, Manhattan, KS 66505-6001 (phone: 913-532-5560).

Celebrate Health Ministries (annual conference). Iowa Lutheran Hospital, 700 East University Avenue, Des Moines, IA 50316.

Harvesting Our Potential, Rural Women's Gathering (annual gathering in February). PrairieFire Rural Action, 550 Eleventh Street, Suite 200, Des Moines, IA 50309-2685.

National Rural Families Conference. Division of Continuing Education, Conference Office, Kansas State University, College Court Building, Manhattan, KS 66506-6001 (phone: 913-532-5575).

Prairie Festival. The Land Institute, 2440 East Water Well Road, Salina, KS 67401.

Rural Ministry Conference (annual conference in early March). Center for Theology and Land, University of Dubuque and Wartburg Theological Seminaries, 2000 University Avenue, Dubuque, IA 52001 (phone: 319-589-3117).

Organizations

Center for Rural Affairs, P.O. Box 405, Walthill, NE 68067 (phone: 402-846-5428).

Center for Theology and Land, 2000 University Avenue, Dubuque, IA 52001. (University of Dubuque and Wartburg Seminaries) (319-589-3117).

Churches' Center for Land and People, Sinsinawa Mound, Sinsinawa, WI 53824 (phone: 608-748-4411).

Health Ministries Association, 1306 Penn Avenue, Des Moines, IA 50316 (phone: 515-263-8556).

Heartland Center for Leadership, Rural Enhancement Program, West River Mental Health Center, Rapid City, SD 57701 (phone: 402-474-7667).

Iowa Lutheran Hospital, Minister of Health/Pastoral Care Education Program, 700 East University Avenue, Des Moines, IA 50316.

The Land Institute, 2440 East Water Well Road, Salina, KS 67401.

National Farm Medicine Center, Marshfield Clinic, 1000 North Oak Avenue, Marshfield, WI 54449-5790 (phone: 715-387-9298).

PrairieFire Rural Action, Inc., 550 Eleventh Street, Suite 200, Des Moines, IA 50309 (phone: 515-244-5671).

Rural Clearinghouse for Education and Development, Kansas State University, Manhattan, KS 66506 (phone: 913-532-5560).

Rural Concerns, 10861 Douglas Street, Urbandale, IA 50322 (phone: 800-447-1985).

Rural Information Center, National Agricultural Library, Room 304, Beltsville, MD 20705 (phone: 800-633-7701).

Periodicals and Newsletters

Agricultural Notes. Division for Outreach, ELCA, 8765 West Higgins Road, Chicago, IL 60631 (phone: 312-380-2669).

Breaking New Ground. Breaking New Ground Resource Center, Department of Agriculture, Purdue University, 1146 Agricultural Engineering Building, West Layfayette, IN 47907-1146. Designed to create awareness and cultivate independence of farmers and ranchers with disabilities.

Buzzworm: The Environmental Journal. Buzzworm, Inc., 2305 Canyon Boulevard, Suite 206, Boulder, CO 80302 (phone 303-442-1969).

Catholic Rural Life. National Catholic Rural Life Conference, 4625 Beaver Avenue, Des Moines, IA 50310-2199.

Center for Rural Affairs, P.O. Box 406, Walthill, NE 68067-5428, publishes a newsletter surveying events affecting rural Nebraska.

Chestnut Sprouts. Chestnut Ridge Farm, Creekside Press, P.O. Box 331, Abingdon, VA 24210 (phone: 703-628-6416). Monthly newsletter publicizes upcoming events at Chestnut Ridge Farm, describes life on the farm, and also carries essays by Richard Cartright Austin on such topics as agricultural economics, the North American Free Trade Agreement, and a proposal to help tobacco farmers make the transition to alternative crops.

Chickadee Chatter. Mission at the Eastward, RFD 3, Box 3897, Farmington, ME 04938. The newsletter of Mission at the Eastward, ministry of the Presbyterian Church in Maine.

Common Ground. The National Catholic Rural Life Conference, 4625 Beaver Avenue, Des Moines, IA 50310-2199 (phone: 515-270-2634).

Earthkeeping News. North American Conference on Christianity and Ecology, 1522 Grand Avenue, #4C, St. Paul, MN 55105.

The Five Stones: A Newsletter for Small Churches. The Reverend Anthony G. Pappas, editor, The First Baptist Church, Box D2, Block Island, RI 02807.

Gaining Ground. Wisconsin Conference of Churches, 1955 West Broadway, #104, Madison, WI 53713 (phone: 608-222-9779). Published four times per year to help facilitate the flow of information about rural concerns in Wisconsin's religious community.

Gleanings: News from Broom Tree Farm. R.R.1, Box 165, Irene, SD 57037 (phone 605-263-3165). Broom Tree Farm is a nonprofit corporation whose mission is to provide a renewal center for pastors and church professionals on a working farm. It is a place of rest, healing, nurture, education, conservation, and counseling.

Good News. Evangelism and Church Development Ministry Unit, Presbyterian Church (USA), 100 Witherspoon Street, Louisville, KY 40202-1396 (phone: 502-569-5246 or 502-569-5228).

The Land Report. The Land Institute, 2440 East Water Well Road, Salina, KS 67401. Published three times a year.

The Land Stewardship Letter. Land Stewardship Project, 14758 Ostlund Trail North, Marine, MN 55407 (phone: 612-433-2770). Published four times a year.

Net Results: New Ideas in Church Vitality and Leadership. National Evangelistic Association, Net Results Research Center, 5001 Avenue N, Lubbock, TX 79412-2993. Twelve issues per year, it contains ecumenical articles from pastor's experiences.

The North Country Anvil. North Country Anvil, Inc., P.O. Box 37, Millville, MN 55957 (phone: 507-798-2366). North Country Anvil, a nonprofit organization, publishes this forum for readers, writers, artists.

Prairie Journal. PrairieFire Rural Action, 550 Eleventh Street, Suite 200, Des Moines, IA 50309-2685.

Rural Development Perspectives. ERS-NASS, 341 Victory Drive, Herndon, VA 22070. Published by the U.S. Department of Agriculture in Washington, D.C., this newsletter presents research on various aspects of rural life that are important to consider when formulating rural policies and programs.

Rural Roots. Brescia College Center for Ministry Support, 717 Frederica Street, Owensboro, KY 42301-9988 (phone: 502-686-4234). A journal for Catholic rural ministers.

Seasons: The Inter-Faith Family Journal. The Inter-Faith Committee on the Family in cooperation with The Archdiocese of Milwaukee, P.O. Box 07912, Milwaukee, WI 53207-0912. The goal of this newsletter is to provide a forum for the sharing of information and resources across denominational lines, and to establish communication among our faith communities around our common concern for families and family life. Published three times per year around a family theme.

The Small Church Newsletter of the Missouri School of Religion. Missouri School of Religion, P.O. Box 104685, Jefferson City, MO 65110-4685.

Videotapes

The videotapes described below are available from the Center for Theology and Land, University of Dubuque and Wartburg Theological Seminaries, 2000 University Avenue, Dubuque, IA 52001 (phone: 319-589-3117).

Churches in Transition: Evangelism and Mission deals in a documentary format with ways that several churches have responded to changes in their communities. Twenty-eight minutes.

The Connecting Link describes how parish nursing can connect rural people in need to the church and the community. Twenty-four minutes.

Down to Earth Theology: Ministry for Sustainable Communities. A selection of excerpts from presentations made at a major conference on ecology and theology. The environmental crisis is examined from a spiritual perspective. Thirty-two minutes.

Healthy Communities: The Role of the Rural Church. The question of what makes a healthy community is examined by rural residents. This video is a good companion piece to the "Planting the Seeds of Community" Bible study series and also the monograph "Building Healthy Communities." Thirty-six minutes.

Searching for Tomorrow presents several rural church experts who offer insights into the practice of rural ministry past, present, and future. Thirty-one minutes.

Worship and Educational Materials

Agria, Mary, and Paul Peterson. *Planting the Seeds of Community: A Bible Study for Revitalization in Rural America.* Dubuque, Iowa: Center for Theology and Land, 1993.

Churches' Center for Land and People. *Seasons of Celebration: Monthly Ways to Celebrate Our Lives, the Land, Scripture's Word, God's Presence.* Sinisinawa, Wisc.: Churches' Center for Land and People, 1995.

Dawes, Gil, and Alexander Rhoads. *Plenty in the Land: A Church Curriculum on Corporate Agriculture.* Des Moines: PrairieFire Rural Action, 1992.

Discipleship Alive! St. Louis: Christian Board of Publication, n.d. Thirteen sessions, with leader's guide. A course on becoming our planet's keepers.

Earth Stewardship Packet. Akron, Pa.: Mennonite Central Committee Global Education and Information Services, 1992. Study and worship resources.

Kapfer, Richard. *And God Said: A Christian Study of Ecology and the Care of God's Creation.* St. Louis: Concordia Publishing House, 1992. Five-session Bible study of the first three chapters of Genesis.

Newman, Toni, ed. *Worship from the Ground Up: A Worship Resource for Town and Country Congregations.* Dubuque, Iowa: Center for Theology and Land, 1995.

Speak to the Earth and It Will Teach Thee (Job 12:8). Philadelphia: Friends General Conference Bookstore, 1987. Five first-day school lessons and additional resources.

Notes

About This Book

1. Jackson W. Carroll, Carl S. Dudley, and William McKinney, eds., *Handbook for Congregational Studies* (Nashville: Abingdon Press, 1986), 11.

1. Introducing Rural Ministry: Congregational Studies in Perspective

1. The other aspects of congregational studies are detailed in the preface.
2. Indeed, Rockwell Smith found that an understanding of social context was highly valuable in producing churches that both grew rapidly and had a strong sense of mission. See Rockwell Smith et al., *The Role of Rural Social Science in Theological Education: With Particular Application to the Town and Country Ministry in the Methodist Church* (Evanston, Ill.: Bureau of Social and Religious Research, Garrett Theological Seminary, 1969).

2. Understanding the Rural Context

1. See, among others, Anthony Pappas, *Entering the World of the Small Church: A Guide for Leaders* (Washington, D.C.: The Alban Institute, 1988), chap. 5.
2. Gary Farley, "Some Facts About Rural and Small Town Population/Places," *The Baptist Program* (1988).
3. Cornelia Butler Flora et al., *Rural Communities: Legacy & Change* (Boulder: Westview Press, 1992), 14.
4. Ibid., 23.
5. Kathleen Norris, *Dakota: A Spiritual Geography* (New York: Ticknor & Fields, 1993), 1-3.
6. These figures are drawn from the report of the National Agricultural Statistics Service, Economic Research Service, USDA (Washington, D.C., 1994).
7. These figures are drawn from a report of the Agricultural Statistics Board (Washington, D.C., 1994), *Statistical Abstracts of the United States.*
8. Norris, *Dakota,* 29-31.
9. Ibid., 51.
10. "How Wal-Mart Hits Main St.," *U.S. News and World Report,* 13 March 1989, 53-55.
11. Patrick Rains, "Flight or Fight: The Town That Took on Wal-Mart—and Won," *American City and County,* November 1992, 50.
12. Edward O. Welles, "When Wal-Mart Comes to Town," *Inc.,* July 1993, 80.
13. Tony Parker, "Failure: Stanley Fricke," in *Bird, Kansas* (New York: Alfred A. Knopf, 1989), 269-74.
14. Richard Thompson, "Get Along But Don't Go Along," in *Caretakers of Creation: Farmers Reflect on Their Faith and Work,* ed. Patrick Slattery (Minneapolis: Augsburg, 1991), 57-69.
15. William P. Browne et al., *Sacred Cows and Hot Potatoes: Agrarian Myths in Agricultural Policy* (Boulder: Westview Press, 1992), 30-31.
16. A. V. Krebs, *The Corporate Reapers* (Washington, D.C.: Essential Books, 1992), 41.
17. National Research Council, *Alternative Agriculture* (Washington, D.C.: National Academy Press, 1989), 8.
18. Marty Strange, "Control Corporate Farming," *The Des Moines Sunday Register,* 8 May 1994, sec. C, p. 1.

19. James Walsh, "Innovative Practices Allow Flexible, More Profitable Lives," *(Minneapolis) Star Tribune,* 4 December 1994.

20. Jan Flora et al., *From the Grassroots: Profiles of 103 Rural Self-Development Projects* (Rockville, Md.: U.S. Department of Agriculture, 1991).

3. Who Are We? Identifying the Spirituality of Rural Congregations

1. Neill Q. Hamilton, quoted in *Handbook for Congregational Studies*, ed. Jackson W. Carroll, Carl S. Dudley, William McKinney (Nashville: Abingdon Press, 1986), 19.

2. As rural churches go about the task of making community issues the focus of Christian education and preaching, varied Scripture-based tools and resources are available to them, including the Center for Theology and Land's fifty-two-week Bible series *Planting the Seeds of Community*, which puts the problems of modern rural life into a Christian context. See table 3.1 on pp. 60-61.

3. Carroll, Dudley, and McKinney, eds., *Handbook for Congregational Studies*, 23. See also the whole of chapter 2 in that source. The *Handbook* is a very valuable resource in that it explains how congregations can study themselves and provides many useful tools for such self-examination. We commend its use, although it is not particularly geared to rural or smaller churches.

4. David Ray, *The Big Small Church Book* (Cleveland: Pilgrim Press, 1992), 31.

5. Ibid., 29.

6. *The Christian Century* published a number of articles from 1993 to 1995 that revisited historic churches the magazine had highlighted two decades earlier. These were fascinating in terms of the identities that they revealed; for example, Trinity Lutheran Church, Freistatt, Missouri (December 1, 1993), and New Hope Presbyterian, Connor Prairie, Indiana (August 24-31, 1994).

4. Program: The Congregation Expressing Itself in Action

1. James F. Hopewell, *Congregation: Stories and Structures* (Philadelphia: Fortress Press, 1987), 5. Hopewell writes, "Word, gesture, and artifact form a local language—a system of construable signs that Clifford Geertz, following Weber, calls a 'web of significance'—that distinguishes a congregation from others around it or like it. Even a plain church on a pale day catches one in a deep current of narrative interpretation and representation by which people give sense and order to their lives."

2. Craig Nessan, *A Theology of the Congregation,* unpublished manuscript, 1996.

3. The Center for Theology and Land has produced a Worship Resource Supplement especially designed for rural and smaller congregations including hymns, prayers, and orders of worship. You may request a copy by calling 319-589-3117.

4. Cathi Braasch, former Director of Rural Ministries for the Evangelical Lutheran Church in America, shared this insight with us.

5. For a report of these findings, see Jung and Kirst, *Revitalization in the Rural Congregation: What We Know, What We Need to Know,* Occasional Studies in Rural Ministry II (Dubuque, Iowa: Center for Theology and Land, 1995). To order a copy call 319-589-3117.

6. Jackson W. Carroll, Carl S. Dudley, and William McKinney, eds., *Handbook for Congregational Studies* (Nashville: Abingdon Press, 1986), 11.

7. D. Finck, "Farmers Are Still Killing Themselves," *Farm Journal*, October 1990, 37.

8. Deborah Cronin, *Can Your Dog Hunt?* (Lima, Ohio: Fairway Press, 1995), 7-8.

9. Ibid., 11-12, 14-15.

10. Tex Sample, "Worship and the Language of the Heart," keynote address at the 1995 Rural Ministry Conference in Dubuque, Iowa (audiotape available from the Center for Theology and Land, phone 319-589-3117).

11. Our thanks to Randy Posslenzny, of International Missions in Hong Kong, for sharing this story and for granting us permission to use it.

12. Our thanks to Gary Farley of the Southern Baptist Convention's Home Mission Board for these ideas.

5. Understanding Process: Leadership and Style in the Rural Congregation

1. Jung and Kirst, *Revitalization in the Rural Congregation: What We Know, What We Need to Know*, Occasional Studies in Rural Ministry II (Dubuque, Iowa: Center for Theology and Land, 1995), 22. You may request a copy of this resource by calling 319-589-3117.

2. Alvin J. Lindgren and Norman Shawchuck, *Let My People Go: Empowering Laity for Ministry* (Schaumburg, Ill.: Organization Resources Press, 1988), 5.

3. Ibid., 55-67.

4. See Roy Oswald, "How to Minister Effectively in Family, Pastoral, Program, and Corporate Sized Churches," *Action Information* 17, no. 2 (March/April 1991): 1-6; and Arlin Rothauge, *Sizing Up a Congregation for New Member Ministry* (New York: Episcopal Church Center, n.d.).

5. Oswald, "How to Minister Effectively in Family, Pastoral, Program, and Corporate Sized Churches," 3. See also Oswald, "When Membership Declines," *Action Information* 17, no. 3 (May/June 1991): 1-5.

6. In effect, we are attempting to build a theory of process in the rural congregation on the foundations of mission and spirituality. This area of process is underdeveloped in congregational studies, and yet it is at the heart of the clergy-laity relationship. The key seems to be to encourage clergy to measure *their* success by how well *laity* lead the congregation and nurture growth in spirituality and outreach.

7. Loren Mead, *The Once and Future Church* (Washington, D.C.: The Alban Institute, 1991).

8. See Kevin Phillips, *The Politics of Rich and Poor* (New York: Random House, 1990), esp. 13, 17.

9. Richard Thompson, "Get Along, But Don't Go Along," in *Caretakers of Creation: Farmers Reflect on Their Faith and Work*, ed. Patrick Slattery (Minneapolis: Augsburg, 1991), 67.

10. Even the closest neighbors and friends may not realize that a family is on the verge of bankruptcy until the auction notices go up or a family member commits suicide, as we see in Jane Smiley's *A Thousand Acres* (New York: Alfred A. Knopf, 1991).

11. Anthony G. Pappas, *Entering the World of the Small Church: A Guide for Leaders* (Washington, D.C.: The Alban Institute, 1988).

12. See David R. Ray, *Small Churches Are the Right Size* (Cleveland: Pilgrim Press, 1982); and Nancy Foltz, *Caring for the Small Church: Insights from Women in Ministry* (Valley Forge: Judson Press, 1994).

13. See the valuable chart on congregational structure in Nancy Foltz, *Religious Education in the Small Membership Church* (Birmingham: Religious Education Press, 1990), 38-41.

14. Pappas, *Entering the World of the Small Church*, 82.

15. See Scott Gustafson, *Ministry with the Power of Jesus* (Lawrenceville, Va.: Brunswick Publishing, 1991).

16. See Gary L. Harbaugh, *God's Gifted People: Discovering and Using Your Spiritual and Personal Gifts* (Minneapolis, Augsburg Fortress, 1990); Roy Oswald and Otto Krueger, *Personality Type and Religious Leadership* (Washington, D.C.: The Alban Institute, 1988); Olaf Isachsen and Linda Berens, *Working Together: A Personality-Centered Approach to Management* (Coronado, Calif.: Institute for Management Development, 1991).

17. For more information about McIntosh's paradigm, contact The McIntosh Church Growth Network, 3630 Camellia Drive, San Bernadino, CA 92402. Ask for volume 3, number 5, of their newsletter.

18. See Loren Mead, *The Once and Future Church*.

19. Lindgren and Shawchuck, *Let My People Go*, 5.

20. Smiley, *A Thousand Acres*, 208, 210-11.

6. Building Community:
Strategies for Empowering Rural Congregations

1. The authors thank the following individuals for their invaluable contributions to the views and insights presented in this section: Sister Miriam Brown, Sinsinawa, Wisconsin; Mary Farwell, Clinton, Iowa; pastors Craig Bowyer, formerly of Lost Nation, Iowa; Don Dovre, Ryan, Iowa; N. David Guetzke, Wyoming, Iowa; Peggy Ogden-Howe, Cedar Rapids, Iowa; and Bill Peters, Olin, Iowa.

2. Anthony G. Pappas, *Entering the World of the Small Church* (Washington, D.C.: The Alban Institute, 1988), chap. 4.

3. See Mary Agria, *Building Healthy Communities: Stories of 12 Communities in the Midwest* (Dubuque, Iowa: Center for Theology and Land, 1995). This monograph presents the model rural communities and congregations who were involved in the Empowering Community Development project and took such Spirit-led leaps of faith.

4. Cornelia Butler Flora et al., *Rural Communities: Legacy and Change* (Boulder: Westview Press, 1992), 4.

5. See Kenneth Haugk, *Antagonists in the Church: How to Identify and Deal with Destructive Conflict* (Minneapolis: Augsburg, 1988).

6. See Roy Oswald, *Clergy Self-Care: Finding Balance for Effective Ministry* (Washington, D.C.: The Alban Institute, 1991). Oswald suggests that rural pastors care for themselves in part by viewing laity as partners.

7. Carl Dudley, *Making the Small Church Effective* (Nashville: Abingdon Press, 1978), 16.

8. *The Connecting Link*, a twenty-five-minute video and study guide on parish health ministry, may be ordered from the Center for Theology and Land, 2000 University Avenue, Dubuque, IA 52001 (phone 319-589-3117).

9. Conrad Phillip Kottak, "Culture and 'Economic Development,'" *American Anthropologist*, September 1990, 723-31.

10. We thank Pastor Watts Rozell for his advice in writing this section.

Index